D1543736

PUBLIC ASSEMBLY FACILITY MANAGEMENT: PRINCIPLES AND PRACTICES

FIRST EDITION

PUBLIC ASSEMBLY FACILITY MANAGEMENT: PRINCIPLES AND PRACTICES

Principal Author
Peter J. Graham, Ed.D.
Professor
Department of Sport & Entertainment Management
College of Hospitality, Retail and Sport Management
University of South Carolina
Columbia, SC

Executive Editor
Ray Ward, CFE
President
Dakota Enterprises
Granite Bay, CA

Contributing Editors
Don Hancock, Ph.D.
Dexter G. King, CFE
Robert J. Stewart, CFE

INTERNATIONAL ASSOCIATION OF
ASSEMBLY MANAGERS, INC.

Printed and Published by
International Association of
Assembly Managers, Inc.
635 Fritz Drive, Suite 100
Coppell, TX 75019
www.iaam.org

ISBN 0-9665670-4-8

First Edition

CONTENTS

DEVELOPMENT TEAM

IAAM Body of Knowledge Task Force (1999-2004)

This textbook is the product of the steadfast commitment by the men and women of the Body of Knowledge Task Force who have dedicated four years to this project. Their devotion to enhancing the public assembly facility industry and passion for sharing this knowledge are hallmarks of these professionals. On behalf of those who will benefit from the fruit of their labor, IAAM gratefully acknowledges their contribution.

Frank E. Russo, Jr., CFE,
Chair 2002-04
Vice President
Global Spectrum
Glastonbury, CT

Debbie Kling
General Manager
Bank of America Centre
Boise, ID

Patrick K. Fitzgerald, CFE,
Chair 2000-02
Senior Director of Facility Operations
Cavaliers/Gund Arena Company
Cleveland, OH

Robert E. Seitz, CFE
General Manager
Topeka Performing Arts Center
Topeka, KS

Dexter G. King, CFE
Executive Director
International Association of
Assembly Managers, Inc.
Coppell, TX

Rodney J. Smith
General Manager
Denver Performing Arts Complex
Denver, CO

Lynda Reinhart
Assistant Director
Stephen C. O'Connell Center
University of Florida
Gainesville, FL

Robert J. Stewart, CFE
Reno, NV

Ray Ward, CFE
President
Dakota Enterprises, Inc.
Granite Bay, CA

PREFACE

If ever a book was written in response to popular demand, this one is! Once little more than a three-credit course in a sport management undergraduate or graduate degree program, the discipline of public assembly facility management has become an entity unto itself with industry professionals, professors, and students literally clamoring for a comprehensive textbook that meets the teaching needs of the academic community and serves as a reference book for industry practitioners.

The initiative for and driving force behind this book is the International Association of Assembly Managers (IAAM) and the IAAM Foundation (IAAMF) under the leadership of IAAM Presidents Carol Wallace (1999-2000), Frank Poe (2000-2001), Lionel Dubay (2001-2002) Joe Floreano, CFE (2002-2003), and Mike Kelly, CFE (2003-2004); and IAAM Foundation Chairs Bob Mayer, CFE (1999-2000), Frank Roach (2000-2001), Dot Lischick, CFE, (2001), Steve Pelham (2001-2003) and Peggy Daidakis (2003-2004).

IAAM/IAAMF created the "BoK" or Body of Knowledge Task Force in 1998. The BoK Task Force held its first meeting in January 1999. More than three years of hard and dedicated efforts resulted in creating the "core competencies" and chapter outlines; interviewing and hiring the University of South Carolina to author the book; monitoring and editing the various chapters; and generally serving as the guiding force behind the entire process.

The result is, for the first time, a comprehensive textbook on the principles and practices of public assembly facility management that incorporates the body of knowledge of the industry. This publication was first printed in a Beta edition in 2003. Nine institutions of higher education used the text during academic year 2003-2004. Constructive criticism was received from both students and professors, which the BoK incorporated into this current edition.

This text represents the completion of just the first phase of the IAAM's efforts to reach into the university community by encouraging, participating in, and endorsing master's degree programs in public assembly facility management and also providing teaching resources for undergraduate and graduate degree programs.

This text will also serve as the basis for future publications and teaching aids to develop the basics of each chapter in this text into a much more detailed and complete treatment of each subject, emphasizing several practical case studies, checklists for managers, and relevant supplemental materials that will broaden the overall knowledge base for students, professors, and public assembly facility management professionals. In addition, these materials are a part of the IAAM's plan to strengthen the Certified Facilities Executive (CFE) certification process and training programs such as the Public Assembly Facility Management School at Oglebay Resort in Wheeling, W.VA.

Few textbooks have been written that received input and support from such a large group. In addition to IAAM's Body of Knowledge Task Force, many others have made substantive contributions. Technical reviewers have included Dick Walsh; Frank Roach; Bill Cunningham, CFE; Lionel J. Dubay; Susan Fobes; Bob Mayer, CFE; Alice Marini; John Page; Greg Deveraux; Xen Riggs; Chris Bigelow, FCSI; Dan Saunders, CFE; and Brad Mayne, CFE. Helpful IAAM staff support was received from Dr. Don Hancock and Dana Glazier. Book design and layout was provided by Debbie Billman Shannon, and copyediting and project management by Julie Herrick. In addition, important contributions from the University of South Carolina were made by Dr. Patricia G. Moody, Dean of the College of Hospitality, Retailing and Sport Management, Dr. Tom H. Regan, Department of Sport and Entertainment Management Chair, Dr. Laura Sawyer, and John Bolin. Thanks to all.

Frank E. Russo, Jr., CFE
Chair, IAAM Board of Education and Body of Knowledge Task Force
June 2004

Peter J. Graham, Ed.D.
University of South Carolina
Columbia, SC

Ray Ward, CFE
Dakota Enterprises
Granite Bay, CA

ACKNOWLEDGMENT

Financial support for the *Public Assembly Facility Management: Principles and Practices* has been provided by the International Association of Assembly Managers Foundation. Without their support, this textbook would not have been possible.

The Foundation is committed to raising funds to support the public assembly facility profession through programs of research, professional development and education.

The following IAAM Foundation Board of Trustees, past and present, has provided leadership and vision for this project.

1

OWNERSHIP AND GOVERNANCE OF PUBLIC ASSEMBLY FACILITIES

CHAPTER OUTLINE

INTRODUCTION

Throughout the world, the public is being asked to provide significant amounts of money in order to build public assembly facilities. More and more these modern "cathedrals" define a city's image and provide the necessary means to compete for the highly desirable big business of sports and entertainment, conventions and tourism.

Public assembly facilities such as arenas, stadiums, convention centers, and theatres evolved out of the need by social communities to build permanent structures for public assembly — for political and commercial activities, religion, sports, spectacles, artistic expression and for commercial and educational assemblies. In modern life, a community responds to requests for new public assembly facilities by first exploring their feasibility, considering factors such as economic, social, and political viability.

On any given day, literally thousands of public assembly facilities worldwide are open and serving the public because their communities responded to the need. Through the presentation of sport and entertainment events as well as conventions, meetings, and trade shows, the benefits of public assembly facilities to the social, educational, and economic environments of communities are being realized.

Public assembly facilities by their very nature meet a number of important needs that justify the investment of public funds. Simplistically, they provide both social and economic stimulus for a community. The social stimulus is normally a "quality of life" benefit provided to the community, while the economic stimulus is realized through the new spending and a resulting "multiplier" of economic activity. When public assembly facilities are considered "troubled," management may be perceived as lacking competence, but very often there is a lack of definition as to what is the purpose of the facility. It is a community asset, but is it intended to be a

- civic center for community events?
- sports and entertainment center?
- convention center/trade show center/attraction?
- economic impact driver?
- all of the above?

At what cost is the community willing to build and operate a public assembly facility? Is it to be a

- net income generator (usually exclusive of debt service and long-term capital improvement fund)?
- *break-even operation?*
- *subsidized operation?*

Does public policy match the public's willingness to subsidize? Clear and realistic determination of intentions provides community leaders with answers to questions on whether to build and how to govern, manage, and operate the facilities. Each of these public assembly facilities is a partner in the larger industries of

- sports and entertainment, including the arts.
- meetings, conventions, consumer shows and trade shows.

Each public assembly facility must find its place within the local, regional, national, or international markets in which they compete; these markets often are intensely competitive. And though there may exist a dramatic variation in size, function, and mission for each venue, their primary purpose remains constant: providing service to the public. (NOTE: The terms venue and facility are synonymous and are frequently used interchangeably). This chapter addresses basic concepts, governance of public assembly facilities, and introductory management issues.

TYPES OF PUBLIC ASSEMBLY FACILITIES

A public assembly facility is a physical entity. Ownership, governance, management, and operations are described as being public or private. There are many different types of public assembly facilities. Therefore, in the discussion that follows, the term public assembly facility (ies) will refer to all public and private facilities designed to accommodate people wishing to assemble for a common purpose. Thus, the term public assembly facility (ies) includes, but is not limited to, amphitheatres, arenas, auditoriums, conference centers, congress centers, convention centers, exhibition halls, performing arts theatres, stadiums, and special event facilities. The following definitions are drawn from the IAAM's *1994 Industry Profile Survey* (IPS):

ARENA - an indoor facility with fixed and/or portable seats surrounding an open floor area, which can be set with different event configurations. May have a permanent stage or use portable staging when necessary. *more personal, intimate*
Typical Events - basketball, hockey, other sports, concerts, ice shows, circuses, *most profitable* other family shows, and miscellaneous other major events. These facilities may also have occasional conventions, trade shows, and meetings, but they are not primarily convention and exhibition centers, as defined in the IPS. *10 - 20 Thousand Seats*

AMPHITHEATRE - an open-air facility with a stage, usually some permanent seating, and some lawn seating area. *Low Maint ~ easy to run*
Typical Events - concerts, stage presentations, community events, and miscellaneous other events. *Not as profitable*

AUDITORIUM/THEATRE - an indoor performing arts facility or concert hall usually with some type of permanent stage and permanent seats on a raked (sloped) floor, or may have a center or thrust stage with either permanent and/or portable seating. *Not as profitable 2,000 - 5,000 Seats*
Typical Events - concerts, symphony, drama, dance, touring Broadway shows, ballet, opera, stage presentations, and other community events. These facilities

may also have conventions, trade shows, and meetings, but they are not primarily convention and exhibition centers, as defined in the IPS.

CONVENTION CENTER/EXHIBIT HALL/TRADE SHOW CENTER - an indoor facility with large exhibit areas, supplemented by various sized meeting rooms. *Most lose money because of different focus on.* **Typical Events** - conventions, trade shows, consumer shows (e.g. boat, home, auto, etc.), banquets, receptions, meetings, major local events, and others. Trade fairs may also own and tour shows. In the IPS questionnaires, a distinction was made between those facilities that were primarily convention centers and those exhibit halls that were part of a complex. *Economic impact on City* *good investment for gout!* *rather than local economy*

Exhibition halls are most often part of a convention center and may contain up to 1,000,000 or more square feet of contiguous flat-floor space and ceilings 25 to 35 feet in height. However, the vast majority are more likely to have floor space in the 60,000 to 100,000 square foot range.

STADIUM - a large facility, either open-aired or domed, with fixed seats, or bleachers surrounding a "field area." *60,000 – 70,000 seats* **Typical Events** - baseball, football, soccer, motor sports, major concerts, spectacles, major civic events, and others. A large domed facility with full-field football/soccer capability is considered a stadium even though its event schedule may include exhibits, basketball, family shows, and other arena-type events.

COMPLEX - a combination of two or more of the above facility types, presenting typical events as indicated. Typically, a complex has single management and combined financial reporting. *more efficient, share resources, ie labor, mgmt, HR* Other types of public assembly facilities include:

CONFERENCE CENTERS are primarily designed for small-scale meetings and conferences. They typically provide state-of-the-art educational meeting rooms and may also provide sleeping rooms.

CONGRESS CENTERS generally are found in Europe where conventions are referred to as congresses. Most of these centers do not have special-purpose or dedicated exhibit space. However, because they are designed to accommodate multiple-hosting duties, they normally contain one or more raked floor, fixed-seat theatres.

SPECIAL EVENT FACILITIES such as tennis and bowling stadiums, velodromes, curling rinks, horse and dog racetracks, and motor speedways are examples of structures designed to accommodate a specific activity or event. These facility types like all public assembly facilities are on occasion used to host activities or events not related to their primary purpose.

Other Types of Facilities: museums, parks, Zoo's, Nature Ctrs,

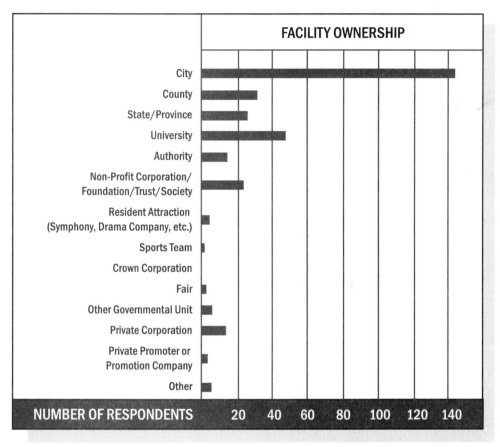

FIGURE 1-1

2003 IAAM Industry Profile Survey

GOVERNANCE OF PUBLIC ASSEMBLY FACILITIES

Public bodies (most often local government) finance, construct, and manage the majority of public assembly facilities and thus this form of ownership is by far the most common. (See Figure 1-1). Governance of these facilities is normally the responsibility of some type of board whose members are often appointed by the chief elected officials or city council. When facility managers are considered department heads by the involved public administration, they report directly to an elected or some other city official.

While there are a variety of possibilities for the ownership, governance, and day-to-day operating management of public assembly facilities, these can be described in certain basic formats. (See Figure 1-2). There are five basic forms of governance of public assembly facilities:

- Elected public body (e.g., city council, county supervisors, recreation districts, fair districts, etc.). While the reporting lines may be through an appointed official, (e.g., city manager, department head) it is the city council, etc. that makes the final decisions (budgets, policies and sometimes events that require specific advance approval in order for the public assembly facility manager to enter into a contract for the event). An "advisory" board may or may not exist but it has no authority. The "advisory" board simply represents the "voice of the community."

- Elected public body with an independent board (e.g., authority, commission, facilities district, etc.). The board would likely be appointed by the public body, receive its authority from the public body and have some reporting responsibilities (and perhaps some approvals such as budget) to that body.

- Public non-profit or not-for-profit corporation or commission or authority. This arrangement might typically have more independent authority yet would have to have at least an operating agreement with the owner (the public body).

- Private non-profit corporation. This arrangement involves the creation of the private corporation that then enters into a legal agreement with the owner. The board of directors is elected internally by the corporation, as are replacements.

- Private corporation, limited liability company or partnership.

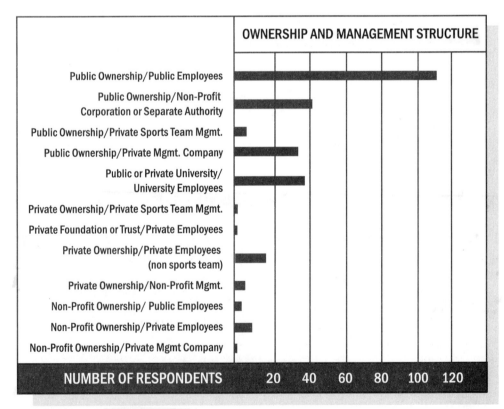

2003 IAAM Industry Profile Survey   FIGURE 1-2

Under each of the governance forms, the responsible entity can hire employees direct-ly to manage and operate the facility. They also have the option of contracting with a *private management* company, sport team, or resident company to manage and operate the facility. In all arrangements, concessionaires or third-party vendors might be contracted to provide certain services. These services could include food/beverage concessions and catering, parking operations, cleaning, general facility maintenance, and/or smaller more specialized services like elevator and scoreboard maintenance.

In order to be effective, all forms of governance and management should be philo-sophically entrepreneurial and seeking a best possible bottom line status given the mis-sion statement. In governmental and non-profit operations, different terminology may be used, but profit is nearly always desired, if not stated as an objective. Public agencies may describe this objective to be *self-sustaining* or to obtain a *net operating surplus*.

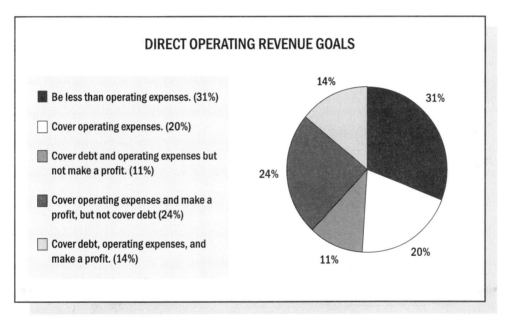

DIRECT OPERATING REVENUE GOALS

■ Be less than operating expenses. (31%)

☐ Cover operating expenses. (20%)

▨ Cover debt and operating expenses but not make a profit. (11%)

■ Cover operating expenses and make a profit, but not cover debt (24%)

☐ Cover debt, operating expenses, and make a profit. (14%)

FIGURE 1-3

Figure 1-3 displays the results of the *2003 IAAM Industry Profile Survey* addressing the expectations of the facility owner regarding facility financial performance. The results are aggregated to include all facility types and sizes. Simply, the results go from an expec-tation that the operating expenses will be (1) subsidized to (2) operating break-even to (3) operating break-even plus debt service but no profit to (4) operating profit to (5) operating break-even plus debt service and making a profit.

The base understanding when reviewing expectations is to remember they are goals and are not always attainable. While aggregated numbers and percentages are helpful in providing generalities, there are many elements in play that effect a manager's ability to reach specific goals. These include the building's size, shape, type, age, location and ability to host a variety of events. The demographics of the area play an important role. The programs presented in the facility need to match the needs and desires of the expected patrons.

The political situation is sometimes a critical element. In public assembly facilities, the owners are usually represented by elected officials. The facility is sometimes thought of as the community's "baby," and the expectations are high for success. When this is put into financial terms, reality might challenge desire.

A clear understanding of expectations is important. Why was the facility built? What are the limits of its program offerings? To what extent is the community willing to support this asset, both financially and through attendance at events?

When such operating objectives become difficult, private management companies may be able to help the owner/public leaders achieve the desired results. These results may be to achieve an actual operating profit, to minimize actual operating losses, and/or to provide a desired event program. The fee and incentive bonus the private management company receives are expenses of the facility's operating budget. To the extent the fee and incentive compensation exceed the private management company's cost of providing the contracted services, it has a profit. Its contract often includes an incentive compensation bonus for achieving predetermined and predefined success.

There is no reason a public assembly facility cannot be successfully operated by a public body if

- there are clearly defined goals.
- the approach is business-like, bottom-line oriented.
- bureaucracy knows the need for an entrepreneurial, marketing-oriented approach.
- the facility and operation are relatively non-political and freed of factors that cause instability, loss of confidence, and lack of competitiveness.
- in effect, the facility's operation is treated as a public enterprise or as if it were a private organization and as free as possible from bureaucratic restraints.

Of major concern, regardless of the form of organization decided upon, is the giving-up/retention of authority and control on the part of the owner (public body). If public-body-operation is selected, the control is totally with the owner. It is still possible to have conflicts between departments, board members and elected officials. It is possible to have an independent governing board using public employees to operate a facility. If the facility is operated as a department of government, control is essentially complete, but governmental entities often do not operate well in a competitive, sales, and marketing-oriented environment due in part to charter and similar legislative restrictions.

A private non-profit or not-for-profit corporation is a further step along the path between 100 percent public and 100 percent private management. If a private management approach is selected, the public body's give-ups and retentions are a function of the contract between the owner and the operator. Whether this is important or not can only be decided by each locality. Private management has proven to be an effective way for government to maintain overall control but to delegate management, marketing, and operations to a private-sector company, thereby allowing for a more entrepreneurial and competitive approach.

The more risk a private operator assumes, the more authority, management control, and performance incentives will be required. The assumed risk is probably a major factor for both parties in deciding and agreeing whether or not to go to a privately managed operation. Risk, from the owner/*governing body* view, relates to the ultimate responsibility for the success or failure (however defined) of the public assembly facility's results, both economic and programmatic, and confidence that the desired results can best be obtained with private management. The private management company's view relates to its ability under the contract to actually manage the operation day-to-day, to make decisions, and to have the legitimate opportunity to earn the performance incentives. The owner, on the other hand, must be sure that benchmarks for incentive income are high enough so as not to make them automatic.

Increasing numbers of publicly owned public assembly facilities are governed by an authority or commission created by the government entity. The facility's owner generally makes appointments to the governing body. This governing format is valuable in that it enables the facility management to operate with greater flexibility and effectiveness, especially in the areas of personnel management, payroll, purchasing, contract approval, sales and marketing and generally just being able to negotiate competitive "deals." A governing authority, whether associated with a public jurisdiction/department or operating through a non-profit corporation or authority, offers greater local control and opportunity for more successful management of facilities.

Given proper authority, these types of boards usually attract dedicated community leaders who bring needed business expertise and bottom-line perspective to the process. In the operating agreements with various types of independent boards (may also be state enabling legislation that allows local municipal ordinances), public agencies can establish policies and controls that protect the public's rights while at the same time developing the framework for effective management.

Of principal concern with any type of public governing structure is the authority that is granted to the board to conduct the business of the facility. If a powerless advisory board were created, one that must depend upon "city hall" for virtually every decision, then it would be better for "city hall" to act directly. Qualified business leaders and citizens are reluctant to devote their time and energy to public bodies if their input is meaningless.

ACADEMIC INSTITUTIONS AND NON-PROFITS

Academic institutions such as colleges and universities, whether public or private, own and operate on-campus facilities such as performing arts centers, stadiums, arenas, and conference centers. Although administrative responsibility of specific facilities may be aligned under applicable departments (e.g., student affairs, business and finance, or athletics), governance of collegiate facilities may also be delegated to an advisory committee comprised of elected and/or appointed representatives of the faculty, administration, and student body. However, ultimate governance authority rests in the hands of the chief executive officer and the institution's governing board.

Some public assembly facilities, particularly performing arts centers, may be owned and operated by private non-profit organizations. With this type of ownership and management, governance is dictated by the organization and those responsible for its governance may be either elected or appointed from the organization's membership. It is important to realize when discussing non-profit organizations that the non-profit designation is only a tax status. Profit as a motive is a state of mind — of intention as to what the economic results should be.

PUBLIC OR PRIVATE

There are no automatic answers as to the issue of whether a facility should be publicly or privately managed. Each situation is unique. The governing body has to make the hard decisions as to what it wants its facilities to be and how much control it is willing to delegate to another entity. The public body has to determine if the return for the expenditure necessary to have a private firm manage the facility is cost effective in terms of dollars, activity, program, and fulfilling the facility's public purpose.

In some cases, private owners, usually major league sport franchise owners, invest substantial amounts of their own capital to build a new arena or stadium. In such cases, local governments may assist with the development of these privately owned facilities by granting reduced tax liabilities and providing other incentives including financial investment of public funds and infrastructure development. In these cases, the team usually has full management control of the venue.

EXAMPLES OF OWNERSHIP AND GOVERNANCE

**DEPARTMENT OF A CITY/
COUNTY/STATE GOVERNMENT**

- Denver Performing Arts Complex (Denver, CO)
- Dallas Convention Center (Dallas, TX)
- Rose Bowl (Pasadena, CA)
- Indiana Convention Center (Indianapolis, IN)
- Springfield Civic Center (Springfield, MA)
- Cintermex Convention and Exposition Facility (Monterrey, Mexico)

AS A PUBLIC AUTHORITY OR COMMISSION

- Georgia World Congress Center (Atlanta, GA)
- Charlotte Coliseum (Charlotte, NC)
- Cumberland County Civic Center (Portland, ME)
- Spokane Arena (Spokane, WA)

NON-PROFIT ORGANIZATIONS OR FOUNDATIONS

- Embassy Theatre (Fort Wayne, IN)
- Wisconsin Exposition Center (West Allis, WI)

**GOVERNMENT OWNED BUT PRIVATELY
MANAGED OPERATION**

- Sovereign Bank Arena (Trenton, NJ)
- Bakersfield Arena and Civic Center (Bakersfield, CA)
- Everett Regional Events Center (Everett, WA)
- Eagan Convention Center (Anchorage, AK)

PRIVATELY OWNED AND OPERATED

- Bass Hall (Ft. Worth, TX)
- Madison Square Garden (New York City, NY)
- MCI Center (Washington, DC)
- Staples Center (Los Angeles, CA)
- Bank of America Centre (Boise, ID)

WITHIN A UNIVERSITY

(Managed by a private management company)
- Dean Dome, University of North Carolina (Chapel Hill, NC)

(Managed as a university department)
- Joyce Center, Notre Dame University (South Bend, IN)
- Frank Erwin Center, University of Texas (Austin, TX)

FIGURE 1-4

When a public assembly facility is government owned but privately managed, the governance arrangement and relationship applied will be defined by the contract agreement between the two parties. Generally, the owner will delegate administration of the contract to a contract administrator (city manager, department head, etc.) or group (authority commission, non-profit organization, etc.) to provide oversight. The purpose of this oversight is for communication and accountability, but not for dictating specifically how private management will be carried out. The contract for private management services will stipulate the term, conditions, scope of service, and consideration of the agreement. In situations of this nature, a strong working relationship is maintained between the management firm and the representative(s) of the owner or the governing body. If not, the remedy may be to contract with a different firm or to take the management operations *in-house*.

(Figure 1-4 presents examples of public assembly facilities that exist within the various forms of ownership and governance). Despite the differences of ownership and operation described above, the public assembly facility manager almost always reports to a higher authority, i.e., an organization or body that represents the ultimate owner. There is a clear need in the public assembly facility industry for each facility to have some type of a board that offers policy guidance, funding, community advocacy and public relations, performance reviews, and counsel and advice in key areas of facility management.

The manager is in charge of the day-to-day operation, not the governing body. The governing body oversees the management and programming of the facility and sets policy. The manager implements the policies. According to Peter Drucker, "without such an organ of review, top management has no way to control itself. It has no true legitimacy. But management also needs someone to talk to…" (Drucker, 1973, p. 631). Drucker further states that boards are also necessary to step in and remove top management for appropriate reasons such as incompetence, unsatisfactory performance, misfeasance or malfeasance, or simply to effect a change in overall direction and philosophy.

Whether a public assembly facility manager's governing body is a city council, county commission, non-profit organization, separately appointed or elected governmental authority, or a private board, the manager needs certain types of expertise at the board level to help guide the organization by establishing policies at least in the following areas:

- Audits
- Financial management and reporting
- Human resource/performance evaluation
- Advertising and marketing
- Law
- Communications/Public Relations

A valuable asset for any governing board is access to the "movers and shakers" in the community. Sometimes, a simple telephone contact can initiate a solution, stop a problem, or at least create a contact point for beginning discussions on an issue.

Fundamentally, public assembly facility managers working for a public body must effectively deal with an administrative department or some form of governing board in

PUBLIC ASSEMBLY FACILITY MANAGER'S DESIRED KNOWLEDGE, SKILLS AND ABILITIES

- Knowing the laws affecting your venue.
- Knowing the public purpose and mission, community needs and expectations.
- Knowing and maximizing the market and community assets.
- Helping to redefine the mission-as often as necessary.
- Establishing clear goals and objectives.
- Knowing and respecting the power of your board because they:
  - Hire and fire the general manager.
  - Approve annual operating and capital budgets.
  - Authorize annual audits.
  - Approve booking and scheduling policies.
  - Approve rental rates and fees.
  - Approve major contracts and long-term tenant leases.
  - Approve new positions, labor contracts, etc.
- Managing-up: learning how to influence and count votes to promote your recommendations while providing a complete evaluation of the issues.
- Remembering - it's not your building, it's theirs.
- Remembering your community responsibilities.
- Remembering your board members at usual and not so usual times, not just when you need something.
- Engaging in constant and effective communication.

- Becoming involved in the community and building a broader-based constituency through groups such as the:
  - Chamber of Commerce.
  - Convention and Visitors Bureau.
  - Arts and Sports Council.
  - Hotel/Motel Association.
- Inviting board members to events to "learn about the business" by walking around with you or other key staff members.
- Striving for improvement in the following performance areas:
  - Effective application of sound business principles.
  - Technical competency.
  - Oral and written communications.
  - Customer service.
  - Being decisive and action-oriented, yet also knowing when to back off and move on.
  - Sensitivity to diversity's value and opportunities.
  - Sensitivity to legal issues and restraints.
  - Risk management.
  - Multi-task orientation.
  - Problem solving.
  - Making things happen.

AVERAGE EDUCATION OF FACILITY MANAGERS

Doctorate	0.9%
Other Post-Graduate Degree	2.2%
Masters Degree	22.1%
Bachelors Degree	54.0%
2-Year College	18.1%
High School	2.7%
Less than High School	0.0%

13.5 percent of facility managers have completed the CFE program.

IMPORTANT AREAS OF STUDY FOR UNDERGRADUATES

Among IAAM active members surveyed in 2002, these areas were cited as most important:

1) Event Planning/Facility Operations
2) Customer Service/Research
3) Accounting/Finance

AVERAGE EXPERIENCE

Years in Facility Mgmt:	20.5
Years at Current Facility:	10.5
Years in Current Position:	7.75

81 percent of facility managers are more than 41 years of age.

order to be effective — and to survive. In many cases this is much easier said than done due to the fact that most governmental offices or boards consist of members elected by the community or appointed by the local legislative bodies (e.g., city councils) for a specified time period. Thus, the public assembly facility manager is always striving to develop positive relationships with new members while maintaining established relationships with continuing members. Given the nature of politics, this can at times prove to be a very difficult and delicate task.

While all public assembly facilities act in some form as economic drivers for the community, many of them can be mired in a straight-jacket of government rules and regulations that render them impotent and ineffective in their mission and role and unable to successfully compete. The bureaucratic processes that may work effectively for departments delivering only taxpayer services (e.g., street repairs) are more often than not totally inappropriate for managers who must deal with issues concerning sales, marketing, customer satisfaction, and intense competition.

Regardless of the facility's governance structure, achieving the public purpose through successful management outcomes is dependent upon effectively earning client and public confidence. Whether publicly or privately managed, facilities must be competitively focused, and able to respond and adjust to prevailing market shifts. It takes extraordinary skill, dedication, and perseverance to cost-effectively manage a public assembly facility.

Within either a public-sector or private-management environment, the principles outlined in Figure 1-5 will assist in the development of characteristics essential to being a successful public assembly facility manager. Development of these characteristics will also prove valuable when striving to build an organizational consensus and an atmosphere of cooperation while keeping the organization focused on its main purposes — the maximization of event activity, attendance, and revenue generation.

COMMON OPERATING DYNAMICS

Common threads of operating dynamics exist among all facilities. Some of these commonalities are event booking and scheduling, event management, parking, crowd management, ticketing, advertising, concessions and catering, facility maintenance, and marketing and sales. Thus, regardless of a facility's size, mission, governance, management, or organizational structure, clear similarities in operating dynamics exist. For example, the manager of an arena and the manager of a performing arts center are both concerned with crowd management and risk management. Some of these commonalities date back to ancient history. Many of the operational areas considered vital by the manager of the Flavian Amphitheatre (Roman Colosseum) when staging gladiatorial combat in A.D. 80 are also considered vital to the manager responsible for staging a rock concert in a modern amphitheatre, or other type of public assembly facility.

Rarely does a public assembly facility operate in a single purpose environment. Twenty-first century governing bodies and managers, therefore, need a commanding knowledge of how these operating dynamics affect their facility as well as understanding the effect they have on their competitors.

Successful facility governance demands fiscal diligence and creativity. However, before establishing fiscal objectives, the financial expectations of the owner must be defined and fully understood. Is the mission of the facility to make an operating profit — profit being defined as a surplus of operating revenue over operating expenses? If so, what level of profit is desired? Is the mission's objective only to generate income sufficient to break-even from operations or should the profit be large enough to also cover debt service? Are operating losses acceptable? If they are, to what extent will the public fund the facility and program? How will any shortfall be funded? Only after these and similar questions have been resolved can the governing body begin to establish realistic and mission-based fiscal goals and objectives as well as event programs to achieve them.

Recognizing the financial impact that public assembly facilities provide, some communities create special taxes or taxing districts to subsidize operating budgets of public assembly facilities. An example of such an approach is the hotel/motel "bed" or transient occupancy tax (TOT). Another approach is an entertainment district tax or ticket surcharge. Regardless of the method, these supplemental funding approaches reflect a recognition by the community that there are other far-reaching, "quality-of-life" values that the facility provides to community members.

Public assembly facility managers and their governing boards must be willing to consider a reasoned gamble based on their risk tolerance level and legal requirements. Thus, like other entrepreneurs, the facility manager might be allowed to organize, operate, and assume the risks inherent in both in-house and *co-promoted* events. (Chapter 3 — Scheduling Facilities and Booking Events provides additional material on this topic.) Since the success of the public assembly facility hinges on the business and political acumen of its manager, it is imperative for the owner and governing body to employ managerial personnel who possess business skills and political insight. The owner through the governing body must then cultivate and nurture an appropriate entrepreneurial environment that will enable the manager to exercise those business and political skills.

COMPETITION AND FLEXIBILITY

The public assembly facility industry has grown, and continues to grow at a significant rate. A by-product of this growth pattern has been intensified competition. The combination of increased growth and intense competition has heightened the need for prudent financial investments in public assembly facilities and utilization of efficient management practices in order for the facility to serve its constituents in a financially responsible manner. A community's elected or appointed officials and administrators are responsible for the delivery of community services and the use of public tax dollars to pay for them according to prescribed regulations, rules, and policies in order to achieve the vision and to accomplish the mission.

It is unlikely that a public assembly facility can be financially successful if its manager is handicapped by governmental policies and procedures that make it difficult, if not impossible, to conduct the facility's business in a competitive, business-like manner. Public assembly facility governing bodies must strive to free their managers from constraints that inhibit the application of sound and reasonable business practices.

EXAMPLES OF MISSION STATEMENTS

THE AIR CANADA CENTRE IN TORONTO, ONTARIO:

Vision and Values
Excite our fans
Inspire our employees
Bring pride to the community
...and we all win

Champions:
By teamwork, relentless determination and pride of tradition.

Fans:
By delivering fun, value, and extraordinary hospitality.

Employees:
By being a dynamic and exceptional place to work.

Community:
By being a good citizen, partner, and role model.

HONG KONG CONVENTION AND EXHIBITION CENTER:

We live and work by a vision and mission "centered" on you.

Our Vision:
To be the best exhibition and convention centre in Asia internationally renowned for excellence and hosting the world's greatest events.

Our Mission:
To enable HKCEC's customers to consistently experience value and levels of service beyond their expectations through individual and team commitment to quality using innovative and creative operating techniques.

ORANGE COUNTY PERFORMING ARTS CENTER:

- To present the finest in performing arts to our community - a balance of quality international, national and regional performances of symphony, dance, musical theatre and opera.

- To broaden the base of understanding, appreciation and support for the performing arts in the community.

- To nurture the development of regional arts organizations that make The Center their performance base.

- To operate, maintain and endow this multi-purpose facility in accordance with the highest professional standards for both the audience and the performing arts.

FIGURE 1-6

 ## MISSION STATEMENTS

All public assembly facilities and their governing boards should have a well-thought-out, concise, and clearly written *mission statement* (See Figure 1.6 for examples). A facility's mission statement is a result of a collaborative process involving the facility's owner, governing body, and its manager and staff. If the professional staff is not included, the mission statement is being developed without the input and knowledge required to ultimately implement the plan.

The process is collaborative in the sense that through directed iterations, the collaborating group arrives at consensus on the facility's mission. By engaging in this group process, vital information is gained and shared relevant to the different perspectives of those involved. Subsequently, the probability of identifying and eliminating inaccurate or unrealistic expectations is significantly enhanced.

The ultimate goal of developing vision and mission statements is to produce statements specifying the facility's purpose. However, the resulting document also provides a basis for the governing body when making policy decisions regarding issues of scheduling, booking priorities, tenant oversight, reporting, budget development and competitive marketing strategies.

A clearly defined facility mission statement and accompanying objective(s), consistent with the vision, is the best foundation for effectively positioning this unique economic driver, the public assembly facility. The addition of effective operating policies and procedures that allow the facility's operating management team business flexibility to navigate and maneuver within the industry's competitive marketplace is necessary for the facility to reach its maximum potential.

SUMMARY

As with many business occupations, public assembly facility management is both an art and a science. However, public assembly facility management is unique due to its complicated need to find a way to blend public ownership and control with the tools needed to operate the enterprise in a competitive manner. The successful facility manager must know how to continuously and effectively navigate these tricky waters. Working hard to help the governing body appreciate the necessity for a business orientation and to provide the atmosphere required to achieve success are some of the manager's most critical responsibilities.

Public assembly facilities are important contributors to a community's social and economic development. These facilities vary in type and purpose and may be publicly or privately owned. In as much as public bodies fund most public assembly facilities, the governing boards of these facilities are typically composed of members appointed by the chief elected official or some other community official or body.

There are five basic forms of public assembly facility governance. With each form, the responsible entity can hire necessary personnel to manage and operate the facility. Each governance body should embrace an entrepreneurial philosophy and along with the facility manager strive to make a profit. Of course, financial operating results should correlate with the facility type and its owner's expectation regarding financial performance.

Contracting private management is an effective way for government to maintain overall control of a facility while delegating the actual management, marketing and operation of the facility to a private-sector company. However, when greater risk is assumed, the private operator will seek greater authority, management control and success incentives.

Academic institutions and non-profit organizations may have different governance structures. Nonetheless, the governance authority ultimately resides in the hands of the chief executive officer and the institution's/organization's governing board. It is important to understand that the term non-profit actually relates to tax status and not profit motivation.

Facility managers are in charge of the day-to-day operation, not the governing board. The governing board oversees the management and programming of the facility and sets its policy. The manager implements the policy.

Managers working for a public body must be able to effectively deal with an administrative department or some form of bureaucratic reporting structure. The manager must constantly strive to develop and maintain positive relationships with all departmental and board personnel. Given the basic difference in the nature of a public assembly facility versus governmental departments as well as the nature of politics itself, this may be a difficult and delicate task.

Regardless of type, all facilities have many common operating dynamics. Managers must possess an understanding of these dynamics and how they affect their facility as well as the effect they have on their competitors.

Successful governance requires financial diligence and a good measure of creativity. Some communities create special taxes or taxing districts designed to raise money specifically to subsidize public assembly facility operating budgets. Other communities impose an entertainment district tax or surcharge on ticket sales to accomplish the same financial assistance goal.

Competition within the public assembly facility business is fierce. Success is dependent upon governing boards allowing the facility manager to operate the enterprise in a business-like manner.

Each public assembly facility should have a mission statement created and periodically revised by its governing board. This document will clearly identify the purpose of the facility and provide a basis for the governing body when making policy decisions regarding issues of scheduling, booking priorities, tenant oversight, reporting, and budget development.

REFERENCES AND ADDITIONAL READINGS

Drucker, Peter. 1973. *Management: Tasks, Responsibilities, Practices*. New York, Harper & Row, p. 631.

Greenburg, Martin J. 2001. *The Stadium Game*, 2nd ed. Milwaukee, WI: ScheerGame.

IAAM (International Association of Assembly Managers, Inc.). 1994. *1994 IAAM Industry Profile Survey*. Coppell, TX: IAAM.

_____. 2003. *2003 IAAM Industry Profile Survey*. Coppell, TX: IAAM.

Jewell, Don. 1998. *Privatization of Public Assembly Facility Management: A History and Analysis*. Melbourne, FL: Krieger Publishing Company.

Petersen, David C. 2001. *Developing Sports, Convention and Performing Arts Centers*, 3rd ed. Washington, DC: Urban Land Institute.

2

ORGANIZATION AND MANAGEMENT

CHAPTER OUTLINE

INTRODUCTION

The challenge for all public assembly facilities is to organize for success. While at first glance this may seem simple, it is easier said than done. This challenge is compounded by the fact that most public assembly facility managers are under pressure from the owner to maximize both the event days the facility is in operation and the revenues generated while minimizing the cost to do so. In order to accomplish these objectives, the public assembly facility manager must manipulate variables such as time, space, monetary resources, and staffing.

The dynamic nature of the industry makes staffing very difficult because the manager must be able to assemble an "elastic" workforce in order to adjust to the different labor demands associated with each event booked. At the same time, the manager must be able to motivate a relatively small group of full-time employees to work extraordinarily long hours that very often fall on evenings, weekends, and holidays. In addition, to assemble an "elastic" workforce, the manager must be able to call upon the services of a large number of part-time and contractual service employees who are available on an "as needed" basis. All employees, full- and part-time alike, must be trained in their specific job responsibilities and must understand the need to be customer service oriented at all times. Although the assembly and maintenance of such a work force is difficult, it is necessary if the public assembly facility is to operate at peak performance.

VARIABLES FOR SUCCESS

There are a number of variables that will determine the success or failure of a public assembly facility. Quality management should be rated highest on the list. Aggressive marketing of the facility can influence the number of events that a facility hosts. But it is only through quality management that contracted services with tenants, event producers, and patrons can be delivered in a manner that meets or exceeds each group's expectations. Following the adoption of the public assembly facility's mission statement, it is the governing body's responsibility to create a top management team possessing the insight, intelligence, experience, and energy to bring the public assembly facility's mission objectives to fruition. Building such a management team may be referred to as "organizing for success." It is accomplished by first hiring a general manager. Although the title may be different among facilities, the major management functions are quite common.

The environment or setting in which a public assembly facility exists will affect the nature of its organization. A publicly owned assembly facility might be organized as a government department similar to city services departments such as public health or water and sewer. In this organizational context, the facility's general manager might be classified as a public employee who reports directly to another public official. An example is the facility manager being a department head reporting to a city manager.

Support services for a public assembly facility could be provided through various other departments. In such instances, the facility would be subject to the public agency's policies related to human resource management, purchasing, accounting, contracting for outsource services, etc. Some municipalities establish departments such as public events, parks and recreation, or facilities administration headed by a general manager and employ civil service personnel to operate it.

Regardless of the form of organization, it is necessary that all public assembly facility operations are able to identify the actual costs of running the facility and to ensure that the facility's management personnel abide by the governing body's rules and regulations. In some arrangements, the public assembly facility may be somewhat autonomous with its own dedicated staff and have the ability to outsource a variety of support services.

For the same reasoning as other public bodies, university public assembly facilities may be organized as a distinct, independent university department with its manager enjoying the same rank as other department managers within the institution. The manager might report through the institution's business affairs, student affairs, or athletics division. The general manager would follow general university procedures when dealing with personnel, banking, accounting, purchasing, and contracting with outside service providers. In these situations the university's physical plant may provide support services that are *billed back* or the assembly facility may self-operate independently.

Many publicly owned facilities operate under an authority or commission that is responsible for developing facility policies. The facility manager is given the power and responsibility for implementing these policies. Facilities organized in this manner allow the authority or commission the opportunity to take a more active management role. At the same time, the governing body should maintain focus on policy and oversight; generally, better results are achieved if governing boards are not involved in the day-to-day operations of the facility. The authority or commission must abide by the guidelines and regulatory statutes governing its operation. Those guidelines and regulations may differ depending upon where geographically the public assembly facility is located. In short, the authority or commission format is designed to minimize, as much as its governing statues will allow, the "red tape" that often goes hand-in-hand with governmental procedures.

Eliminating or reducing "red tape" allows the general manager the opportunity to operate the public assembly facility in much the same manner as executives in the private sector operate their businesses. Generally, the authority or commission form of operation is less politicized and decisions can be achieved in a more expeditious manner than when having to involve other governing councils in the deliberative process.

Whether ownership is public or private, privately managed public assembly facilities tend to be organized along the lines of dynamic entrepreneurial operations and are less subject to non-entrepreneurial government guidelines. Regardless of ownership, privately managed public assembly facilities tend to encounter less resistance to the implementation of competitive business concepts than their publicly managed counterparts. At one time, publicly operated assembly facilities were organized with a strong emphasis on protecting public assets and providing a venue for community activities. However, as publicly managed facilities strove to match the economic achievements of privatized public assembly facilities, this strategy gave way to placing more emphasis on gaining maximum net operating surplus or reducing subsidies. The difficulty is balancing profit and community service.

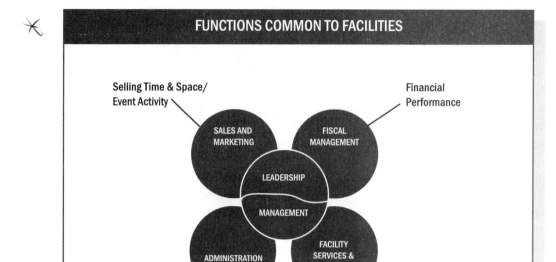

FIGURE 2-1

FUNCTIONS COMMON TO FACILITIES

Exactly how a facility is organized is determined by factors such as ownership, purpose and mission, and facility type. Nonetheless, all general managers face common tasks. (Figure 2-1 illustrates functions common to facilities). The five core functions evident in each facility are 1) administration, 2) sales and marketing, 3) facility services/operations, 4) fiscal management, and 5) leadership/management. While different public assembly venue configurations have special aspects that may make them unique, these five functions are vital to their operation.

The competitive nature of the public assembly facility business mandates that successful managers have the capacity to be strong, deliberate leaders in order to ensure the achievement of established performance objectives and effective management of the "time and space" elements. Successful managers are leaders who also effectively influence all aspects of the facility. The central and key element is the leadership/management of the facility; that is what ties these functions together.

While these functions exist in all venues, staffing and budget allocations may differ widely depending on the nature of the public assembly facility. Smaller venues have fewer employees and many of them are responsible for more than one function. In larger facilities each function may have one or more individuals assigned to it on a full-time basis. Other variables affecting the number of part- or full-time employees assigned to each of these units include the number of events, event types and sizes, and the audience demographic and dynamics.

For example, hosting a Rolling Stones concert in a stadium environment might well require hundreds of staff, including uniformed security officers, peer security staff, first aid staff, concessions workers, box office staff, a media credentialing team, stage crew, plus other personnel such as ticket takers, ushers, matrons, janitors, and parking lot attendants. On the other hand, a piano recital held in a smaller public assembly facility might only require the services of the house manager, a security guard, and a stage manager. Nonetheless, the operating dynamics are similar regardless of an event's size. The only difference is found in the scale of application.

(Figures 2-2 and 2-3 present possible organizational charts illustrating the relationship of positions and their reporting lines typically found in a public assembly facility). While all of these functions/tasks must be performed, it is not unusual that individuals may be assigned to more than one of these areas. The functions/tasks may be basically common with all facility types, but the actual organizational structures will vary significantly depending on variables including facility size, location, type of event, form of governance and organization, and the facility's physical aspects.

FIGURE 2-2

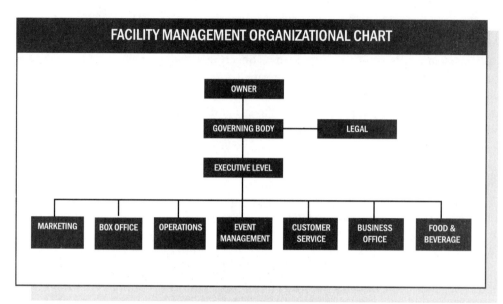

FIGURE 2-3

ADMINISTRATION

Regardless of facility ownership, the on-site management personnel are typically under the supervision of a general manager who may also be known as executive director, managing director, vice president and general manager, etc. This individual must wear a multitude of hats and must be a conduit between the facility and the community; a liaison between the governing body and the facility's staff; and, an administrative supervisor, mentor, and leader. Although balancing available resources to achieve the facility's mission is the general manager's primary responsibility, a successful manager must also become the governing body's prime resource, the user's partner, the staff's leader, and the patrons' advocate and sympathetic ear. (Figure 2-4 outlines daily operational areas pertinent to all types of facilities).

HUMAN RESOURCES

The human resources (HR) function, often referred to as personnel, is extremely important to public assembly facilities. Only the largest public assembly facilities have full time HR directors. More often, this function is shared by several departments with responsibility for activities such as the recruitment, hiring, and termination of employees; the maintenance of all personnel records; ensuring that the organization is in compliance with all government rules and regulations affecting employees; and for filing all required reports to government agencies. In those public assembly facilities that have personnel directors, they would be involved directly or indirectly in managing employee performance evaluations and mediating disputes between employees and/or supervisors. In con-

OUTLINE OF DAILY OPERATIONAL AREAS PERTINENT TO ALL TYPES OF PUBLIC ASSEMBLY FACILITIES

ADMINISTRATION

- Preparing reports and presentations for owners.
- Monitoring the operating budget.
- Overseeing daily building activities.
- Service contracts and tenant leasing issues.

BOOKINGS AND EVENT SCHEDULING

- Rental and rate schedules.
- Promoting and co-promoting events.
- Negotiating individual lease issues.

EVENT MANAGEMENT

- Detailed event production-meetings and facility walkthroughs.
- Providing event services as needed.

SALES AND MARKETING

- Marketing facility to prospective tenants, shows and events.
- Marketing facility to general public, government, business, industry, etc.
- Marketing of events.

FOOD AND BEVERAGE/ CATERING/MERCHANDISE

- Customer service and sales.
- Inventory management.
- Food handling safety.

BOX OFFICE AND TICKETING

- Training, quality control, supervision.
- Use of electronic ticketing inventory and financial controls.

SAFETY AND SECURITY

- Crowd Management.
- Providing building safety and security.
- Emergency Preparedness..
- Risk Management.
- Customer and employee safety and security.

HUMAN RESOURCES/PERSONNEL

- Staff recruitment and training.
- Resolution of personnel issues.
- Application and enforcement of employment regulations and statutes.
- Record keeping.

OPERATIONS/ENGINEERING

- Physical plant repair and maintenance.
- Facility equipment maintenance and repair.

HOUSEKEEPING

CUSTOMER SERVICE

- Providing for customer comfort and satisfaction.
- Resolving complaints.
- "Meet, greet, and direct."

FIGURE 2-4

sultation with the accounting/payroll department, the personnel department may maintain benefit records such as sick days, vacation time, tax deductions, and medical and dental insurance enrollments and keep the employees informed of any changes to their retirement program.

TYPICAL JOB DESCRIPTIONS

Similarities exist not only in the organization of the basic functions of public assembly facilities, but also in individual management positions. For example, all facilities, regardless of configuration, have an individual (e.g., general manager) who oversees the total operation of the facility. This individual, no matter the title, is the chief hired hand. While ownership and governing structures, facility type, geographical location, target

DESCRIPTIONS OF MANAGEMENT POSITIONS ADAPTED FROM IAAM POSITION DESCRIPTION HANDBOOK

GENERAL MANAGER

- Initiates and provides direction for planning administration and operational management of facility.
- Responsible for physical plant facilities and equipment.
- Responsible for finances and personnel, consistent with goals and directives of corporation.
- Provides leadership and direction to subordinate operating departments, management, and staff.
- Coordinates and executes plans and directives.
- Continues liaison with corporate staff, industry associates, governing agencies, communication mediums, and public.
- Determines and establishes organizational structure and personnel staffing requirements; imposes and directs the structure for effective and efficient utilization of personnel.

OPERATIONS MANAGER

- Provides overall administrative planning.
- Provides direction and policies to operating managers.
- Assures highest quality service program to assure rebooking of events.
- Ensures an effective and cost-efficient program by controlling the operating budget.
- Coordinates all elements of facility operation.
- Directs operation of personnel, payroll, billing, insurance, accounting, budget, data processing, and purchasing.
- Plans and directs operation and maintenance of mechanical, electrical, HVAC, custodial, grounds, event set-up and changeovers, sound, lighting, stagehands, security, traffic control, and patron services.

FOOD AND BEVERAGE DIRECTOR

- Under general direction of General Manager.
- Oversees all aspects of food and beverage service provided by facility.

SALES AND MARKETING DIRECTOR

- Reports to General Manager.
- Works with minimum supervision and direction to initiate contact with promoters/presenters/producers/planners.
- In cooperation with the General Manager, is responsible for booking and scheduling of the facility.
- Works to enhance image of facility and promote good will in community through media releases and promotions.
- Communicates daily with the General Manager to discuss new ideas to promote the facility.
- Manages group sales.
- Manages media/public relations.
- Manages sales of commercial rights.
- May manage in-house ad agency.
- Oversees content development for website.

BOX OFFICE SUPERVISOR

- Reports to Finance Director.
- Responsible for day-to-day affairs of box office and supervises ticket selling and cash management functions in coordination with promoter and building personnel.
- Assists the Finance Director as required.
- Directs operations of finance department and box office.
- Supervises the box office, accounting, payroll, and pay parking program functions.

FINANCE DIRECTOR/BUSINESS MANAGER

- Reports to General Manager.
- Supervises ongoing accounting procedures relative to operation of the facility.
- Prepares routine financial and operational reconciliations, reports, and settlements.
- Maintains formal accounting systems, including accounts payable/receivable, payroll, purchasing, insurance/risk management, internal audits, and event settlements.
- Supervises organization of accounting records and files.
- Supervises preparation of regular reports and reconciliations including event settlement.
- Prepares budget-related materials.
- Supervises office support staff and employee relations.
- Maintains log of wage analysis, project lists, and purchase orders.

EVENT MANAGER

- Position reports directly to the Director of Operations.
- Plans, organizes, and controls events within facility as assigned and prepares event outlines and scaled drawings of event areas; coordinates equipment distribution and event billing.
- Oversees all event coordination tasks after events are booked through their conclusion.
- Ensures tenant requirements are met and facility rules, regulations, and policies are adhered to.
- Assists tenants in planning their own events.
- Serves as a liaison between the facility and tenants.
- Assists in revising operational plans; recommends changes in personnel and procedures.

SPECIAL POSITIONS

- Stage Manager
- Groundskeeper
- Loading Dock Foreman
- Information Technology Coordinator
- Patron Services Manager
- Concierge, VIP Areas
- Party/Special Event Attendants

FIGURE 2-5

market, and the facility's mission are variables that affect the management philosophy for a specific facility, all managers must, nonetheless, assume some common responsibilities. How these activities are organized and managed will affect both the quantity and type of business available to and booked by the facility. (Figure 2-5 provides various descriptions of management positions).

SPECIAL POSITIONS

Some positions are only found in certain types of public assembly facilities because they serve a specific purpose related to program or facility type. Included in the special category are positions such as computer system administrators, graphic designers, special project coordinators, and volunteer coordinators. Facilities that rely heavily on computerized booking/scheduling, accounting, payroll, and/or ticketing may need an on-site information technology (IT) and computer systems administrator to deal with data lines, computer/printer installations, software installation, equipment maintenance and repair, system expansion and upgrading, and any other issues related to these operations, including in-house and external ticket outlets. In most instances, this employee would also be responsible for issues related to the Internet. It is also possible to have all, or a portion of each of these functions provided by outside vendors.

VOLUNTEERS/VOLUNTEER DIRECTOR

It is not unusual for performing arts and auditorium facilities to use a significant number of *volunteers*. The use of volunteers is generally restricted to *front-of-house* activities such as ushering, greeting and ticket taking. For example, university performing arts and auditorium facilities, particularly those with a strong student participation mission, will often employ someone either part- or full-time to supervise the student volunteers. Many community-based theatre workshops engage the services of volunteers to assist in their operation. In such instances, a coordinator of volunteers might be hired, or a member of the management team may be assigned the task of organizing, training, and supervising the various volunteers

However, facility managers must be cognizant of all rules and regulations governing the use of volunteers especially if the facility is a *union shop*. A large percentage of public assembly facility employees are unionized. Whether or not volunteers may be used and under what conditions is addressed in the union contract. Unions might view volunteers as threats because the unpaid volunteer is filling a position that could be filled by a paid union member.

It is critical that the public assembly facility manager and the director of human resources be conversant with the terms of all union contracts and abide by those terms. It is also important that good communications exist between venue management and union representatives. Many issues can be resolved with minimal disruption if both the facility management and union representatives are able to work together in a friendly, respectful, and cooperative atmosphere to achieve a mutually agreeable resolution to issues.

TECHNICAL SERVICES DIRECTOR

Virtually all performing arts centers and auditoriums employ a director of technical services who is responsible for a host of activities that directly influence each performance. Setting up stage equipment; directing stagehands before, during, and after the performance; striking equipment; designing and building props; and the development of lighting diagrams are some of the technical director's responsibilities. The complexity of these tasks requires the services of an individual who is dedicated to the job, who possesses significant technical knowledge, and who is very familiar with the facility.

Some special positions exist today either because of societal changes or changes in the way business is conducted. For example, technological advancements have expanded communication vehicles to include cell phones, e-mail, instant messaging, multiple party conference phone calls, fax machines, video conferencing, and personal digital assistants. Even the delivery of postal materials has experienced a tremendous transformation. Using either government or privately operated postal services, it is possible to have letters and packages delivered to almost any city worldwide within one day. The availability and common use of these communication vehicles, many of which were once considered luxuries, have created a new set of communication expectations by public assembly facility users. Therefore, it is important for technical support staff to provide ancillary operations, such as a business center in a convention center, that support and provide for the customer's communication expectations. More and more business centers are becoming a part of a larger percentage of public assembly facilities.

DEVELOPMENT DIRECTOR

Effective fund raising may make the difference between a budget deficit and financial solvency for many public assembly facilities. It is imperative that facility managers understand the necessity and importance of external fund raising as well as developing other ancillary revenue sources. Managers who lack the time or requisite skills must recognize the need to hire a development director in order to maximize their facility's potential for attracting external funding at the local, regional, and national levels.

During periods of fiscal austerity, government organized and funded public assembly facilities, and those operated by non-profit organizations, tend not to receive sufficient financial resources to fully operate and manage their venues. Consequently, these underfunded entities are confronted with either raising additional capital to meet the full funding requirements of their public assembly facility or cutting back on their program offerings and/or services provided. The search for supplemental monies has resulted in a tremendous increase in the competition for the awarding of financial support through government and private sector grants, endowments, and philanthropic foundations.

Many public assembly facility managers have discovered that in order to successfully compete for these various awards, they must employ an individual whose prime, if not sole, responsibility is to secure external funding. This person is frequently referred to as a development director and is often based in the marketing department. A growing source of external funding is through the solicitation of program and event sponsorships and the awarding of naming rights to the public assembly facility, rooms within the facility, and to individual sponsored programs.

Businesses, corporations, and private individuals willing to pay a specified amount of money to have a particular building, room, program, or event carry their name may exist within a public assembly facility's geographic region. For example, the Fleet Center in Boston, Massachusetts, is named for the Fleet Mortgage Company while the Delta Center in Salt Lake City, Utah, is named for Delta Airlines. The Koger Center for the Arts is named after Ira and Nancy Koger, who donated a significant amount of money for the facility's construction at the University of South Carolina.

Another example might be a symphony performance being sponsored by a corporation doing business in the geographic area. Sponsorships of this nature provide excellent advertising opportunities along with projecting a sense of good corporate citizenship. Foundations often sponsor particular programs or events.

There is a potential downside to this form of fund raising in that the purchaser of the naming rights or the sponsor of an event may lose their financial standing and not be able to fulfill their financial agreement. Or, in some instances, the sponsor may become entangled in social or legal issues that may seriously diminish their appeal to the community and the customers of the public assembly facility. The same situation also can occur with a long-term advertiser.

LUXURY SEATING DIRECTOR

Many newer public assembly facilities provide luxury seating in the form of suites or boxes. Individuals or corporations may lease these special seating areas for significantly higher prices than regular ticket purchases would cost. However, in paying the higher fees, the suite or box holder is able to use the seating to entertain personal or business guests in a special environment. Thus, the availability of these special seating areas allows the facility to generate significantly greater money per seat than they could from "regular" seating. The significance of this potential revenue stream is illustrated by virtue of the fact a specific organization exists for this field — the Association of Luxury Suite Directors (www.alsd.com).

Included in the category of full-time employees are usually general managers, department managers, supervisors, administrative, operations, and maintenance personnel. Event staffs are typically made up of part-time employees trained to perform in certain supervised roles during events such as ushers, ticket takers, ticket sellers, stagehands, concession workers, decorators, caterers, banquet servers, parking attendants, housekeepers, security, and customer service representatives. However, in larger facilities, and depending on the program, some departments using mostly part-time positions may also require a number of full-time positions. These might include ticket sellers, stagehands, security staff, and parking attendants.

SALES, MARKETING, ADVERTISING AND PROMOTION

Regardless of type of public assembly facility, the effective use of marketing, advertising, and promotion is crucial in order to favorably present the venue to potential users and customers. Marketing is a term that is often used interchangeably with other related terms such as promotion and advertising. The term marketing has been defined in many ways. However, when used within the content of public assembly facility management, marketing can be interpreted to include the process of searching out and identifying potential business for a facility (see Chapter 4 for the American Marketing Association's definition of marketing). Marketing also might include involvement in the process of negotiating an agreement for and/or booking an event.

It can be argued there are two basic areas addressed by marketing in the public assembly facility industry. One is the marketing of the facility and its program generally. The second area is the marketing to groups or marketing a specific event or series of events (e.g., season tickets). The latter marketing effort is directed toward target audiences, advertises specific activity, time, place, dates, prices, etc. This is where the more typical tasks of advertising and promotion are involved.

Marketing the facility itself is directed at potential users, the community in general, owner's representatives (e.g., city councils), and appropriate industry members. In addition, it is very important to market the facility and its programs internally to staff, the governing body, owners, and other major stakeholders. These individuals need to understand the vision, mission, goals, and objectives of facility management and how it applies to the specific facility. The operating and event staffs are the individuals on the front line interacting with the patrons. They can "make or break" the facility's image, program, and ultimate success.

FISCAL MANAGEMENT AND THE BUSINESS DYNAMIC

Every facility has a business dynamic that includes budgeting, financial accounting, fiscal management, payroll, purchasing, and inventory control. These functions may be under a department called the business office, administration, finance/accounting department, or some other name. The accounting and auditing aspects of revenue-generating activities normally come under the direct supervision of this business office. Business offices often provide accounting and auditing services to the public assembly facility's ticketing activities, especially if financial transactions with the tenant are tied to ticket sales, event contracting, and settlements.

Public assembly facilities, regardless of type, should have a business office, or at least one designated individual, available and prepared to handle large amounts of cash. Collecting and accounting for cash, checks, and credit card revenues from ticket sales, making bank deposits, and completing post-event financial settlements with event promoters are typical activities performed by business offices or the facility's designated individual. The designated individual might be the box office manager, the food and beverage manager, the merchandise manager, or the parking manager. Other business office responsibilities may include the preparation, distribution, collection, and *reconciliation* of cash boxes used in the concessions and ancillary sales operation, or these tasks may be handled directly by the involved department (e.g., box office). The ultimate responsibility lies with the facility manager.

Cash has traditionally been the most frequent form of payment for concessions, parking, and merchandise by patrons at public assembly facilities. Ticket sales, however, are moving toward electronic and credit purchase and the consuming public's prolific use of credit cards to pay for telephone, online, and on-site purchases has resulted in many public assembly facilities accepting this form of payment also. (This will be discussed further in Chapter 5 — Ticketing and Box Office Management.)

OPERATIONS AND PHYSICAL PLANT

Along with general maintenance and housekeeping duties of the physical plant, the public assembly facility's operations department is usually responsible for the facility's heating, ventilation, and air conditioning (HVAC); groundskeeping; security and life safety; and a unique unit often referred to as the event production or stage unit. For most touring attractions, it is not economical to bring their own production personnel such as loaders, riggers, stagehands, deck hands, and forklift operators. Consequently, public assembly facilities are expected to provide these personnel to meet the production needs of those events requiring such services.

Thus, the facility operations become the critical unit ensuring that "The Show Must Go On." In busy facilities with frequent *changeovers* of multiple types of events, (e.g., basketball, hockey, concerts, rodeo, wrestling, motor sports, and exhibitions) a skilled and motivated operations department carries enormous responsibilities in meeting the facility's contractual obligations and need for competent and quality customer service. (This is covered in depth in Chapter 9 — Facility Services and Operations).

SAFETY

For all events involving the general public, safety is a major responsibility of the public assembly facility manager. Although patrons may appear to be the primary focus of such concern, it is important to understand that the public assembly facility manager must also take appropriate and reasonable measures to ensure the safety of the facility's staff, tenants, vendors, and any other occupants. The local fire department may assign a fire marshal to review and approve all floor plans for shows with exhibits that use an exhibit hall or meeting room or stage events using flashpots or pyrotechnics. This is done to ensure that the aisles are wide enough to handle the anticipated attendance, that exits are kept clear of exhibit materials or other barriers, and that other safety issues of this nature are addressed and satisfied. When a fire marshal is assigned to a public assembly facility, the facility may pay a fee for the service. The facility in turn may pass this charge along to the user.

While the stage or operation manager is responsible for managing the production labor force, including casual labor, the house security manager is responsible for the management of security personnel. Besides the normal uniformed and, perhaps, plain clothed security personnel, ticket takers, ushers, vendors, and parking personnel, by virtue of their direction and crowd control functions, the house security manager also has a role in creating and maintaining a safe environment. Some public assembly facilities outsource their security operations. The decision to outsource or alternatively to provide in-house security staff depends on a number of variables such as cost, programming, and the ability to provide sufficient personnel in an efficient and effective manner. Other forms of security such as night patrols (e.g., watchmen) unrelated to specific facility events, first aid, and emergency evacuation might also be the responsibility of the security unit. Facility managers must also work closely with local fire and police departments as well as local hospitals and emergency medical providers to ensure proper and complete safety and security for all in attendance at the facility.

WORKING WITH REGULATORY AGENCIES

In order to have an established, organized, consistent relationship with regulatory agencies, it is important to have policies and procedures in place. (Figure 2-6 is a sample policy). A policy such as this could apply to all agencies/organizations with regulatory power applicable to public assembly facilities. If a law or valid regulation included the

---

**SAMPLE INTERNATIONAL CENTER
REGULATORY AGENCY POLICY/PROCEDURES**

Date: _____

The following policy statement and procedures are effective immediately:

POLICY

1. It is the policy of the International Center to be in compliance with all laws, rules and regulations as they apply to occupational health and safety.

2. It is the policy of the International Center to cooperate with (agency) in the latter's fulfilling its duties and obligations under the laws, rules and regulations.

PROCEDURES

- (Name, title) has been designated the primary person for the implementation of International Center's health and safety programs.

- The (title) will meet with (agency) inspectors at mutually convenient times to review and/or respond to appropriate items.

- It is necessary (agency) inspectors make an appointment to meet with the (title) and/or other employees prior to coming onto the International Center's premises.

- Only the (President, General Manager) or the (designated primary person) may schedule other employees to meet with (agency) inspectors.

Employees are directed to refer all questions and requests to the (designated primary person) unless otherwise directed.

FIGURE 2-6

right to entry at anytime by authorized personnel, that would, of course override the facility policy. Even so, the facility should have policies and procedures in place that make it clear to employees and others who might become involved that the facility intends to comply while at the same time having orderly, cooperative procedures in place.

✗ MANAGERIAL LEADERSHIP

No matter how the facility management is organized, operating a public assembly facility on a daily basis is very demanding and requires a manager who possesses a unique intelligence combination of a strong IQ (traditional intelligence quotient) and an equally strong EQ (emotional intelligence quotient). These combined forms of intelligence provide the ability to acquire the knowledge base from which the manager can draw upon in order to skillfully manage. Public assembly facility managers who are not capable of quickly recognizing and appropriately responding to existing or foreseeable situations, especially when under pressure, will not survive. Good managers tend to be people-oriented, inquisitive, eager to learn and apply new management and business principles, and intensely devoted to fulfilling their job responsibilities. And in today's competitive environment, the successful manager must also be intelligent, responsive, knowledgeable, persistent, flexible, ethical, and an excellent motivator and leader of superior staff. (Figures 2-7 and 2-8 provide examples of codes of ethics applicable to public assembly facility managers).

Successful facility managers possess an extensive understanding of each managerial function associated with the operation of a public assembly facility. Very importantly, they also understand how the facility is organized and how that impacts the operational alternatives. Managers of this stature have acquired their knowledge and experience through varying scenarios. In some cases, a manager may have "come up through the ranks," advancing from an entry-level position to higher or different positions within the organizational structure and then eventually being elevated to facility manager. This form of career development generally ensures that the individual has had personal involvement with many of the facility's operational units and, in all probability, has had the opportunity to work with facility contractual agreements and the process of conducting financial settlements.

Other managers may have developed their careers by starting at mid-level management positions such as facility operations, marketing, or promotions and then being promoted to facility manager. Although "on-the-job training" has proven an effective way to gain information, it is neither the only nor perhaps the most efficient method. Similar to trial and error, on-the-job training can sometimes be painful and expensive compared to a well-structured training program. It is critical that the facility's management structure be organized in such a way to include strong, consistent, effective training programs. These programs need to be customized to the job functions, education, and experience levels of the employees involved. Cross training by moving personnel around the various departments is an excellent way in which to impart and continue institutional knowledge within the staff. However, even though there is an element of on-the-job training in all management career development routes, other educational opportunities exist that can impart lifelong learning.

INTERNATIONAL CITY/COUNTY MANAGEMENT ASSOCIATION
CODE OF ETHICS

1. Be dedicated to the concepts of effective and democratic local government by responsible elected officials and believe that professional general management is essential to the achievement of this objective.

2. Affirm the dignity and worth of the services rendered by government and maintain a constructive, creative, and practical attitude toward local government affairs and a deep sense of social responsibility as a trusted public servant.

3. Be dedicated to the highest ideals of honor and integrity in all public and personal relationships in order that the member may merit the respect and confidence of the elected officials, of other officials and employees, and of the public.

4. Recognize that the chief function of local government at all times is to serve the best interests of all of the people.

5. Submit policy proposals to elected officials; provide them with facts and advice on matters of policy as a basis for making decisions and setting community goals; and uphold and implement local government policies adopted by elected officials.

6. Recognize that elected representatives of the people are entitled to the credit for the establishment of local government policies; responsibility for policy execution rests with the members.

7. Refrain from all political activities which undermine public confidence in professional administrators. Refrain from participation in the election of the members of the employing legislative body.

8. Make it a duty continually to improve the member's professional ability and to develop the competence of associates in the use of management techniques.

9. Keep the community informed on local government affairs; encourage communication between the citizens and all local government officers; emphasize friendly and courteous service to the public; and seek to improve the quality and image of public service.

10. Resist any encroachment on professional responsibilities, believing the member should be free to carry out official policies without interference, and handle each problem without discrimination on the basis of principle and justice.

11. Handle all matters of personnel on the basis of merit so that fairness and impartiality govern a member's decisions pertaining to appointments, pay adjustments, promotions, and discipline.

12. Seek no favor; believe that personal aggrandizement or profit secured by confidential information or by misuse of public time is dishonest.

Reprinted with permission of the International/City County Management Association, 777 N. Capitol St. NE, Ste. 500, Washington, DC 20002. All rights reserved.

FIGURE 2-7

CREATIVE ENTREPRENEURS

Even though a facility's mission may not emphasize the creation of new revenue centers or new revenue streams, skilled facility managers will focus energies toward becoming creative and entrepreneurial in seeking out opportunities that will serve to maximize the facility's resources and thereby generate additional income. The creative manager knows how to package a public assembly facility in a way that is attractive to businesses, promoters, and patrons. And the entrepreneurial manager knows how to devise and implement marketing and promotional strategies capable of producing favorable financial results. Increasingly, bottom line financial data are used to evaluate both the manager's and the facility's success or failure. Consequently, both the manager and the facility run the risk of elimination if they do not achieve the economic expectation and thus become an economic drain on their funding source(s).

IAAM CODE OF ETHICS

- Strive for continued improvement in the proficiency and usefulness of service.

- Maintain the highest ideals of honor and integrity in all public and personal relationships.

- Emphasize friendly and courteous service to the public and recognize that the function of the building is at all times to serve the best interest of the public.

- Exercise fair and impartial judgment in all Association and professional business dealings.

- Maintain the principle of fairness to all.

- Have a firm belief in the dignity and worth of service rendered by the building and have a constructive, creative, and practical attitude.

- Refrain from any activity that may be in conflict with the interest of the employer.

FIGURE 2-8

EFFECTIVE COMMUNICATOR

Effective communication is a key element in successful facility management. Public assembly facility managers must be able to effectively communicate with distinct groups: the owner(s) and governing body, staff, users, attendees and the community at large. It is the manager's responsibility to develop and maintain direct and efficient two-way lines of verbal and written communication with each of these groups.

The successful manager is a team leader who can work effectively in the present environment while envisioning and preparing for the future; is a consummate advocate of the public assembly facility and its potential; and is aggressive in striving to achieve announced goals. Managers' visions should both inspire and motivate all within the organization. In addition, the successful manager is not only efficient and productive but also skilled in dealing with delegation of responsibilities, discipline, organization, and creativity. The successful manager announces and abides by a personal code of ethics and demands the same from all employees. The successful public assembly facility manager leads by example.

PROFESSIONAL ASSOCIATIONS AND CONTINUING EDUCATION

The International Association of Assembly Managers (IAAM) (www.iaam.org) offers numerous professional development programs designed to create the knowledge and develop the professional skills of both current and aspiring facility managers.

Participation in these programs and similar programs of allied industries also assists the student with developing an expanded network of colleagues. (Appendix D includes contact information for IAAM and related industry groups).

Programs are available for individuals employed in entry-level public assembly facility positions seeking to develop a career path as well as for the executive level managers wishing to expand their professional education. The IAAM's Public Assembly Facility Management School (PAFMS) at Oglebay Resort in Wheeling, West Virginia, is the only program of its type in North America. Its courses focus on providing the student with information central to the operation and purpose of each function within a public assembly facility. The Senior Executive Symposium held at Cornell University in Ithaca, New York, is focused towards the needs of executive managers. The IAAM also presents the Leadership Institute that is designed to fill the gap between the PAFMS program and the Senior Executive Symposium by focusing on the development of leadership rather than managerial skills. The dynamic nature of the public assembly facility business perpetuates the need for each of these programs in order to disseminate new concepts and practices designed to increase management consistency, effectiveness, and efficiency throughout the industry.

The IAAM also offers a professional certification program. This program involves the study of extensive industry information assembled by the IAAM which serves to expose the manager to core knowledge components instrumental in successfully managing a facility. To attain certification from this program, candidates must complete the core study component and then successfully satisfy a personal interview and a comprehensive written examination. Successful candidates are accorded the professional status of Certified Facilities Executive (CFE). The CFE designation is intended to say three important things about facility executives: they are skilled managers, are committed to the industry, and are pledged to continued professional growth and development. Managers who have completed the CFE program are recognized by those within and external to the industry as experts in their profession.

Other educational meetings are devised to address specific topics in response to current events. For example, following terrorist attacks of September 11, 2001, on the New York City World Trade Center, the Pentagon in Washington, DC, and the downing of American Airlines flight #93 in Pennsylvania, the IAAM developed several special seminars that focused on security and crowd management. These were a continuation and expansion of IAAM's crowd management programs. It is crucial that public assembly facility managers understand how current events may serve as a catalyst for change, sometimes rapid change, with respect to the principles and practices associated with public assembly facility management. Finally, a host of management conferences dedicated to the various facility types (stadiums, arenas, performing arts venues, convention centers, university venues) concerning specific and timely topics are also available. Advanced technology has allowed some of these seminars to be delivered through audio-Internet conferencing, a format that enables the participants to verbally and visually interact with those presenting the seminar.

The IAAM is divided into districts. Each district sponsors an annual district meeting and seminars on contemporary management issues for middle management and operations personnel. Members are encouraged to participate in these seminars. The IAAM also sponsors an annual conference and trade show that features internationally recognized speakers, panel discussion sessions, and workshop activities focusing on topics of importance to the public assembly facility industry.

In addition, the IAAM and the IAAM Foundation have fostered a direct relationship with higher education through assistance with the designing of college curricula, development of study materials, and making available financial grants for the conduct of industry specific research. Entry into this realm of education by the IAAM is significant because, in the past, colleges and universities had independently developed facility management courses that were included among required core courses for degree granting curricula such as sport management, sport and entertainment management, sport administration, art administration, performing arts management, and convention and meeting planning.

SUMMARY

The public assembly facility is a complex organization that requires the delicate balancing and leveraging of many relationships. Managers of public assembly facilities must be effective leaders who are self-motivated and focused. They must be well equipped through knowledge, education, and experience to accept the challenges presented by new events, new technology, and changing societal practices and standards and using them as vehicles to enhance both the image and productivity of the facility.

The public assembly facility manager understands it is neither safe nor productive to subscribe to the "build it and they will come" theory. While the building may serve as the physical site for accommodating events, it is the quality and efficiency of the personnel employed by the facility that determines the satisfaction level perceived by the facility's various users. This team must be carefully constructed employing both full-time and part-time personnel possessing varied skill sets and who understand their role in providing a positive experience for all users.

It is extremely important to understand that personnel employed in the lowest level position on the organizational chart typically have the greatest number of personal contacts with the facility's users. And quite often it is these individuals, many of whom may be part-time employees, who establish through their interaction the basis for an event attendee's positive or negative perception of the public assembly facility and the events it presents.

To re-emphasize, the public assembly facility manager is responsible for the organization's five core functions: administration, sales and marketing, facility services/operations, fiscal management, and leadership/management. Additionally, the manager must act as a leader to ensure that each function area is properly staffed and that it performs at the level necessary for the facility to achieve its performance objectives.

Simply put, organizing for success starts at the top of the organization. Public assembly facility managers committed to this principle are well on the way to developing an efficient team of employees and to establishing a positive relationship with all of the communities involved.

REFERENCES AND ADDITIONAL READINGS

Allison, Michael and Jude Kaye. 1997. *Strategic Planning for Nonprofit Organizations: A Practical Guide and Workbook*. Hoboken, NJ: John Wiley & Sons, Inc.

Bryson, John M. and Farnum K. Alston. 1995. *Creating and Implementing Your Strategic Plan: A Workbook for Public and Nonprofit Organizations*, 2nd ed. San Francisco: Jossey-Bass.

Bradford, Robert. 1995. *Simplified Strategic Planning: A No-Nonsense Guide for Busy People Who Want Results Fast!* Worcester, MA: Chandler House Press.

Cohen, Allan R. 2002. *The Portable MBA in Management*. Hoboken, NJ: John Wiley & Sons, Inc.

Condrey, Stephen E. (Editor). 1998. *Handbook of Human Resource Management in Government San Francisco*: Jossey-Bass.

Cox, Terry B. 1996. *Managing in a Competitive Environment Participant's Guide (Performance Through Participation)*. New York: Van Nostrand Reinhold.

Desseler, Gary. 2002. *Human Resource Management*, 9th ed. Upper Saddle River, NJ: Prentice Hall.

Drucker, Peter F. 1992. *Managing the Non-Profit Organization: Principles and Practices*. New York: Harper Business.

Ellis, Susan J. 2002. *The Volunteer Recruitment (and Membership Development) Book* 3rd ed. Philadelphia, PA: Energize Books.

Fogg, C. Davis. 1994. *Team-Based Strategic Planning: A Complete Guide to Structuring, Facilitating and Implementing the Process*. New York: AMACOM.

George, Stephen and Arnold Weimerskirch. 1998. *Total Quality Management: Strategies and Techniques*. Hoboken, NJ: John Wiley and Sons, Inc.

Jewell, Don. 2003. *Public Assembly Facilities*, 3rd ed. Coppell, TX: International Association of Assembly Managers, Inc..

Lee, Jarene F., Julia M. Catagnus and Susan J. Ellis (Editors). 1998. *What We Learned (The Hard Way) About Supervising Volunteers. Collective Wisdom Series.* Philadelphia, PA: Energize Books.

Little, Helen. 1999. *Volunteers: How to Get Them, How to Keep Them.* Naperville, IL: Panacea Press.

Robbins, Stephen P. 2002. *Essentials of Organizational Behavior*, 7th ed. Upper Saddle River, NJ: Prentice Hall.

Wilber, Robert H. (Editor). 1997. *The Complete Guide to Nonprofit Management.* Hoboken, NJ: John Wiley and Sons, Inc.

3

SCHEDULING FACILITIES AND BOOKING EVENTS

CHAPTER OUTLINE

INTRODUCTION

Since time and space are the primary commodities of the public assembly facility, it is essential to understand the value of these assets and their perishable nature. Accordingly, the scheduling calendar which manages the facility's space and time is the most important tool for the booking manager to utilize in controlling these assets. This instrument and its inventory of dates must be closely managed with uncompromising integrity and accuracy to maximize profitability and minimize negative client relations.

This chapter examines the principles and practices of scheduling and booking events, industry relationships, and the processes that are required to secure event activity. Discussions include the development and sequencing of the scheduling calendar, fitting events into the calendar, and the involvement of the convention and visitors bureau in sales. Issues related to the establishment of scheduling priorities, the First Amendment rights of the United States Constitution, and the holding and contracting of dates are discussed. Attention is also directed toward booking errors, block booking, the potential risks and liabilities associated with scheduling and booking, and other aspects of the scheduling and booking processes.

CLIENT/TENANT RELATIONS

Two key ingredients to successful facility management are leverage and relationships. Nowhere is this statement more appropriate than in the booking and scheduling of the public assembly facility, particularly the relationship element. Financial risk hovers over every attraction, performance, show, or event. However, few facility managers are positioned, either financially or politically, to take on the role and associated financial risks of the commercial event promoter, at least not on a consistent basis. Exceptions are the performing arts facility managers who, more out of necessity than choice, frequently assume the role and risks of the promoter. For some performing arts events, the cost of talent combined with production and advertising expenses frequently exceed box office receipts. Yet, if the performing arts facility is to stay in operation, the manager must assume the risk of incurring a financial loss with the hope of making up the difference through donations from benefactors or from the next performance. An alternative would be to keep the facility *dark*. While electing this alternative might represent the best financial decision, it might also be in direct conflict with the facility's mission statement and financial expectation.

A large number of public assembly facility owners envision the bulk of their business will come from renting or leasing facility space through short-term contracts to private promoters for the purpose of staging an attraction for which booth space or rights to admission are sold. In this business model, the facility gains income from the rental/lease fees as well as from the *ancillary revenue streams* generated by the attraction, such as parking, food and beverage, catering, and novelty sales. The promoter assumes responsibility for the expenses associated with delivering the act, such as rental/lease fees, equipment charges, advertising and promotion costs, taxes, talent costs, etc. The promoter only makes a profit when receipts are greater than the expenses.

Many conferences, conventions, meetings, assemblies, concerts, trade shows, and exhibitions are presented through variations of this model. The straight rental/lease model is popular with public assembly facility managers because it shields the facility from financial risk and assures net income if the lease is properly managed. However, for this model to work, it requires a willing promoter. Since there are far more facilities available for rental/lease than attractions to present, it is extremely important that the public assembly facility manager cultivate and maintain a positive relationship with each event promoter. Without an event promoter, the facility manager has but two choices: assume the promoter's role and the associated financial risks or keep the public assembly facility dark. While the underlying premise of the above statement is valid, it is not applicable in all instances. It does not matter how many facilities are available regionally, nationally, or worldwide. What does matter is how many public assembly facilities within the market area are capable of presenting the event, and to what extent it is incumbent for the promoter/artist to even appear in the market area.

Some promoters and presenters believe there are no bad shows, just bad deals. This belief points to a number of important facets in the facility manager-promoter relationship. For example, rather than purchase a strong concert performance, the promoter could lease the facility at a predetermined percentage of ticket sales, pay all expenses, and realize all of the net profit or loss. However, it might be a better deal for a promoter to purchase a weak concert performance (in terms of potential ticket sales) and then enter into a contractual agreement with the facility through which the promoter receives a reasonable guarantee, a percentage of the net profits, and, co-promotes/partners with the facility (in which case the facility and the promoter share the financial risks and rewards).

CALENDAR

Traditionally, calendar scheduling and booking activity was done using a master calendar often known in some operational environments as the "black book/bible." The calendar was usually a large volume of loose-leaf sheets, each depicting a single date and (if multiple venues) designated space. Today, more often that not, this processes involves a very different instrument. The computerization of this function has ingeniously combined many roles and functions into database software that will copy fields of information from initial entry into a multitude of documents. (Figure 3-1 depicts a typical booking/scheduling calendar).

Managing the calendar is one of the most critical roles of the public assembly facility and must be assigned to a capable individual(s) who is detail-oriented, personable, and creative. Although the scheduling and booking function depends and survives on the free flow of communication among staff, management should limit control of dates to minimal staff; one is ideal.

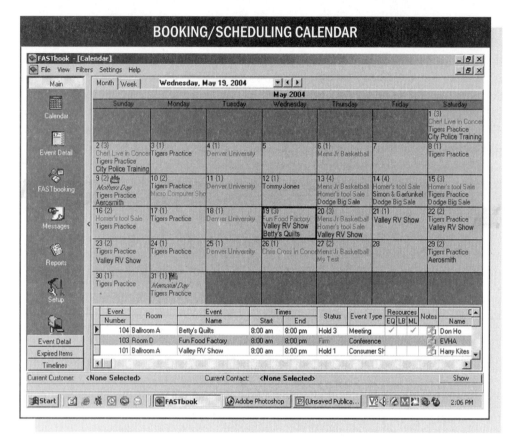

Courtesy of Event Software   FIGURE 3-1

SCHEDULING

Scheduling facilities and booking events are interrelated management processes common to all public assembly facilities. Scheduling may be interpreted in more than one way. From one perspective, scheduling is the reservation process for making all event dates fit with each other. For example, the process is employed when dealing with sports teams and series or theatrical productions in order to make sure the event dates fit with each other. Put another way, scheduling from this perspective is the "strategic planning and decision-making involved in determining the type of events and the timing of their use of the facilities." (Smith, 2003) From a second perspective, scheduling is perceived as the process of providing the best possible mix of events for a facility or the community.

Perhaps the key distinctions are that scheduling involves the creation of a game plan of events desired and those normally scheduled during the year. Booking is putting the plan into play. More generally, however, booking refers to the act of blocking specific space within a specific facility for a specific date at a specific time for a specific purpose for an agreed upon compensation. All facilities book space in some manner, regardless of whether they have the capability to promote or co-promote events.

Achieving a diversified program can only be accomplished through appropriate and proper scheduling. Thus, scheduling is the process of fitting events into the times and spaces available within a facility's calendar. Events must fit the facility physically, its purpose, and the community it serves. Care must be taken at all times to ensure that events are compatible with local, regional, and national holidays; vacation patterns of area residents; or special days celebrated within the community. In addition, all other activities outside the community but within the region that might impact an event's success must be taken into consideration when developing the public assembly facility's schedule.

For example, scheduling a symphony orchestra performance on the same evening when 80,000 people will be attending a collegiate football game in an adjacent community may affect either or both events, depending on how many people are loyal fans of both the symphony and the college team.

Nonetheless, the core fact is public assembly facilities are in the business of selling the perishable commodity of time and space. All activity by the facility manager and the facility's staff is focused on this singular objective. Nothing else happens if this is not accomplished. Once an opportunity has passed, it's gone forever.

USER PRIORITIES

Scheduling determines the calendar sequencing of events — sequencing designed to provide the best possible mix of events to meet the needs of the community, the user, and the public assembly facility. A diversified event program, properly scheduled and effectively presented, requires a clear understanding of expectations of the events, the events' consumers, and the public assembly facility's governing body coupled with an understanding of the facility's physical plant and/or personnel limitations. Priorities given to primary tenants or facility users can help ensure a high level of event activity without giving such users exclusive rights. In most cases, priority policies and criteria are defined and written to include time-sensitive thresholds.

A number of variables, such as facility ownership and governance, the community's social and economic climate, the community's demographics, and the availability of attractions as well as ancillary support capabilities, can offer direction and guidance concerning an appropriate event mix and schedule. In addition, the existence of precise facility vision and mission statements should provide strong guidelines. Attempting to host event types considered unsuitable for the facility and community or that may conflict with the facility's prime tenants could produce negative reactions. However, if vision and mission statements are properly developed and disseminated, the public assembly facility's governing body, its managers, and consumers should have a general sense of what constitutes an appropriate attraction for the facility. (Figures 3-2 and 3-2-1 depict a booking priority for a convention center and performing arts complex).

For example, a properly developed mission statement for a privately owned, for-profit amphitheatre might direct management toward a broad mix of commercially viable, popular entertainment events, while a convention center's mission statement emphasizing downtown revitalization and hotel use would point to conventions, conferences, multi-day meetings, and trade show activities.

BOOKING PRIORITIES FOR A CONVENTION CENTER

FIRST scheduling priority is given to conventions, trade shows, corporate meetings and similar activities that use a minimum of 1,500 room nights during the event and that are not normally open to the general public.

SECOND scheduling priority is given to conventions, trade shows, consumer or public exhibitions and corporate meetings using more than 100,000 square feet and less than 1,500 room nights. Second priority will also be given to events which book either the ballroom plus a minimum of 48,000 square feet of exhibit space, or the ballroom when accommodating a minimum of 600 person banquet function.

THIRD scheduling priority is given to smaller consumer or public exhibitions, local corporate meetings, special events, banquets, and other activities which primarily draw from or appeal to the general public and/or local attendees.

Scheduling for second priority events will not be confirmed more than 18 months in advance; third priority events will not be confirmed more than 12 months in advance. Both second and third priority events are subject to change to accommodate first priority events unless a License Agreement has already been executed by The Center.

FIGURE 3-2

BOOKING PRIORITIES FOR DENVER'S DIVISION OF THEATRES AND ARENAS

GENERAL

The Director reserves the authority to grant reservations at any time but recognizes that certain priorities have been and are created as contractual or historical priorities including but not limited to, the National Western Stock Show, the Colorado High School Activities Association, and certain established annual events. The Colorado Symphony in Boettcher Concert Hall, Denver Center Attractions in the Buell Theatre, Opera Colorado in the Quigg Newton Denver Municipal Auditorium have right of first refusal in their respective venues. Only Opera Colorado may reserve dates up to 5 years in advance.

Scheduling policy is designed to obtain maximum utilization of the facilities and provide fair and equitable availability to a broad spectrum of sports and entertainment presenters. All events are inclusive of load-in, production, rehearsal, performance, and load-out.

a. Ten (10) weeks each calendar year shall be available for use at the City's discretion in each facility.
b. Multi-week - multiple performance events have first priority.
c. Week long multiple performance events, 6 or more, have second priority.
d. Multiple performance events, 2 or more, have third priority.
e. Single performance events have fourth priority.

Reprinted with permission by the Theaters and Arenas Division of the City of Denver.

FIGURE 3-2-1

Understanding a public assembly facility's mission can also assist in resolving booking priority conflicts and revenue distribution issues when they arise. A facility manager caught between a popular basketball coach demanding more practice time and a local entertainment promoter with a "hot" concert should be able to rely on the public assembly facility's mission statement for guidance in establishing and adhering to booking priorities. Of course, any existing contracts may determine which party gets the date. A strong mission statement can be used as the foundation to effectively deter those who would seek to use the facility for unsuitable purposes.

The key to setting some type of priority policy lies in the designated use of the facility. For example, if a performing arts facility is built to serve the local arts community (such as the symphony, ballet, theatre groups, and so forth) then those groups should be given certain priority to reserve space. Priority should be given to convention activity in a convention center, particularly if room/bed tax funds are used to retire the construction debt or to pay operating expenses. On the other hand, the university basketball team should be given priority in a campus arena, if the construction of that facility was for the team.

Priorities given to primary facility users can help ensure a high level of event activity without giving such users exclusive rights. In most cases, priority policies are defined and written ... if not, they should be!

Since community needs and tastes are subject to change, a facility manager must continually monitor them and adjust the public assembly facility's programming accordingly. Thus, as a community's programming interests and social standards evolve, the facility's mission statement should be revisited and changed so that it reflects the needs of the contemporary community. By paying close attention to both the community's evolving needs and available business, the facility manager can guide the facility's governing body, clients, and consumers toward the formation of a revised mission. Revitalization often necessitates adopting an entirely redefined focus and mission statement.

CONVENTION BUREAUS

While common to all facility types, scheduling for convention business is slightly more complex because the decision-maker(s) must take into consideration the event's short-term impact upon the community in order to assess any effect it may have on the community's long-term needs. Strategically, collaboration among the convention center's general manager, the convention and visitors bureau (CVB), representatives from area hotels, and the local hospitality industry is most important. Typically, the CVB, operating as the marketing arm for long-range events, will market the convention center's calendar for scheduling of events more than a year or eighteen months in the future.

Frequently CVBs and/or hotels will arrange for group housing accommodations. This process ensures the necessary housing for attendees is available for specific dates of scheduled conventions, conferences, multi-day meetings, and trade shows.

It is paramount that public assembly facility managers accept the responsibility for cooperating with other community entities in an effort to coordinate their facility's use with existing community wide, long-range goals. At the same time the facility manager may be committed to traditional annual events for which the facility was built. In most cases, a priority is given to the scheduling of dates based on the impact the event has on the number of *hotel nights* that can be guaranteed by the attendees or delegates that accompany a given convention. These major conventions are scheduled with lead times of eighteen months to three years or longer and are actually placed on the facility's calendar before smaller conventions, conferences, multi-day meetings, and trade shows.

✈ BOOKING

Booking is the process of identifying desired events or activities appropriate for the public assembly facility and the community, contacting owner(s) or promoter(s) and engaging in negotiations leading to a contract with the event or activity to appear in the facility. From the perspective of both the public assembly facility manager and the event or activity's promoter, determining the "when," the "where" and at "what cost" are the prime decisions in the booking process.

A promoter will not contract with a facility for the appearance of an event or activity until first assured the venue is appropriate, available, and economically viable. In similar fashion, a trade show promoter is not able to attract exhibitors without knowing the specific date(s), location(s) and costs of the show. Producing an event might include

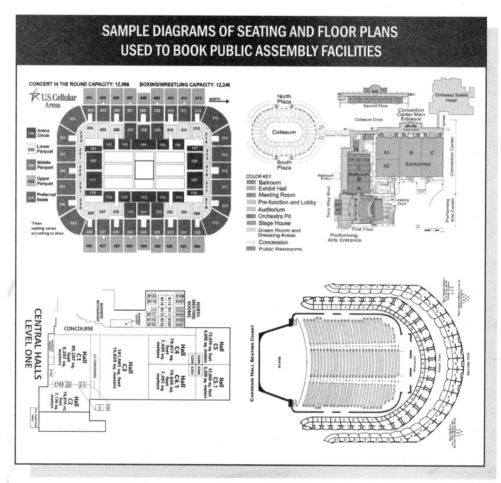

Clockwise from top left: arena, complex with multiple facilities, theater, and exhibit hall.

FIGURE 3-3

advertising, ticketing, marketing and promoting, staffing, and rentals needs. All of these are critical to the success of the event and hinge on the booking process. The end of the booking process is the beginning of the production process and the ultimate deliverable outcomes by facility operations. (Figure 3-3 illustrates some sample diagrams of seating and floor plans used to book public assembly facilities).

QUALIFYING THE EVENT

Whether the public assembly facility promotes the event itself (contracts for the event to happen and accepts all of the financial risk), co-promotes the event (contracts for the event but shares the financial risk with other entities), or leases the facility (rents space to a tenant/client thereby not incurring any direct financial risk), the public assembly facility's booking manager responsible for scheduling and booking must answer several common questions, including:

- Is the event consistent with the facility's values and expectations?
- Are the date(s), time(s), and space(s) requested available?
- Does the event fit?
  a) Is the facility large enough (or too large) to accommodate the event's space requirements?
  b) Can the facility provide specialized support for the event and reconfigure to meet the event's needs (ice for hockey or dirt for a rodeo or acoustics for a symphony)?
- Will the event conflict with a prime tenant or any other activity?
- Can the facility meet the demands of the event such as staffing, changeover, etc?
- Does the person seeking to book space in the facility have the necessary experience, authority, and financial resources?

(See Figure 3-4 for a typical booking memo checklist).

It is the booking manager's responsibility to determine if the potential client actually is legitimate and, in fact, can deliver the event in question. In the interest of fairness, consistency, and good business practice, the facility management should have an application process often referred to as a *license application*, for qualifying all new promoters or prospective tenants/clients.

There is a correlation between a facility's success and the processes and procedures by which it accepts business. Experienced, reputable, financially sound promoters are essential. One way to achieve this situation is by pre-qualifying potential users before making a contract offer. (See Appendix A, Figure 3-5 for a sample license application designed to acquire the necessary information). It would probably not be used for former users of the facility. The requested date(s) can still be held on a "tentative" basis during this process. Deadlines must still be met.

Business statements, bank and financial verifications, agency verification of previously negotiated contracts, past experience, and recommendations from the manager of

BOOKING MEMO CHECKLIST

- ☐ Date of inquiry
- ☐ Date(s) of event
- ☐ Specific type of event
- ☐ Areas to be used
- ☐ Hold date(s)
- ☐ Hold status
- ☐ Contact's name
- ☐ Contact's address
- ☐ Contact's phone
- ☐ Contact's fax
- ☐ Contact's email address
- ☐ Set up/Take down schedule

- ☐ Rate quotes
- ☐ Showtime
- ☐ Projected attendance
- ☐ Staffing requirements
- ☐ Equipment needs
- ☐ Show running time
- ☐ Name of artist/show
- ☐ Ticket on sale date
- ☐ Ticket prices/house scale
- ☐ Complimentary/trade tickets (tickets provided in return for goods or services)

FIGURE 3-4

former contracted venues are several ways to help determine the applicant's qualification to book an event. There are a number of reasons why potential promoters or meeting planners will request a hold on a date(s) even though they may lack the authority to actually deliver the attraction. While most of the reasons are legitimate, the public assembly facility manager needs to be prudent about over committing date inventory frivolously without establishing control processes that protect from fictitious holds.

Does the person making the inquiry have the experience and resources to produce the event and the ability to contract the talent and book the space? Utilizing the permit application process, the booking manager can shield the public assembly facility from many problems that might typically arise from dealing with an inexperienced or unscrupulous promoter. At the same time, the booking manager should assist, help develop, and encourage new promoters as much as possible.

Booking managers need to evaluate if there are unusual risks and liabilities associated with a proposed event. They must seek as much information as possible about a specific attraction in order to determine its potential risks and legal, social and physical liabilities. Is the proposed event one that will cause controversy in the community? Potential controversy, however, should not necessarily result in an automatic rejection. Disallowing an event deemed "inappropriate" by the facility's governing body might be illegal based on the laws and statutes of the legal jurisdiction under which the governing body operates. In addition, denying the event may ultimately prove expensive and embarrassing if the promoter seeks relief in the courts.

Refusing to book an event solely based on the management's or governing body's perception of its content might be construed as a violation of the promoter's and the event's right to free speech which in the United States is guaranteed under the First Amendment of the United States Constitution. Court charges, assessed penalties and fines, and a damaged relationship between the facility's manager and the event's promoter frequently result from hasty knee-jerk decisions.

In matters of taste, treading softly is generally the prudent course of action. Three critical issues booking managers must determine about each inquiry received are: Is the proposed event safe? Is it legal? If not, can it be made safe and/or legal? If an attraction can be made safe and legal and is not in direct violation of the public assembly facility's policies and procedures, the booking manager should give the application the same consideration accorded all other inquiries.

Booking the facility actually involves more than simply "answering the telephone." Booking the facility is about relationships, relationships of trust and accountability as partners. Booking begins with an event's promoter contacting the public assembly facility's booking manager for *avails* (available dates). It is the booking manager's responsibility to ensure future business by cultivating potential event owners and promoters. A competent, experienced booking manager will seek to create new and/or alternative opportunities.

The facility should provide an environment that encourages maximum profit with minimum risk. Essential elements in nurturing the relationship between an artist's or event's promoter and the facility's booking manager include maintaining close contact with these individuals and being constantly aware of available touring attractions and potential convention/conference/multi-day meeting/trade show clients. Public assembly facility clientele must experience a sense of trust and partnership if the relationship is to yield productive outcomes.

BOOKING PROCESS AND TERMINOLOGY

Over the years, the booking process has spawned a unique vocabulary that allows brief but efficient communication between exhibitors, artist's managers, booking agents, and promoters. Which unique aspects of a vocabulary are used is partially a function of the event and facility type. Facility management personnel assigned booking responsibilities must quickly learn the nomenclature and the ensuing processes associated with each if they are to be effective.

A promoter may *reserve* (hold) space in a facility at three distinct levels: *tentative, confirmed* (contract out) or *contracted*. While different facilities or facility types may have different names for these levels (for example firm, pencil in, definite, etc) and some may have intermediate levels, ultimately there remain only three distinct categories.

The booking agent attempting to route an event (booking agent jargon for getting from place to place in the most expeditious manner) will ask the booking manager to place a tentative hold for an open date(s) on the facility's calendar. This tentative hold simply tells the booking manager that the event is interested in appearing in the public assembly facility.

Once the booking manager agrees to hold a specific date, the promoter automatically assumes the event will occur on that date(s), that there are no scheduling conflicts, that the facility will host the event, and that the date(s) will remain on hold for a predetermined period of time and not be reassigned to any other event without agreement with the event's owner or promoter.

The booking manager, by placing this hold on a date(s), signifies the belief that the promoter is serious about producing the attraction and also that the promoter will release the date(s) promptly whenever it is deemed no longer viable. Of course, there is the possibility that a promoter may not release a hold under these circumstances.

Experienced managers have a policy of deadlines whereby holds are automatically released (for example, I'll hold for xx days and then make the date available to others.) It is very common for multiple dates to be held by different promoters for the same act. Therefore, it is extremely important that holds are act-specific. If a date is being held by promoter A for act Z and promoter A loses act Z to promoter B, then promoter A also loses control of the date. Whoever gets the act gets the date.

Booking facilities and scheduling routes are difficult tasks. There are many moving parts that must come together. As a result, while it is prudent for a public assembly facility manager to have the automatic cut-off built into the hold date(s), the intelligent manager should be willing to extend that date upon request whenever the event is desired and the booking process is viable and continuing. Granting extensions is also beneficial in maintaining a good relationship with the promoter.

Once routing is completed and the exact date(s) have been chosen for the event, the booking manager should be notified so any unused held date(s) are released and returned to inventory. When a hold is confirmed, a contract is issued with a deadline for its return along with a rent deposit. When the signed contract and deposit are returned, the event's status becomes "contracted." (See Appendix C, Contract Components). Any remaining holds for the now confirmed event are released at the point of contracting and the dates are reclassified as open and offered to potential users as the process begins anew.

CHALLENGING HOLD DATES

Prospective tenants desiring a date(s) held by another promoter might ask the booking manager for a second hold or issue a challenge for the date(s) sought. (See Figure 3-6 for a tentative hold process). A second hold enables the requesting promoter to immediately gain top priority if the event promoter currently possessing the hold date(s) relinquishes it or doesn't meet the facility's timelines. When a challenge occurs, the facility's booking manager contacts the promoter who has the first hold on the date and announces that another promoter is seeking the same date(s). The tentative hold promoter then must either enter into a contract for the date(s) within 24 (48, 72) hours or remit a non-refundable deposit within 24 hours in order to keep the tentative hold status. If the original promoter does neither, the date(s) are relinquished and awarded to the challenger. The facility may require the challenger to remit a deposit, up to the minimum rental fee, prior to contacting the first hold promoter to ensure the challenge is a legitimate one and not just a means to control dates. The challenging promoter should be required to immediately go to contract if the date(s) becomes available. It is not unusual for concert promoters, for example, to attempt to tie up facilities with tentative holds. If successful, the promoter is then able to go to the act/artist's agent with that leverage to gain an advantage in competing with other promoters for the act/artist. Facility managers might follow a policy that sets the date aside, for whoever gets the act, when a major act/artist is known to be touring. A key consideration is that facility managers structure the process so that they control the facility's schedule and do not allow others to gain that control.

A challenge may only be issued against a "tentative" hold. If a contract has been sent to a potential user for a date(s), that promoter has until the stated deadline to sign and return the contract along with any required deposit. Of course, if the deadline is missed, the date(s) becomes available for the facility manager to allocate as desired.

PROMOTER	REQUEST	ACTION
PROMOTER "A"	Requests tentative hold on date(s).	Grants tentative hold if date is available, attraction desired, user qualifies and basic contract terms agreed. Hold has deadline to go to contract and is subject to challenge.
PROMOTER "B"	Challenges Promoter "A's" hold on date(s). (Assume Promoter "B" meets criteria for contract). Manager may require "B" to provide a non-refundable deposit and understand that s/he will have to go to contract immediately if the date(s) becomes available.	Manager notifies Promoter "A" of challenge and gives a short deadline to receive contract, sign and return with deposit. If "A" cannot, or will not, commit to contract, manager may declare tentative hold is cancelled and available to Promoter "B."

Sample process of a tentative hold   FIGURE 3-6

NOTE: Promoter "A" should be told that if Promoter "B" does not meet his/her deadline, the tentative hold will be reinstated for Promoter "A" with the same original timeline. E.g. Promoter "A" is originally given a ten-day hold. The challenge by "B" occurs on day two and the facility cancels "A's" tentative hold on the third day. If "B" fails to perform, "A" should again have the tentative first hold with seven days to perform. Of course, in all instances, the facility manager sets the deadlines. Circumstances will determine how much time and leeway to give to promoters during this process.

HOLD SPACE/DATE SEQUENCE

Giving specific deadlines for potential users to provide/return information, contracts, deposits, etc., increases the facility manager's abilities to control the dates and the process. If a deadline is missed, the date(s) become available to commit to other potential users. (See Figure 3-7 for the process of holding space/date).

The public assembly facility industry is one of leverage and relationships. The booking process is a prime example because of the level of trust that must exist between booking managers and promoters for the system to work. The importance of clearly defined book-

HOLD IS:	PROCESS SEQUENCE	PROCEED OR STOP
TENTATIVE	Inquiry - Is date available? Is attraction desired? Potential user qualifies? Basic contract terms agreed? Give "tentative hold" for X days (subject to challenges)	YES NO ____ ____ ____ ____ ____ ____ ____ ____ If answers are all YES, proceed. If any answer is NO, stop at that point. No hold is given.
CONFIRMED (Contract Issued)	Promoter qualified. Contract terms agreed. Contract issued. Return required in X days. Deposit required with contract.	Stop process if any deadline is not met unless promoter has requested and manager agrees to an extension of time.
CONTRACTED	Contract signed & returned. Deposit returned with contract (Subject to bank clearance). Facility signs contract.	Contract follow-up: internal processes to prepare for event and production begins.

Sample process of holding space/date.   FIGURE 3-7

ing policies and procedures can never be overstated. While no formal agreement may exist that requires booking managers and promoters to abide by the rules, there are definite penalties, in this relatively closed professional area, for those who do not. If a promoter cannot trust a booking manager's word, the promoter has little choice but to bypass the facility. Conversely, booking managers may require a non-refundable deposit for a tentative hold date(s) if they believe a routing agent lacks the proper understanding of and respect for the booking process or is unwilling to abide by the spoken, or unspoken, rules. As within any select community, word "gets around" quickly about who is or is not trustworthy.

DATE PROTECTION

A public assembly facility manager attuned to the community market may decide the local economy is unable to support two or more similar attractions offered in close proximity to each other. For example, booking two circuses in the same month or two country concerts in the same week is generally not considered a wise practice except possibly in a unique or the largest of markets. To avoid such conflicts and preserve financial viability, some public assembly facility governing bodies have instituted scheduling criteria requiring a reasonable degree of separation between similar attractions. Policies of this nature are termed "protection policies" and are designed to facilitate box office success for all parties. Traditional touring family shows commonly request protection from similar events.

Clearly outlined and fairly enforced protection policies tend to be good tools for enhancing the success of an event. (See Figure 3-8 for a sample date protection and event spacing policy). However, providing protection as a matter of policy can also be the root of problems. For example, a booking manager, working with a policy that provides a two-week window of protection, books a small attendance, local wrestling card. Shortly thereafter the manager discovers an opportunity exists to host a major national professional wrestling show. But, in order to book the major show, the two-week window of protection policy would have to be violated. What should the manager do: abide by the protection policy and lose the bigger production or ignore the policy and schedule both events? A situation of this nature requires a manager to demonstrate a delicate touch and creative flexibility. Possible best solutions include the facility manager offering to reschedule the lesser event for a later date, perhaps at a reduced rental rate. If this approach is not acceptable, the manager might then offer to buy out the lesser act.

Under the circumstances, it might be considerably more prudent for the public assembly facility and its manager to lose money than credibility. Like the proverbial elephant, promoters have long memories and they converse with each other. It is possible the lesser event might refuse to relinquish its date(s) while the larger event insists on having its event booked even though the date(s) violates the protection policy and failing to do so, the larger event plans to seek judicial relief based on restraint of trade. (See Figure 3-9 about a convention center sued for restraint of trade). Whenever conflicts occur, public assembly facility managers must use their relationships, leverage and negotiating skills in an attempt to craft a resolution acceptable to all parties.

SAMPLE DATE PROTECTION AND EVENT SPACING POLICY

DATE PROTECTION POLICY
When comparable events request the same dates, preference on dates is given in order of requests. The Civic Center will attempt to provide protection before and after events to competitive shows.

EVENT SPACING POLICY
Event spacing shall apply to events which have twenty percent (20%) or more similar exhibitors, as determined by The Center; are charging an admission to gain entry to the show and/or are open to the general public rather than being limited to a well-defined class of persons who normally belong to a trade or professional association.

Similar shows renting the entire ballroom or more than 30,000 gross square feet of exhibit hall space and which are actively competing for specialized and specific local markets shall maintain the following clearance periods prior to the first show day and following the last show day of booked events:

- 45 Days: Public/Consumer shows; e.g., boat shows, RV shows, home shows, car shows, sportsmen shows, nursery/garden shows, business/office/computer shows, etc.
- 30 Days: Hobby/arts and crafts; e.g., antique shows, food shows, collectibles, auctions, bridal shows, career fairs, etc.
- Events not falling into any of these event categories will be spaced at the discretion of The Center.

FIGURE 3-8

CONVENTION CENTER SUED FOR BOOKING PRIORITY POLICY

In June of 1996, a trade show organizer, Brett Enterprises, sued the New Orleans Metropolitan Convention and Visitors Bureau in Federal court, claiming the CVB and convention center conspired "to restrain trade and to monopolize advance bookings at the center. Mr. Brett claimed that the CVB and the center jointly monopolized the market for convention and exhibition hall space in the New Orleans area by virtue of their control over an essential facility. The convention center claimed that its booking policies were immune from antitrust liability under the state action doctrine of Federal case law that says antitrust laws do not apply to state action or official action directed by the state. The Ernest N. Morial Convention Center, like many convention centers, is governed by a state statute creating an authority to acquire, construct, and maintain projects for the economic growth and development of New Orleans.

In its ruling, the U.S. District Court stated that:
"The Authority's alleged refusal to give advance booking dates at the Convention Center to trade show producers who do not attract a large number of hotel room users is a foreseeable result of its legislatively granted authority. ...Simply put, the Louisiana statutes authorize the Exhibition Hall Authority to establish priorities for the use of the Convention Center, and it was foreseeable that the Authority would conclude that a priority for advance bookings should be given to shows that will generate the most revenue for itself and the local area. Moreover, requiring a minimum number of hotel rooms allows the Authority to assure the bondholders that there will be a predictable level of hotel occupancy tax revenues to pay off the bonds."

FIGURE 3-9

The open date inventory of a public assembly facility's event calendar is sometimes referred to as avails. These dates are constantly discussed by potential users and booking managers in person or via fax, phone, or e-mail. Computer software programs may allow viewing of the facility's calendar through the public assembly facility's Internet home page. Some of these computer calendar programs also permit prospective users to view the event calendar, initiate reservation inquiries, and gather rental rate information without ever having to talk with the facility's booking manager!

BLOCK BOOKING

It is critical to the success of attractions that travel and play several, or many facilities, that the routing be as efficient as possible. This may involve several elements, such as the time necessary to move staging and production equipment including sound and light consoles, costumes, video production often used in musical concerts, circus animals, etc., in and out of the facility.

Sometimes a manager is not able to attract a desired event to only his/her facility. Cooperation and coordination with other facilities in the general area or region presents an opportunity to entice the event because of the availability of the multiple locations. In effect, the facilities are engaging in cooperative marketing of the area with the hoped for end result being several bookings in a logical touring sequence that will be beneficial for the facility and the event. The result is block booking. The block is a combination of the participating facilities with necessary dates available and willing to book the event.

Experienced managers understand that to be successful, the key to block booking requires planning well in advance so the participating facilities will have available dates that can be used to create logical and efficient tour routes.

Once the group agrees to work together and entices the event to come to the area/region, they can individually book it as they would normally. If the facilities choose to be in the position of a landlord, this is not uncommon. There is another option, and one that might more likely be used by performing arts centers or auditoriums that elect to market and book as a block. That is, they may simply buy the show (or a part thereof) and take on the role of the promoter, including the added risks. In such instances, it would not be uncommon to assess the participating facilities, on a pro rata basis, for their share of the costs to buy the attraction since they have different seating capacities, population, etc, and therefore may be able to develop more or less revenue than others in the group.

Regardless of whether the facilities act as landlords or buy the event, there can be significant benefits from having common sponsors, promotional efforts and advertising campaigns. Ideally, block booking results in providing financial incentives to both the facility and the touring attraction.

Promoters have applied this strategy for years, block booking tours throughout their regional market places, thus effectively spreading a promotion company's overhead costs over a greater number of performances. Additionally, the promoter is able to realize benefits from synergies in sponsorship and promotion campaigns.

Block booking is a frequent topic at industry meetings, especially of performing arts managers and presenters. Also, booking agents for touring attractions may advertise to facilities in a region that discounts are available if their act is booked in the same time period in a nearby but separate market.

During the early eighties, in the lightly populated territory of the intermountain northwest United States, a group of nine buildings in tertiary markets joined together to form Tours West. This block booking effort met with some success by simply heightening general awareness of the region and its markets. Although each facility made its own individual decisions regarding attraction purchases, booking agents and promoters began to pay more attention to the group market potential of this tour circuit. Following the 1999 National Basketball Association (NBA) lockout in the United States, several facilities joined together to form what eventually became known as the Arena Network with the singular purpose of leveraging touring attractions. This loose knit association, made up principally of major league facilities with anchor tenants in major league ice hockey and basketball, as well as several university facilities, contributed financial support to the hiring of an individual to represent them in block booking the facilities and buying attractions.

BOOKING PITFALLS

One of the best safeguards against costly booking and scheduling errors is to carefully restrict the number of staff members allowed to engage in discussions with potential promoters and further restrict the number empowered to actually book an event. Ideally, the safest approach is to have the final approval restricted to one individual. An agent or promoter who asks the public assembly facility's office receptionist to "reserve the last Friday in February" is requesting that a tentative hold be placed on that date and probably believes, or at least claims to believe, the receptionist has the power to authorize the hold. In this important area of booking, less is better. All parties must understand that ultimately minimizing the number of individuals sharing the booking responsibility reduces the chance for mistakes to occur.

Regardless of the scheduling and booking method employed, it is always possible for double booking to occur. Committing the same space to two different clients at the same time is potentially disastrous from both a financial and a relationship perspective. Hopefully, the booking manager will detect the double booking while sufficient time remains to reschedule one of the events. If sufficient time is not available to reschedule or if the option is refused, then it is generally prudent for a financial settlement to be offered.

Almost as disastrous as double booking is scheduling events in a manner that causes them to overlap because sufficient time and/or space has not been provided to allow one event to breakdown and the other to setup. Errors of this nature generally occur when the booking manager has little understanding of changeover logistics or possesses limited knowledge of specific event requirements. For example, booking a symphony too soon after the rodeo may produce some lively discussion regarding the lingering barnyard scent. Not providing for a sufficient airing-out interval between the two events places the public assembly facility manager in a delicate position, one that requires skillful public relations in "mending fences." An open line of communication during the advance consideration of events between the booking manager/department and the event operations staff can go a long way to minimize this type of confusion.

While the scheduling and booking process is generally well controlled, booking errors are inevitable and can range from mildly irritating to catastrophic. Some causes of booking errors include ignorance of the booking process, poor communications between the various parties, lack of appropriate management policies, intentional deception, poor follow up, inattention to details, and allowing unqualified employees to participate in the booking process.

Errors of this nature may be reduced or eliminated if the individual(s) responsible for the booking process is well trained, has experience, pays attention to details, maintains appropriate record keeping, and possesses good listening skills. It is the responsibility of management to train, support, and provide the necessary resources to accomplish the tasks. The development of clearly written booking policies and procedures should be a collaborative effort between the public assembly facility's clients, governing board, and managers. Once established, these policies and procedures must be effectively communicated to appropriate staff members.

Booking Memo

Precise and timely information from clients and promoters is imperative for the success of any event. During the initial contact when a request for a date hold is made, some critical information must be gathered and recorded on the booking memo. Once all necessary information has been gathered, it should be disseminated to all stakeholders.

The booking manager should require information as to the intended use of the space and the name of the artist(s)/show involved (if it is an event with artists). The first question the manager should probably ask is, What is the show — who is the artist? Just being told it is a musical show is not adequate. Is it Bach or is it rock? (See Figure 3-10 for a sample booking memo).

It is important to know the anticipated ticket price and house scale in order to calculate the possible gross potential (GP). This is then a major consideration in quoting the rental rate based on the facility's expected share. The facility's management staff can provide information and local knowledge that is helpful in determining ticket prices and in scaling the house. (These concepts will be discussed further in Chapter 5 — Ticketing and Box Office Management.)

In addition, continued communication with prospective or contracted users and keeping the booking calendar up-to-date and accessible for all department managers to view help to minimize potential problem areas, invites input, and gives the various managers time to prepare for the event.

SAMPLE BOOKING MEMO

Show Date(s): _____

Show Time: _____   If event has more than one show time, refer to event data sheet.

Schedule: _____

Music Genre: _____   Plan (Hall Layout):_____   Expected Attendance: _____

TERMS

Lease Start Date: _____   Lease End Date: _____

Rental Rate: _____

Box Office Rate:

Deposit of: _____to be returned by: _____. A second deposit of _____ due by _____.

Additional Deposit Notes:_____

PROMOTER/AGENT   Signator: _____

Company: _____

Contact: _____   Address:_____

Phone: _____   _____

Fax: _____   Permit App Received / Approved for Use

EVENT TICKETING   Ticket Header

Pricing Scales: _____

_____

_____

Total Capacity Holds: _____

                                                       Discounts: _____

On Sale Date: _____

FIGURE 3-10

All booking managers should have a thorough knowledge regarding the needs of their tenants and events, their facility's specifications and its accommodation limitations, their protection policies, the community's requirements, the expectations of their governing body, and any unique requirement or limitations imposed by government statutes or ordinances on the facility itself or its tenants.

A booking manager must understand that the tour routing process hinges directly upon the event agent's ability to hold a date(s) on a facility's calendar and in so doing be totally confident that the held date(s) will remain reserved under the conditions of the hold. Allowing a promoter to presume facility availability without positive confirmation could derail an entire portion of a touring attraction, or cause major disruption for both the promoter and the attraction. As stated earlier, if the relationship between the booking agent and promoter deteriorates, business is often the first casualty.

Accountability for proper booking is also the responsibility of the promoter or agent. The locking-up of dates based on a remote possibility that an attraction might appear, and/or not releasing non-viable dates, is the height of irresponsibility and demonstrates a lack of courtesy and forethought. Many opportunities have been missed by public assembly facilities because their booking manager was unable to commit a date(s) already being held by another prospective tenant and then later discovered the date(s) would have been available had the promoter or agent holding it been forthright. Some operative concepts in managing a successful booking process should include courtesy, honesty, diligence, knowledge, and trust. Yet, due to increased competition, some agents or promoters may consciously tie-up dates as a means of "protecting" their event. Placing a tentative hold on the calendar of a facility providing a protection policy effectively eliminates similar event competitors from gaining access to that facility during the protection period. For example, placing a tentative hold for a non-existent show two weeks before and two weeks after the original hold would serve to provide an additional month of protection. The established hold policies can address this in a number of ways, including limiting the number of holds that can be placed by each promoter/client for a specified act or by having an automatic expiration date for holds. For example, a tentative hold needs to become contracted out within thirty days and the contract needs to be signed and returned within thirty days. This may vary based upon heavily trafficked markets and/or the lead time or proximity to the proposed event date.

SERVING PATRONS WITH DISABILITIES

In the United States it is necessary to be aware of the needs of these individuals and to ask questions during the booking process that will elicit appropriate information in order to provide for those individuals with special needs. Under the Americans With Disabilities Act (ADA) requirements, individuals with disabilities should receive some special consideration when using the facilities to ensure they do not suffer from discrimination due to their disability. Other countries have similar laws. Older facilities are usu-

---

ADA SAMPLE CONTRACT LANGUAGE

AMERICANS WITH DISABILITIES ACT:

The Center represents and warrants that as a place of public accommodation, it is in compliance with applicable regulations implementing the requirements of Title III of the Americans with Disabilities Act. Auxiliary aids or services required for Licensee's functions, including sign language interpreter, Braille or large print materials, or other auxiliary aids or services, shall be the responsibility of the Licensee. In the event Licensee fails to provide ADA-required auxiliary aids or services, the Center may elect to do so and Licensee shall be billed for such aids or services under Section 2(e) of this Agreement. Licensee may contact the event coordinator for assistance in addressing Center layout, architecture, design, electrical specifications, or other Center features which may be a factor in Licensee's efforts to comply with the Americans with Disabilities Act and its regulations. The Center shall make good faith efforts to assist the Licensee in meeting ADA requirements, and the parties agree to negotiate allocation of any costs, other than auxiliary aids or services, which are incurred by the Center for this purpose.

FIGURE 3-11

---

ally not designed for the physically challenged, but every effort should be made to provide reasonable accommodations whenever possible. (See Figure 3-11 for ADA contract language).

FIRST AMENDMENT ISSUES

A manager may be asked to book an event that, although deemed "safe and legal," is so controversial in nature that hosting it would undoubtedly create problems. Public facility managers and their booking personnel must remember, however, that a "controversial" event may have the same legal protection as any other event. For example, in the United States a controversial event might be protected under the provision of free speech afforded by the First Amendment of the Constitution. (See Figure 3-12 for an example of a facility being sued for violation of First Amendment rights).

While a manager, supported by the facility's policies, may reject any event that might distress either the community or the facility's governing body, the prudent manager will not refuse to lease the facility to a third party unless the intended activity is patently illegal or the manager believes it presents a clear threat to public safety. A facility with a history of leasing its public space to commercial promoters is obligated by that history to continue this practice, without regard to performance content, so long as the building's protection policies remain inviolate, space is available, the event is properly scheduled and booked, and the activity is both legal and safe.

The operative word here is content. Neither the booking manager, the facility's governing body, the law enforcement authorities or the "community fathers" may discriminate against an event or attraction based strictly on its content. For instance, a facility

IN THE NEWS

MARILYN MANSON SHOW CANCELED IN SOUTH CAROLINA IN 1997
April 11 -- Columbia, South Carolina has told Marilyn Manson they don't want his type of music in their town, forcing cancellation of a concert that had been scheduled for April 20, 1997. The University of South Carolina and the concert promoter, Cellar Door Productions, canceled the show using a buy-out clause in the contract. State Treasurer Richard Eckstrom, who learned about the band at church, led pressure from religious and political groups to force the cancellation. South Carolina's state legislators introduced a bill to ban the use of any state facility for a concert by Marilyn Manson, and shortly afterwards, the cancellation was announced.

MARILYN MANSON GOES TO COURT AND WINS IN NEW JERSEY
April 28 -- Marilyn Manson's attorney filed a lawsuit against the New Jersey Sports and Exposition Authority for refusing to sell tickets to the June 15, 1997, Ozzfest at Meadowlands if Manson was a part of the show. Paul Cambria, the band's attorney, said the plaintiffs allege that the New Jersey Meadowlands is violating Manson's First Amendment rights. The ban on Manson was later overruled in court, finding that banning Manson would violate his First Amendment rights, even though concerns over crowd control and "community standards of decency" were made. Ozzfest went on as planned with Manson as a part of the show.

FIGURE 3-12

leasing space to traditional religious congregations cannot legally forbid religious cults from use of the same space even though a majority in the community might disapprove. In this instance, the booking manager would be on more solid legal ground by simply denying use of the public assembly facility for all religious activities rather than trying to accept some while rejecting others. This can be an issue where each answer creates two questions: (1) What is the stated purpose and mission of the facility? (2) What is the power of the religious community?

CONTRACTING

Once the promoter agrees with the conditions of use for a public assembly facility and the hold is confirmed, the booking manger, using the information previously record-ed in the booking memo, will issue a contract. The specific details of the agreement should be itemized succinctly and include, but not be limited to, the name of the event or attraction, the date and times of occupancy, the contract space or premise, and finan-cial deal. Additional language should be included stipulating such items as deadline for contract return, expiration dates, lead time for delivery of insurance and performance rid-ers, overtime charges, merchandizing rights and fees, equipment service and labor rate card references, etc., along with applicable boiler plating that establishes fundamental performance expectations while occupying the facility. This initiative will constitute an offer. Before the agreement becomes legally binding, the recipient must accept the offer and provide consideration in the form of a deposit or collateral.

When the signed contract and deposit are returned, the event's status becomes con-tracted and the event management process begins. (See Appendix C - Contract Components). While it may appear the public assembly facility has nothing to lose in a straight rental scenario, it is very important for the commercial promoter to also enjoy success. The long-term success of many public assembly facilities depends upon repeat business, and the only way for that to happen is for the facility owners to adopt operating philosophies that allow both the public assembly facility and the event promoter a reasonable chance to succeed. If promoters are successful, they tend to come back. If they're not, they'll go elsewhere or they go out of business. Success breeds success.

Creating the proper business relationship with each of the facility's clients is the responsibility of public assembly facility management. Although there are various types of clients, such as promoters, presenters, vendors, subcontractors, meeting planners, etc., the objective of developing strong and positive relationships remains consistent. It is important that the public assembly facility manager create a sense of partnership even though the official working agreement between client and facility may not call for the sharing of revenue, expenses, or risk. This particular type of partnering requires the sharing of information and ultimately a sharing of concern for the welfare and success of each other. It also requires an effort by each party to understand the problems and concerns of the other, to be willing to share energy and resources whenever possible, and to be creative in looking for a win-win solution to any problem that may arise.

SUMMARY

The booking and scheduling processes are controls designed to maximize, yet safeguard the facility's two most important commodities: time and space. Efficient management of these elements is vital to maximizing the number of event bookings and the number of potential revenue streams. Booking and scheduling are the processes that result in the programming of a facility's master calendar and should take into consideration the facility's vision and mission statements along with the needs of the community.

However, these processes are by no means infallible. Careless management may result in unnecessary errors, such as double booking or overlapping of events. Careful consideration must be given to the safety and legality of an event as part of the booking decision.

Although a public assembly facility manager may not agree with or like the content of a prospective event, freedom of speech may well prohibit the manager from barring the event based on content alone. The baseline question is, "What is the event manager's role in determining what the taste and values of the community ought to be?" Nonetheless, it is understandable that a manager may seek to protect the public assembly facility from any negative publicity that may be generated as a result of a controversial event. It is also important for the facility's event manager to consider the logistical needs and safety concerns of each event and to determine whether the facility is capable of accommodating the requirements.

REFERENCES AND ADDITIONAL READINGS

Shagan, Rena. 2001. *Booking & Tour Management for the Performing Arts*, 3rd ed. New York: Allworth.

Smith, Rodney. 2003. *Booking and Scheduling,* unpublished manuscript. Coppell, TX: International Association of Assembly Managers, Inc.

Sonder, Mark. 2003. *Event Entertainment and Production.* New York, NY: John Wiley & Sons, Inc.

4

SALES AND MARKETING

CHAPTER OUTLINE

- INTRODUCTION
- THE NEED FOR MARKETING AND WHAT IT CAN ACCOMPLISH
- HOW AND WHY DOES MARKETING APPLY TO PUBLIC ASSEMBLY FACILITIES?
- GETTING THE EVENTS
- THE SALES AND MARKETING DEPARTMENT
- THE MARKETING PLAN
  - EXECUTIVE SUMMARY
  - OTHER COMPONENTS OF THE MARKETING PLAN
  - IMPLEMENTATION
  - MARKETING BUDGET

- MARKETING EFFORTS AT MULTIPLE LEVELS
- THE IMPORTANCE OF RELATIONSHIPS TO SALES AND MARKETING
- RELATIONSHIPS ARE KEY
- THE FACILITY IMAGE
- ADVERTISING AND PROMOTION
- SEASON TICKETS AND SUBSCRIPTIONS
- MARKETING OF PREMIUM ACCESS
  - PREMIUM SEATING AND LUXURY SUITES
  - PRIORITY SEATING
  - NAMING RIGHTS AND ENDORSEMENTS

- SELLING ADVERTISING SIGNAGE AND SPONSORSHIP
- MEMORIAL GIFTS AND DONOR PROGRAMS
- PRODUCT BRANDING AND POURING RIGHTS
- SUMMARY
- REFERENCES AND ADDITIONAL READINGS

INTRODUCTION

Competition is pervasive throughout society. From the boardroom to the classroom to the playing field, the drive to "get ahead" of the competitors is a message that rings true to people of all ages and backgrounds. The old adage "raising your game" refers to the acknowledgement of your opponent's performance level and the need to raise your own to a matching or higher level. Although this phrase is often used in a sports context, it is also applicable to the public assembly facility management profession.

People have more choices than ever when it comes to spending their discretionary income. The performing arts, collegiate and professional sporting events, touring attractions, festivals, and concerts are all viable entertainment consumer options. The common denominator here is that all of these options involve convincing the people to leave their homes rather than watch TV/VCR-DVD and/or MTV.

Most people are no longer restricted to holidays, vacations periods, or weekends to enjoy their choice of entertainment. For example, business travelers may attend a local theatre production. Conference, convention, and trade show delegates may attend a nearby college or professional sports event. Meeting planners often incorporate available concerts, theatrical productions, and athletic events with meeting, conventions, conferences, and trade shows as a marketing tool designed to make the overall program more appealing to prospective attendees.

Another example of change that has occurred is the scheduling of concerts, many of which appeal to the younger demographic segments, on nights other than the once traditional Friday/Saturday, holidays, and school vacation periods. This change is significant as it allows the public assembly facility manager much greater flexibility in booking and scheduling acts and events for these market segments and frees up weekend dates for prime tenant sports franchises thereby generally enhancing attendance at their games.

The examples above demonstrate that entertainment, as well as sports, conventions, and exhibits, enjoy a high priority with large segments of the population. A further analysis of the state of the entertainment industry will help public assembly facility managers better understand how this popularity may affect the overall management strategy for their facility. The tremendous increase in the number of public assembly facilities in the United States beginning in the 1950s was noted earlier. This rapid expansion was largely the result of flourishing suburban communities building their own public assembly facilities coupled with the construction of numerous other facilities as memorials to World War II veterans. Local governmental bodies were eager to invest their financial resources into the development of new public assembly facilities believing they would serve as economic catalysts for their respective communities due to the conventions, conferences, meetings, trade shows, theatrical productions, and sporting events they would bring to the community.

THE NEED FOR MARKETING
AND WHAT IT CAN ACCOMPLISH

What exactly is marketing? Bearden, Ingram and Laforge assert the most widely accepted generic definition of marketing is that proffered by the American Marketing Association (AMA) which defines marketing as "the process of planning and executing the conception, pricing, promotion and distribution of ideas, goods and services to create exchanges that satisfy individual and organizational goals." (Bearden, 1995)

The purpose of this chapter is not to provide detail on effective event marketing campaigns but rather to demonstrate the need for basic facility marketing in order to attract events. While the above noted increase in public assembly facilities created more jobs for people in the community and more activity options for the general public, it also created more competition among those public assembly managers seeking to capture the general public's discretionary expenditures. The expansion of available public assembly facilities along with escalated competition, relatively fewer attractions, shorter concert circuits, and the need to generate profits resulted in the implementation of aggressive sales and marketing strategies. Prudent public assembly facility managers know that waiting for business to appear on the facility's doorstep is nothing short of competitive suicide. Consequently, a well-thought-out and orchestrated strategic marketing plan becomes an absolute necessity if the public assembly facility manager is to achieve success.

Marketing plans may be developed to acquire specific events, to support promotions by building tenants (such as sport teams, symphony orchestra, dance companies, etc.), and to promote the public assembly facility itself. Marketing techniques should serve to bolster relationships with many parties including guests, promoters, *sponsors*, teams, *resident companies*, elected and appointed government officials, and local businesses. They may also help to accomplish business objectives such as increasing the public assembly facility's attendance figures and/or revenues by a defined percentage, or by simply increasing the community's participation in local programs. Business objectives should be written in a manner that facilitates the measurement and evaluation of achievement. Measurement and evaluation are extremely important because they provide the basis for determining success and subsequently revising and refining objectives, if needed.

It is also important that facility management report results of its efforts to political boards and the general public. Data derived from empirical evaluation provides a powerful tool that the marketing department can use in their effort to focus on the purpose(s) for which the facility was built. It follows that continuing "reports" describe and provide factual data that can be used to determine to what extent the purpose(s) is being achieved.

Public assembly facility managers must resist the urge to list objectives such as "to increase awareness" or "to enhance the image." These can be identified and included as "positive/consequent desired results." The prime issue is the meaning of these objectives.

On what basis can they be evaluated or measured? If a manager really wants to increase the community's awareness of the public assembly facility, the first step could be to conduct a study to determine the community's current awareness level. With that measurement in hand, a marketing program designed to raise the community's awareness level could be developed and implemented. A follow-up study would later be conducted to determine the community's awareness level at that point in time. Comparing the pre- and post-awareness levels would then establish whether the marketing program was successful and, if so, to what extent.

In essence, strategic marketing implemented with strategic advertising and promotion will assist the public assembly facility manager in cutting through the marketing, advertising, and promotional clutter that result from increased competition. The objective is to assist in driving business and sales to a higher level and to strengthen guest loyalty within targeted segments of the community.

HOW AND WHY DOES MARKETING APPLY TO PUBLIC ASSEMBLY FACILITIES?

For public assembly facilities such as convention centers, arenas, stadiums, amphitheaters, and performing art centers to maintain their viability, each must secure events to present to their consuming public. Therefore, whenever applying the definition of marketing to a public assembly facility, it is important to first identify the target audiences and the events or facilities to be sold. Most public assembly facilities are concerned with selling facility time and space to promoters for the purpose of producing events. In some instances, the facility sells the tickets to the public in order to "fill seats." More and more public assembly facilities, especially major facilities, are taking over the role of the producer and are assuming the associated risks. In other instances, the facility's role is more that of a landlord. The tenant/promoter, such as a sport team, convention/exhibit firm, resident company, touring show or concert, etc., is responsible for ticket sales that may be handled in-house or contracted out. Whether the facility actually sells the tickets or not, it still should "sell" the facility and the event so the public will want to buy the tickets.

Thus when applying the AMA's marketing definition to the public assembly facility industry, the events produced or the facility itself can be identified as the goods and services that the manager must conceptualize, produce, promote, and ultimately sell to the consuming public, to a promoter/presenter, or to both. The exchange may be represented by rental fees, ticket sales, and *ancillary revenue* from sources such as parking, food and beverage and merchandise. A marketing plan provides a vehicle for managers to drive sales by fulfilling the desires and needs of community residents based on the social and economic demographics and psychographics profile data of the constituent population.

✕ GETTING THE EVENTS

In order to remain viable, public assembly facilities must secure events. Although commonalities exist, the approach to achieving this goal may be somewhat different for facilities focusing on entertainment-oriented events than those primarily hosting conferences, trade shows, meetings and exhibits.

Managers of public assembly facilities primarily hosting entertainment-oriented events seek to book attractions that appeal to one or more segments of their population mix. The public assembly facility manager must be acutely aware of the demographic/psychographics of the population within the facility's potential drawing area. With this in mind, the public assembly facility manager must make contact with the attraction's promoter and indicate an interest in having that particular attraction book their facility. Of course, the opposite occurs whenever the promoter makes first contact seeking an available booking date. Public assembly facilities of this nature may also seek to attract other types of events such as religious meetings, graduations and similar activities for which the facility has available dates and resources to accommodate.

For managers of public assembly facilities that primarily host conferences, trade shows, meetings and exhibitions, the process of attracting and booking events is somewhat different. Key to successfully attracting events to convention centers, meeting facilities and exhibit halls is the development of positive relationships with corporate, government and organization leaders and their meeting planners.

According to Steve Camp (President and CEO of the South Carolina Midlands Authority for Conventions, Sports and Tourism), the process of developing positive relationships requires significant work and planning. Initially, a comprehensive database must be created to identify on a regional basis (in some instances a national or international basis) the leaders and future leaders of the various entities that may become potential users of the public assembly facility. Once identified, plans must be made to have a public assembly facility representative make a "cold call" visit to these individuals in order to provide information about the facility and to "qualify" their events that could be hosted by the public assembly facility. The qualification process is simply one of learning of the event's requirements and verifying the public assembly facility's capability of accommodating those requirements.

Following the cold call, for those entities expressing an interest in possibly booking a qualified event, the public assembly facility manager should schedule a follow up face-to-face visit with the appropriate meeting planner. At that time, an offer should be extended to conduct a familiarity tour of the public assembly facility, to provide introductions to the various hotel/motel managers, etc.

Many entertainment attractions, such as concerts, are regularly booked from days to weeks in advance or to "next year's tour." Some family shows and flat shows contract five to ten years in advance and for the same time frame each year, e.g., the 3rd weekend in April.

Lead time for booking most conventions, exhibits, trade shows and some meetings is often considerably longer. The size of the event (in terms of space requirements, expected attendance, catering demands, and hotel/motel accommodations) usually dictates the booking lead time parameter. Major conventions generally require an advance booking of three to five years (smaller ones, one to two years) in order to properly secure all the arrangements necessary for their success. On the other hand, a small meeting may only require an advance booking of one month, sometimes less, if sufficient facility space and required services are available.

The Convention and Visitors Bureau director should be responsible for working effectively with representatives of the various public assembly facilities, hotels/motels, restaurants, caterers, etc., in order to attract the greatest number of events to the particular community or region and for assisting, to the extent possible, in the financial success of each entity. For example, a large conference may contract for meeting and trade show space with the convention center while locating its convention headquarters and housing its delegates in a particular hotel. Other hotels/motels may be identified as being available for overflow or alternative guest accommodations.

The Convention and Visitors Bureau director should also assist in directing smaller-sized events to those hotels/motels with sufficient meeting space, dining accommodations and guest rooms. Convention centers are generally capable of providing for most catering requests. However, whenever assistance is required in providing for these needs, hotels/motels, local caterers and restaurants may be contracted to provide assistance.

Cultivation of a cooperative spirit among the various public assembly facilities, hotels/motels, restaurants and caterers will contribute toward the success of each. The success of these various entities will in turn produce a positive effect on the economic viability of the community or region in which they exist and the quality of life enjoyed by its residents.

✳ THE SALES AND MARKETING DEPARTMENT

A vital part of many public assembly facilities is the sales and marketing department. While job titles may vary by facility type, overall responsibilities include:

- Assist with booking of events in some but not all instances.
- Assist in the advertising, marketing, and promotions of events.
- Sell group tickets.
- Place event-related advertising.
- Conduct marketing and customer satisfaction surveys.
- Maintain positive on-going media relations
- Arrange for publicity of the facility and its events; achieve consistent, positive and high profile public/industry awareness.
- Place industry advertising for the facility.
- Oversee web site content and design.

- Arrange for the design, printing, and distribution of brochures and other collateral materials.
- Coordinate marketing efforts with local CVB and other appropriate groups.
- Manage and administer any outside advertising agency contract(s).

Ultimately, the job of the sales and marketing department is to induce sales: sell time and space in every facility, sell every ticket to every event, sell ancillary products and sell premium access.

THE MARKETING PLAN

Ideally, every public assembly facility, regardless of type, should have a marketing plan and marketing staff in place. The ideal is seldom achieved. Though larger facilities and programs are likely to have an adequately staffed marketing department, smaller facilities not only may have only one individual responsible for the marketing functions, but that individual may be the general manager. The marketing plan presents a strategy for positioning the public assembly facility within the marketplace in order to maximize its business potential and to accomplish its established performance objectives. A sales plan is part of a marketing plan; it's one of the ways the marketing plan is carried out.

A distinction needs to be made between sales and marketing plans developed for the facility itself and those constructed for promoting specific events held in the public assembly facility. The facility may participate in the marketing of specific events to varying degrees, depending on the relationship between the facility and event producers. The facility may be only in the role of property owner or it may be a co-promoter or even the promoter.

Depending upon the public assembly facility's purpose and mission, the marketing plan may focus on a specific demographic target market group(s) or a specific industry niche. While marketing tactics may vary among organizations, the need for effective marketing has taken on a tremendously important role for all public assembly facility organizational formats. Consumers of leisure time activities and events enjoy a continually expanding number of available options for spending their discretionary monies. This escalation in opportunities serves to further increase the level of competition among public assembly facilities for the available events and patrons. Each public assembly facility, as part of its marketing plan, must address the questions, including the following:

- What makes us different from our competitors?
- Why should event promoters and organizers book our facility rather than a competitor's facility?
- What effective strategies can be employed to maximize ticket sales and attendance?
- What are our strengths and weaknesses?
- What competitive threats exist?
- What competitive opportunities are available?

The marketing plan is an "organizational resume" that focuses on capturing the attention and business of all customers, tenants, clients, and patrons. The elements and creation of the marketing plan are discussed later in this chapter.

Effective marketing can provide competitive advantages for facility users. Marketing efforts designed to maximize business for a public assembly facility may include some or all of the following:

- Selling advertising, sponsorships, and other commercial rights.
- Advertising the facility in industry trade publications as well as in both regional and local media outlets.
- Providing event producers with in-house ad placement and promotional services.
- Assisting with public relations efforts for the facility, its tenants and their events.
- Assisting with media relations efforts.
- Maintaining solid relationships with sponsors.
- Developing and maintaining the venue's web site.
- Group ticket sales promotions.

How does a public assembly facility manager construct a marketing plan? First and foremost, the facility manager should remember that the purpose of the marketing plan is to guide the establishment of *market position* that achieves stated objectives that are in concert with the facility's purpose and mission statements. Stotlar (1993) indicates that all business entities exist to realize such objectives and that the marketing plan is the planning process used to accomplish them.

The manager should examine the facility's mission statement carefully in order to determine what business objectives to pursue consistent with the purpose of the facility. For example, does the mission statement specify that earning a net operating surplus is an objective? And if making a profit is indeed an objective, to what extent or level should it be pursued? Does the mission statement denote a minimum number of event dates that must be booked per year? Are specific events mandated? Information of this nature is extremely useful when determining where marketing energies and resources should be focused.

Numerous books and guides devoted to the process of writing effective marketing plans currently exist. Nevertheless, what the public assembly facility manager needs is a plan that is practical and applicable in a variety of business environments. Most importantly, the plan must be tailored to fit the unique local market condition.

The following material describing components of a marketing plan are taken from Cohen (1987) and are modified to directly address the public assembly facility management industry.

EXECUTIVE SUMMARY

The end portion of the marketing plan is an executive summary that presents a concise overview of the marketing plan. The key is to provide an accurate description of the services and facilities available.

Cohen asserts that even though the executive summary is written last, it is often the first item to be reviewed. It can be likened to a book review or a chapter summary within a text-book. In a corporate environment, CEO's with heavy time constraints often make decisions based solely on the executive summary and therefore require the clearest snapshot of the current status of where the organization is headed with respect to its business objectives. The executive summary should also state financial, personnel and equipment requirements, the facility's competitive advantage, and the anticipated return on investment.

OTHER COMPONENTS OF THE MARKETING PLAN

Introduction - Include a facility and service analysis that answers the basic questions of what you are capable of providing to the user, what unique characteristics your facility or service provides (capacity, parking, state-of-the-art sound and lights, etc.) and precisely how it fits into the users' market. This is often reflected in the vision and mission statements.

Situational analysis - Incorporates the economic climate, geographic attributes, area demographics, demand trends, technological trends (including need to meet them), competitor analysis, and applicable internal aspects of the organization.

Analysis of target markets - Utilizes market segmentation, marketing information systems, and research on consumer behavior and historical buying patterns.

Marketing objectives - Identifies and describes end results such as number of events, number of event days, mix of events, event category and total attendance, per capita results from all revenue sources, etc. Presents desired market share, sales volume/grosses, ticket sales, rental revenue, and ancillary endeavors and revenue generation.

Marketing strategies - Describes in conceptual terms what is to be done to accomplish the objectives of the plan. Points to the path(s) to follow and the specific recommendations for overcoming direct competition.

Implementation and Control - Details start-up costs, public relations, sales, promotions and advertising efforts, on-going budget(s) and cost analysis procedures.

IMPLEMENTATION

The implementation process (Figure 4.1) is the same process a manager would use for all projects, not just a marketing plan. Implementing the marketing plan, then, is basically a four-step circular process performed by the manager(s) following approval from their board, owners, etc. The steps are:

M = MARSHALL resources of labor, equipment, and funds.
A = ALLOCATE resources according to considerations such as need, timing, and effect on the plan.
M = MONITOR the results of the implementation on a continuing basis whether there is to be an endpoint or not. This is the key measurement and evaluation step.
A = ADJUST the plan, marshal new or additional resources, allocate or re-allocate existing resources.

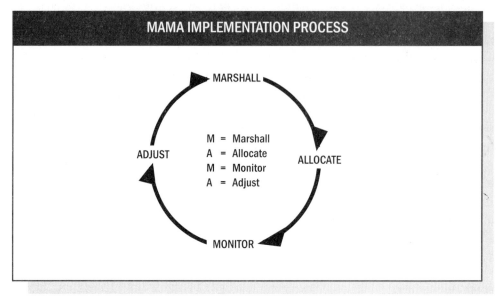

MAMA diagram   FIGURE 4-1

MARKETING BUDGET

Figure 4-2 (in Appendix A) represents a Marketing Settlement Sheet that presents a detailed record of advertising and promotional expenditures associated with a specific event presented in a specific public assembly facility. Expenditures for print, television, radio and outdoor (billboard) advertising as well as those costs associated with creating and producing printed flyers, brochures and post cards are presented. Postage, telemarketing and public relations expenditures are also identified.

Settlement sheets of this nature not only assist in accurately determining the cost of all marketing efforts related to a specific event, they also serve as a guideline for constructing future marketing budgets for the same or similar event presented in that particular public assembly facility or at another facility located within a comparable demographic/psychographic/economic market.

MARKETING EFFORTS AT MULTIPLE LEVELS

Once the marketing strategy and target audience market(s) are determined, the public assembly facility manager must begin to market the facility at the appropriate levels. Public assembly facilities can be marketed on an international, national, regional, and local basis depending on their mission statement and the types of programs and events they desire to present.

In all probability, the public assembly facility will be marketed simultaneously on several levels in which case the manager will need to carefully determine the marketing vehicles most appropriate for each level. For example, a performing arts center may have a world-renowned concert or Broadway production that has the potential to attract an international audience. The same performing arts center may also boast a program menu featuring artists who are especially appealing to local residents. The performing arts center manager must decide how to market each of these events and select those marketing vehicles that will most effectively reach the targeted audience. In many cases, facility managers themselves are the most effective marketing tool available. Their contacts, relationships and personal integrity as business partners often serve as a magnet for event promotional producers.

Print advertising, for example, could be used in international, national, regional, or local marketing efforts depending on the circulation and readership of the available vehicles. Although print media that enjoy a large circulation would seem most desirable, this may not be true if the public assembly manager is seeking to reach a specialized market segment or a niche audience. Quite frequently, preference is given to smaller circulation publications that are targeted toward a readership profile more representative of the market segment(s) sought.

Direct mail and blast e-mails also offer a way to disseminate printed materials to particular population segments. However, the continual increase in the cost of postage must be taken into consideration if large numbers of promotional units are to be mailed. From some perspectives, Internet advertising may be more efficient in terms of accessibility and may prove more cost effective for the number of individuals/ households reached. Aside from providing basic information about the public assembly facility, many facilities offer virtual facility tours through their Internet website along with a schedule of upcoming events and the opportunity to electronically purchase tickets online. Having an Internet website allows prospective guests to access desired information at any time without affecting staffing requirements. Other printed materials such as programs, newsletters, billboards, and newspaper ads and inserts are additional marketing vehicles that can be utilized individually or in various combinations. These same vehicles may be included on the Internet website thereby enabling visitors to view them and to download a personal hardcopy of the desired information at no cost to the public assembly facility.

The key element for the public assembly facility manager is to decide which marketing levels are most appropriate for the facility and to then carefully research the various types of promotional vehicles that may prove effective in achieving the desired results. In so doing, the public assembly facility manager should ask the following questions: Who is the target audience(s)? What marketing vehicles are available and can they effectively reach this target market(s)?

THE IMPORTANCE OF RELATIONSHIPS TO SALES AND MARKETING

When the terms sales and marketing are mentioned, many individuals immediately think of advertising channels and promotional efforts. However, it is important not to overlook the need for nurturing personal relationships with guests, teams, resident companies, government officials, business leaders, meeting planners and association executives, and vendors as well as the general ticket-buying public. It is equally important to understand the positive effect these relationships can have on the "marketability" of public assembly facility managers and their facility. It must be remembered at all times that people do business with people, not just with other businesses. It cannot be stressed too often that the public assembly facility management industry is built on relationships. The personality and management style of the public assembly facility manager is paramount in helping to generate and/or maintain repeat business with promoters and other industry representatives. A public assembly facility may be at the cutting edge in terms of its seating capacity and physical amenities, but generally the most important influence on tenants and promoters to book future dates with the facility is the manager and the facility's staff working diligently to ensure that ticket buying patrons are attracted to the facility and that all aspects of an event "run smoothly."

Yogi Berra once said, "If they don't want to come . . ., nothing on earth can stop them." (Berra). Since public assembly facility managers are generally very knowledgeable about the communities and regional areas in which the majority of potential event attendees reside, it becomes their responsibility to attempt to enhance the public perception of the event-related experience through a strategic marketing program.

RELATIONSHIPS ARE KEY   *Ask Guest Speaker this!*

Creating and maintaining positive relationships with industry colleagues is also very important to the successful public assembly facility manager. Membership and active participation in organizations such as the International Association of Assembly Managers (IAAM) (www.iaam.org) allows the facility manager to interact with colleagues worldwide. The common interests of association members tend to facilitate the creation of friendships and the development of extensive networking. In the process of growing these professional relationships, facility managers have the opportunity to market their facilities, as well as themselves, to a wide cross section of industry members and representatives.

Industry relationships and networking are vital in helping the public assembly facility manager to raise the profile of the facility. While each venue has its own particular characteristics and quirks, most first-time problems encountered by the facility manager are probably not unique and most likely have been experienced by other facility managers. Public assembly facility managers who enjoy strong positive relationships with their colleagues may contact them for assistance or advice when perplexing problems are encountered.

✕ THE FACILITY IMAGE

The public assembly facility industry is a business based on leverage and relationships. Prudent public assembly facility managers understand the cliché "image is everything" and they constantly work to maintain and improve the image of the facility and its scheduled events. The facility manager should become involved in community affairs and should frequently interact with and discreetly educate the public and labor, business, government, community leaders, and other stakeholders about the public assembly facility's business, social, and economic agendas. Facility managers' interpersonal skills play a vital role in determining the level of cooperation and support they receive from these individuals. Inviting potential partners to participate in educational tours of the public assembly facility and working cooperatively with local agencies such as the convention and visitors bureau will also serve to bolster community relationships. The convention and visitors bureau is especially important because it interacts with virtually every business within the community and region, especially the hotel, motel, and food and beverage industries, in an effort to attract events and visitors to the community thereby generating additional revenue for the various entities.

Other alliances the public assembly facility manager should foster include the chamber of commerce, local sport councils, elected and appointed government officials, the media, school associations, and community groups. Participating in promotional efforts catering to community-based groups, such as discounted group ticket sales and reduced rental fees, also contributes to the development and maintenance of strong community relations.

The manager must diligently work to uphold the community's image of the public assembly facility by insuring that it creates a positive impact upon the lifestyle of the citizens residing within the community and surrounding areas. Some considerations include:

- Has every effort been made to ensure the safety of guests while they are in and about the facility?
- Does the facility's programming meet the diverse needs of the community?
- Are community residents employed by the public assembly facility?
- Does the presence of the public assembly facility enhance the economic health of the community?
- Are the public assembly facility and its grounds properly maintained?
- Has the facility manager been successful in scheduling events that minimize dis turbing citizens living in close proximity to the facility?

These are questions that citizens may ask when evaluating the public assembly facility with respect to its being a good community partner. Government officials may also ask these or similar questions when evaluating the management of the facility with respect to its program, financial resources and results, and physical elements. These questions would be particularly applicable if the government owns or operates the facility. The public assembly facility manager must adhere to relevant public concerns while constantly striving to exceed the performance expectations of owners, clients, guests, and the general public.

✗ ADVERTISING AND PROMOTIONS

As previously stated, marketing can help with the achievement of specific objectives of the public assembly facility. While objectives may differ for each, a commonly shared objective is to increase revenues generated through rent, ticket sales (if the rental fee is based on a percentage of the ticket sales), and ancillary service income. Effective marketing is the key to achieving this and all other objectives.

Advertising campaign strategies are an effective method of planning a multiple attack on the target market. Once an advertising and promotion budget amount is determined, the marketing department will need to assemble the resources available to achieve the promotion objective. This exercise begins with evaluating the market demographics of the event and then determining the various methods, times, frequency, and incentives that will be used to reach the target audience. The campaign can involve a number of different strategies included, but not limited to, multiple pricing scales of tickets, *group ticket sales*, *cross-bounce coupons*, etc. Additionally, the campaign may employ special sponsored events with local charities as beneficiaries.. This tactic might drive consumer sales at area business at the same time.

A media blitz using a myriad of different options, e.g., radio, television, print, and billboards, can be used to achieve saturation levels that reach the target audience in multiple ways. Also, utilizing electronic web sites can be an added asset to the arsenal. The frequency and length of these advertising messages along with the optimum choice of schedules for running the ads is an important ingredient to include in the development of the campaign strategy. For some radio advertising schedules, a run of schedule (ROS), i.e., the station selects timing of ads, may be sufficient. (See Appendix A, 4-3). Using the ROS is often much less expensive per exposure and frequently is tied into promotions sponsored by the radio station of one of the event sponsors. For other advertising and promotion efforts, a prime time segment like drive time, specifying the radio spot to play frequently during times people are driving to and from work, may be the preferred tactic.

If increasing the sales of ancillary products is the objective, group ticket sales and cross-bounce coupon strategies are an effective way to increase attendance. Information about these options is normally displayed in the paid advertising. In these cases, the ticket buyer is getting a value-added benefit by either getting a discount or an opportunity to get a discount at a participatory retail outlet or some other partner. These tactics not only help to grow ancillary receipts but also help build a fan base through exposure to new entertainment and events.

✗ SEASON TICKETS AND SUBSCRIPTIONS

Packaging or *bundling* is a concept of marketing that often helps to promote events in public assembly facilities. One of the more common practices of this strategy is the season ticketing or subscription price. Whether it is a string of sporting events or a theatre series, the intent is the same, to encourage fans and patrons to make a long-term commitment by purchasing in bulk. To achieve this, the bulk price for the season ticket or subscription is usually less than the combined individual rates of each event. However, if the event being promoted is in high demand, the price does not necessarily have to be less. A season pass to a series may simply guarantee you an exclusive opportunity that individual purchasers may not have, not a less expensive price. Another method of adding value to season subscriptions is to package a specified genre of talent together and schedule the performances over several event dates. Using this tactic, a creative entrepreneur can produce a subscription series by contracting for a well-known and recognized act/talent and then include in the season package some lesser known talent. The (more expensive) loss leader coupled with acts with less or uncertain popularity as a package can be a very marketable series.

In the United States, some Major League Baseball (MLB) and National Basketball Association (NBA) teams have recently begun using this same basic approach. That is, they are using access to the games with the more attractive opponents to create value. For season tickets, there may be an added cost included in the price for the prime opponents, or there may be no added cost but the fan is induced to buy the season ticket and ensure access to the game(s).

✳MARKETING OF PREMIUM ACCESS

Regardless of the industry, retail sales of inventory can very often be enhanced through creative marketing and value-added packaging and the public assembly facility is no exception. In the sports and entertainment business, exclusive and prestigious commodities that are in limited supply, are often more desirable and attractive than the standard fare. Since time and space is the key commodity of value in the public assembly facility, access and especially premium access to its audience and attraction for clients and patrons alike can garner extraordinary value. These types of sales are an ever-increasing percentage of the facility's revenue pie. Whether it be *golden circle* front row seating or a captured audience for advertisers, exclusive demand for access is a marketable program. The following segment is devoted to discussions of some of the more prevalent concepts being employed in the public assembly facility industry.

PREMIUM SEATING AND LUXURY SUITES

The sale of *premium seating* is becoming the financial mainstay of many public assembly facilities. This marketing concept is based on the premise that individual guests and businesses are willing to pay a premium price for seating in areas that offer added amenities. These added amenities might include proximity, front row seats for an opera or basketball game, sight lines and/or physical comfort. Businesses might purchase these premium seats to entertain clients and others important to their activities.

Luxury suites represent the ultimate in upscale seating. Many businesses lease luxury suites for a specified period. For example, luxury suites at football stadiums are leased on a season or multiple season contract and are available for use during all home games of the prime tenant(s). On the other hand, public assembly facilities that host a variety of events throughout the year generally lease their luxury suites on an annual or multi-year contract. Some public assembly facilities offer leaseholders the opportunity to sublease their suites on a per-event basis. In return for providing this service, the public assembly facility management might collect a commission ranging from 10 to 25 percent of the revenue generated by the sublease.

This service is particularly appealing to suite leaseholders not wishing or unable to attend every event because it allows them the chance to recapture a portion of their leasing costs. It is also appealing to the public assembly facility manager because it provides another revenue stream; it places guests at events who purchase tickets and ancillary products or services (empty seats do not purchase food and beverages); and it provides an opportunity to introduce the suite concept to potential leaseholders.

For sport fans not wishing the luxury of a suite, premium or "club" seats offer an excellent opportunity to enjoy some of the same amenities available to the suite holder but at a lesser price. Depending on the amenities provided, these premium seats might cost from $500 to $3,500 (US) per seat on a seasonal basis. At the same time, depending on the event and facility, a premium seat may cost a considerable amount for a single event. A courtside seat at an NBA game in a major market might cost $1,000 per game. Premium seating tickets for Las Vegas concerts by Luciano Pavarotti and Barbra Streisand have sold for as much as $1,250 - $1,500 each. Premium seating and luxury suite amenities might include preferential parking, food and beverage delivery service to your seat, access to the facility's restaurants and clubrooms, and admission to the facility through a private entrance.

Premium seating and luxury suites have become such important revenue producers that they can drive the design of new facilities, especially amphitheatres, arenas and stadiums. The exclusive concept and added amenities of premium seating have long been an element of performing art facilities. A separate organization exists for professionals in this area — the Association of Luxury Suite Directors (www.alsd.com).

PRIORITY SEATING

The selling of priority seating or *personal seating licenses* (PSL) represents yet another vehicle for generating additional revenue. In purchasing a PSL, fans pay a one-time fee in order to gain "ownership" of a specified seat and they retain "ownership" with the annual purchase of a season ticket for a specified period of time, up to lifetime. Although not limited to sporting events, the PSL can produce significant amounts of new money in markets with rabid sport fans. However, it must be kept in mind that the sale of a PSL only produces one-time money to help offset construction costs rather than annual operating revenue unless the PSL is for a limited period of time and then must be "re-purchased."

In the collegiate setting, the PSL concept is the same, although applied somewhat differently. Rather than selling a PSL, fans are encouraged to become members of the institution's booster club. Most booster clubs offer a variety of membership levels each requiring a specified minimum financial contribution. Each contribution level provides stated benefits with the number and quality of the benefits increasing as the contribution level increases. In the United States, for most NCAA Division I collegiate institutions, it is virtually impossible to purchase "good" seats for football and men's basketball (and in some instances women's basketball) without being a member of the booster club. Booster clubs are not limited to collegiate institutions. In various places in the world, clubs and even professional teams have booster clubs. Generally, season ticket assignments might be based on a formula that takes into account the number of years the applicant has been a member of the booster club, the total amount of contributions during that membership period, and the current membership level. It is not unusual for an upper tier NCAA Division I institution to generate over $10 million (US) annually from booster donations in addition to the revenue garnered from the sale of season tickets to these members (Cohen, 1987).

NAMING RIGHTS AND ENDORSEMENTS

Naming rights associated with events or facilities is not necessarily a new phenomena but the practice has become very sophisticated in the public assembly facility industry. Naming rights provide other avenues for generating additional income. One form is that of providing the named entity with the opportunity to have its name associated with the facility itself. A second form is enabling the named entity to have its name attached to one or more of the facility's scheduled events. In both formats, a specified fee or other agreed upon form of payment is required from the named entity in return for the opportunity to have its name affiliated with and to gain exposure through their association with the facility or event.

Relationships of this nature have become increasingly popular and are generally referred to as sponsorships. Sleight defines sponsorship as a "business relationship between a provider of funds, resources or services and an individual, event, or organization which offers in return some rights and associations that may be used for commercial advantage." (Sleight, 1989).

While sponsorship partners are usually thought to be businesses, they may also be governments or govermental agencies, non-profit organizations, or special interest groups. Media partners can be especially valuable. Sponsors usually enter into agreements that will enable them to achieve specific objectives, business and otherwise, through their association with the facility or the event(s) taking place within it. Sponsorship agreements can be extremely lucrative for the public assembly facility manager because of the money, human resources, physical equipment, or services they can provide.

Although sponsorships have been traced back to ancient Greece, they began to flourish in the early 1900s when American railway companies and Major League Baseball entered into agreements designed to attract additional customers for each business (Stotlar, 1993). In the early 1970s when traditional print advertising streams and electronic media outlets became cluttered, potential customers began to switch television channels to avoid listening to/viewing commercials and they also began to pay less attention to newspapers and magazine advertisements. It was at this point that businesses turned more to sponsorships in an effort to capture or recapture consumer attention.

However, as more and more businesses entered into sponsorship agreements, clutter rapidly followed thereby negating, to some degree, the effectiveness and value of this advertising format. In addition, the cost of sponsorship had become increasingly expensive, and many sponsors and potential sponsors began to express concerns regarding the level of return on their investments. For example, international Olympic Games sponsors pay more than $40 million (US) for official worldwide exclusive sponsorship rights in their product or service line. Yet, some research studies have revealed that when attendees at the Games, along with those who viewed the Games on television, where asked to recall the official sponsors of the Games, they failed to mention many of the legitimate sponsors who had paid substantial fees in order to become affiliated with the Olympic Games. In fact, studies have also revealed that some of the competitors to these official Olympic Game sponsors — competitors who had no official affiliation with the Games but who engaged in "ambush marketing" tactics during the course of the Games — were frequently recalled by both on-site and television viewers as being the official Olympic Games sponsor.

Always seeking to gain a competitive advantage, businesses and other sponsorship partners once again began searching for ways to cut through the marketing clutter. The need for greater recognition and stronger returns on their advertising dollars motivated some business sponsors to drop traditional partnerships so they could invest even greater amounts of money into securing naming rights for public assembly facilities and/or events. Capturing exclusive beverage *pouring rights* at public assembly facilities was a major objective for businesses in the beverage industry. Owners of public assembly facilities soon discovered that selling facility naming and exclusive pouring rights could generate significant revenue because many of the largest and most powerful businesses were in competition for these opportunities. Monies generated in this manner are particularly helpful in defraying the debt service related to the construction of new, or the renovation of existing, public assembly facilities.

To illustrate the increase in the value of naming and pouring values, consider the following: the Carrier Corporation in 1983 paid Syracuse University $900,000 (US) to name its new sports facility the Carrierdome. In 1992, Pepsi Cola paid Penn State University $14 million (US) to become the University's official beverage. Naming rights for the Staples Center (Los Angeles), Bank One Ballpark (Phoenix) and Ford Stadium (Detroit) cost $100 million, $66 million and $40 million dollars (US), respectively.

Payment for naming rights deals is generally negotiated, and they range from a single up front payment (which is particularly helpful when constructing or renovating a facility) to annual payments spread over the term of the contract. Generally, sponsors pay less for single upfront payment contracts than for multiyear long-term deals. Nonetheless, each of these payment formats is beneficial to the public assembly facility. The single upfront payment deal enables the facility to immediately reduce its debt service thereby saving a substantial amount in interest payments. On the other hand, the long-term annual payment deal provides the facility with the reasonably strong likelihood of income over the life of the contract - assuming periodic success with renewals.

Naming and pouring rights deals are not necessarily easy to sell and are definitely not risk free. If the naming sponsor experiences financial difficulty, or if its products/services become the subject of negative publicity, the public assembly facility may not be able to collect the full value of its contract and/or may have to sever the contractual relationship.

Consider the financial woes of Enron Field (Houston) following the business scandal that ensued in 2001 when Enron was accused of engaging in major financial mismanagement. These charges led to the company's bankruptcy, job loss for thousands of employees, tremendous financial losses for all its shareholders, and the removal of its name from the facility. Prudent rights agreements should require the holder of the naming or pouring rights to submit periodic financial statements and annual reports to the public assembly manager so their financial status can be evaluated.

However, in the Enron Field case, submission of these documents would not have indicated any pending problems because data had been falsified. Thus, the lesson learned from the Enron case is that although the potential for gaining significant profits through the awarding of naming and pouring rights may be extremely enticing, the prudent public assembly facility manager, in conjunction with legal counsel, should carefully research and investigate all potential rights holders before engaging in any negotiations that may lead to the signing of a legal agreement.

SELLING ADVERTISING SIGNAGE AND SPONSORSHIP

Sponsorship agreements are not advertising substitutes. They represent but one form of advertising in the development of the public assembly facility's advertising mix and they should be recognized as such. Public assembly facilities should make appropriate space available, within and outside the facility, for *signage* posting. Selling signage space is still a viable form of revenue generation and is generally reasonably priced thereby enabling smaller businesses to become advertising partners.

Selling space on the back of tickets, as well as on the backs of the envelopes the tickets are placed or mailed in, represents yet another excellent marketing opportunity. Businesses wishing to market their products/services will often purchase advertising space in event programs and facility newsletters thereby providing yet another revenue stream. Printed materials produced for dissemination to the facility's guest and the general public, such as guides (much like sport team media guides), seating charts, and schedules listing upcoming events and attractions, offer genuine opportunities for expanding revenue streams.

Some businesses will also pay the public assembly facility for the opportunity to provide event attendees with novelty items such as frisbees and water bottles imprinted with the businesses' name and logo. Baseball teams in both the major and minor leagues are prime examples of sport businesses that capitalize on revenue generation through the distribution of promotional giveaways replete with business advertising.

Virtually every public assembly facility that provides public ice skating, ice shows, and ice hockey sells advertising space for businesses to have their name and logo displayed. These spaces include spots on the ice itself, on the boards surrounding the rink, and on the vehicle used to clean and make new ice surfaces. This vehicle is commonly referred to as a *Zamboni*. However, Zamboni is but one of several brands available.

Scoreboards, announcement boards, and seat cup holders represent additional opportunities for the placement of business advertisements and logos. The possibilities for raising additional monies through marketing/advertising channels are virtually endless, restricted only by the public assembly facility manager's imagination.

With this in mind, the public assembly facility manager must be careful to resist selling too much advertising if clutter is to be avoided. Not only does the presence of too many advertisements produce clutter, it also tends to diminish the facility's attractiveness. In addition, an overload of advertisements makes it very difficult for the facility's guests to recall the names of the advertising partners.

The level to which guests are able to recall advertisers is very important to the advertisers seeking to gain a return on their advertising investment. The guest's level of advertiser recall is also important to the public assembly facility manager seeking to attract new and/or retaining current advertisers. Wise public assembly facility managers will implement periodic research studies to ascertain their guest's recall levels. The resulting data can be very influential when negotiating with current and potential advertisers.

✸ MEMORIAL GIFTS AND DONOR PROGRAMS

Donor programs are designed to attract individuals or businesses wishing to assist the public assembly facility financially or through the provision of goods and services. The difference between *donors* and sponsors is that contributions made by donors are generally altruistic and do not afford the donor any competitive advantage. The return to the donor is more likely to be satisfaction and recognition, such as a plaque at the facility, a room named for the donor, or the like. The "buy-a-brick" program used at the Atlanta Olympic Games is an example of a donor program that has been employed to assist many public assembly facilities generate funds for construction projects.

Institutions of higher education have developed excellent donor programs to solicit contributions from their graduates as well as from the business community, philanthropic organizations, and the general public. Public assembly facilities can institute similar donor programs when seeking contributions from foundations, benefactors, and businesses wishing to "give back" to the community. The performing arts represent one segment of the entertainment industry that has benefited greatly from donor programs.

Public assembly facility managers should consider directing their marketing staff to initiate a donor program, if one is not already in place. Even though donor programs may not seem as profitable as sponsorship agreements, they can create substantial amounts of good will in addition to providing needed revenue or goods and services.

✸ PRODUCT BRANDING AND POURING RIGHTS

Over the past several decades, the food and beverage industry has increasingly focused on the marketing importance of *branding*, and this concept has not gone unnoticed in the public assembly facility management industry. The greater the influence manufacturers and suppliers can have on customers and their buying habits, the greater their profit potential becomes. The emergence of branding concepts into the event scene scenario is a natural evolutionary step in the growth of public assembly facilities. As operating surplus margins become increasingly more difficult to achieve, public assembly facilities have ventured aggressively into this arena.

The ability to provide vendors with exclusive access to audiences is a valuable asset to the public assembly facility and such rights are much sought after by those businesses desiring to reach these target markets. Pouring rights exclusives are a component of the market mix and can be effectively capitalized upon using smart strategies. Beverage contracts providing exclusive pouring rights are not unique. In fact, many public assembly facilities have gained, through the leverage these contracts provide, dedicated funds from the vendor for facility upgrades and improvements. However, alcohol beverage companies in the U.S. are limited in what they can give or include as barter in their pouring rights deals.

SUMMARY

Sales and marketing have been in existence since at least the first century. Society in the twenty-first century is replete with competition. Consequently, successful managers of public assembly facilities must employ effective sales and marketing strategies in order to raise and maintain the viability of their venues. The continual expansion in the number of public assembly facilities has further heightened this competition to the point where only the "fittest" will survive.

Although people have more discretionary time and money than in any other period in history, they also have a much wider array of choices in which to expend these resources. Therefore, it is paramount that public assembly facility managers develop strategic sales and marketing plans for their facility.

The sales and marketing plan must focus on the existing and potential marketplace. The demographic and psychographic profiles of both the community and the region in which the public assembly facility exists must be taken into consideration when developing these plans. And, research designed to evaluate the success, or lack thereof, of these plans must be ongoing.

Effective sales and marketing are highly correlated with the ability of the public assembly facility manager's ability to create and maintain strong relationships. Effort must be taken to cultivate positive relationships with colleagues, owners, community leaders, promoters, vendors, and all other individuals with whom the manager interacts.

Advertising is an important component of the sales and marketing mix and all appropriate media outlets should be utilized. Every sales and marketing avenue must be explored to assess its potential contribution to the economic success of the public assembly facility.

The possibilities for raising additional monies through marketing/advertising channels are virtually endless, restricted only by the public assembly facility manager's imagination. Yet, diligent attention must be paid to insure the absence of promotion and advertising clutter.

REFERENCES AND ADDITIONAL READINGS

Bearden, W., Ingram, T. and LaForge, R. 2004. Marketing: *Principles and Perspectives,* 4th ed. New York: McGraw-Hill/Irwin, p.3.

Berra, Yogi. http://www.yogi-berra.com/yogiisms.htm.

Brooks, Christine M. 1994. *Sports Marketing: Competitive Business Strategies for Sports.* Upper Saddle River, NJ: Prentice Hall.

Burns, Alvin C. and Ronald F. Bush. 2001. *Marketing Research with SPSS 10 CD* 3rd ed. Upper Saddle River, NJ: Prentice Hall.

Bygrave, William D. 1994. *The Portable MBVA in Entrepreneurship.* Hoboken, NJ: John Wiley & Sons, Inc.

Cohen, William A. 1987. *Developing a Winning Marketing Plan.* New York: John Wiley & Sons, Inc.

Hall, Doug. 2003. *Meaningful Marketing.* White Hall, VA: Betterway Publishers.

Hiam, Alexander and Charles D. Schewe. 1998. *The Portable MBA in Marketing.* Hoboken, NJ: John Wiley & Sons, Inc.

Hoyle, Leonard H. 2002. *Event Marketing: How to Successfully Promote Events, Festivals, Conventions, and Expositions.* New York, NY: John Wiley & Sons, Inc.

Kerin, Roger A. and Robert A. Peterson. 2001. *Strategic Marketing Problems: Cases and Comments,* 9th ed. Upper Saddle River, NJ: Prentice Hall.

Kotler, Philip. 2002. *Marketing Management,* 11th ed. Upper Saddle River, NJ: Prentice Hall.

Mullin, Bernard J., Stephen Hardy and William A. Sutton. 1993. *Sport Marketing.* Champaign, IL: Human Kinetics Publishers.

O'Guinn, Thomas C, Chris T. Allen and Richard J. Semenik. 1998. *Advertising.* Mason, OH: South-Western College Publishers.

Perreault, William D. and E. Jerome McCarthy. 1996. *Basic Marketing.* Boston: Richard D. Irwin Publishers.

Ries, Al. 1994. *The 22 Immutable Laws of Marketing: Exposed and Explained by the World's Two*. NY: HarperBusiness.

Shimp, Terence A. 2002. *Advertising, Promotion and Supplemental Aspects of Integrated Marketing Communications*, 6th ed. Mason, OH: South-Western College Publishers.

Sleight, Steve. 1989. *Sponsorship: What It Is and How To Use It*. London: McGraw-Hill.

Solomon, Michael R. 1996. *Consumer Behavior*, 3rd ed. Upper Saddle River, NJ: Prentice Hall.

Stotler, David K. 1993. *Successful Sport Marketing*. Madison, WI: WCB Brown and Benchmark Publishers.

Zaltman, Gerald. 2003. *How Customers Think: Essential Insights into the Mind of the Market*. Cambridge, MA: Harvard Business School Press.

5

TICKETING AND BOX OFFICE MANAGEMENT

CHAPTER OUTLINE

INTRODUCTION

Box office management has evolved from using hard tickets of one kind or another into a highly sophisticated computerized operation. Box office management represents a process of financial accounting and inventory control that warrants careful attention. Providing for the safe, efficient movement of people into and out of public assembly facilities is a key to successful management. For many events, the use of tickets is a critical aspect of this process. This chapter will highlight the various facets of this extremely important process and will discuss the significance for having a properly managed ticketing operation.

HISTORICAL OVERVIEW

In the latter part of the first century, admission into many of the events held at the Roman Colosseum was free to the public. However, social class determined exactly where attendees were allowed to sit. Citizens and their families were allowed to sit or stand closest to the action and in front of soldiers and craftsmen/tradesmen. Slaves and servants were usually relegated to the extreme upper level(s) of the facility.

How did the early colosseum managers communicate the concept of assigned seating to their guests, and how did they avoid oversubscribing the facility when events were presented free to the public? These are certainly interesting questions.

Archeological evidence indicates attendees were issued a predetermined number of colored pottery shards that corresponded to color-coded entrance portals and seating sections in the facility. These pottery shards served as the first control of assigned seating and were the genesis for the evolution that led to today's ticketing process.

The issuance of tickets is almost as old as the management of public assembly facilities itself. Whether in the form of pottery shards, specially minted coins (ducats), pre-written or preprinted hard tickets, or today's computer generated tickets, issuing tickets helps the public assembly facility manager address issues common to virtually every facility type. These issues include managing and controlling admission to the facility and providing a level of financial accountability for the parties involved with presenting and managing the event.

Selling tickets and collecting box office receipts prior to the actual date of an event provide the box office manager with an opportunity to invest those revenues in short-term, interest-generating accounts, thereby creating a revenue stream for the public assembly facility. Selling tickets in advance also enables the facility's manager to staff the event efficiently and effectively. In addition, it provides a vehicle for transmitting information to purchasers related to the event or attraction as well as to the public assembly facility itself.

Bar coded tickets provide the box office manager with an innovative way to gather marketing information about the purchaser. Unused space on the ticket itself presents a valuable opportunity to gain additional revenue by printing paid advertising messages.

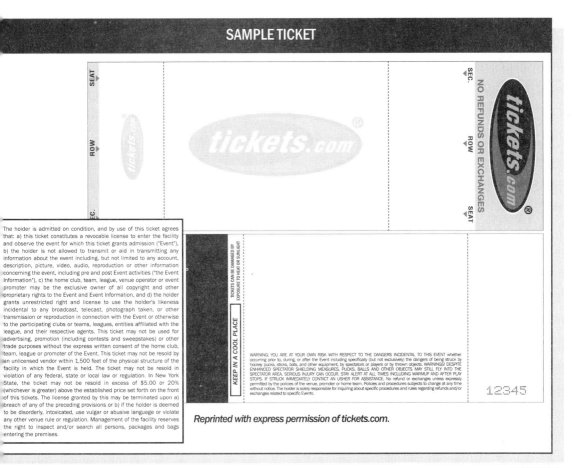

SAMPLE TICKET

The holder is admitted on condition, and by use of this ticket agrees that: a) this ticket constitutes a revocable license to enter the facility and observe the event for which this ticket grants admission ("Event"), b) the holder is not allowed to transmit or aid in transmitting any information about the event including, but not limited to any account, description, picture, video, audio, reproduction or other information concerning the event, including pre and post Event activities ("the Event Information"), c) the home club, team, league, venue operator or event promoter may be the exclusive owner of all copyright and other proprietary rights to the Event and Event Information, and d) the holder grants unrestricted right and license to use the holder's likeness incidental to any broadcast, telecast, photograph taken, or other transmission or reproduction in connection with the Event or otherwise to the participating clubs or teams, leagues, entities affiliated with the league, and their respective agents. This ticket may not be used for advertising, promotion (including contests and sweepstakes) or other trade purposes without the express written consent of the home club, team, league or promoter of the Event. This ticket may not be resold by an unlicensed vendor within 1,500 feet of the physical structure of the facility in which the Event is held. The ticket may not be resold in violation of any federal, state or local law or regulation. In New York State, the ticket may not be resold in excess of $5.00 or 20% (whichever is greater) above the established price set forth on the front of this tickets. The license granted by this may be terminated upon a) breach of any of the preceding provisions or b) if the holder is deemed to be disorderly, intoxicated, use vulgar or abusive language or violate any other venue rule or regulation. Management of the facility reserves the right to inspect and/or search all persons, packages and bags entering the premises.

WARNING: YOU ARE AT YOUR OWN RISK WITH RESPECT TO THE DANGERS INCIDENTAL TO THIS EVENT whether occurring prior to, during, or after the Event including specifically (but not exclusively) the dangers of being struck by hockey pucks, sticks, bats, and other equipment, by spectators or players or by thrown objects. WARNINGS! DESPITE ENHANCED SPECTATOR SHIELDING MEASURES, PUCKS, BALLS AND OTHER OBJECTS MAY STILL FLY INTO THE SPECTATOR AREA. SERIOUS INJURY CAN OCCUR. STAY ALERT AT ALL TIMES INCLUDING WARMUP AND AFTER PLAY STOPS. IF STRUCK IMMEDIATELY CONTACT AN USHER FOR ASSISTANCE. No refund or exchanges unless expressly permitted by the policies of the venue, promoter or home team. Policies and procedures subjects to change at any time without notice. The holder is solely responsible for inquiring about specific procedures and rules regarding refunds and/or exchanges related to specific Events.

Reprinted with express permission of tickets.com.

FIGURE 5-1

✳ TICKETS AS LIMITED CONTRACTS

By legal definition, a ticket of admission is both a *limited contract* and a *revocable permit*. (See Figure 5-1 for sample of language on the back of a ticket). For the ticket holder, it provides physical evidence of permission to enter the facility and a guarantee that the presenter will deliver what has been advertised on the ticket face or by prior advertising or promotion. If the guarantee is compromised, the ticket then becomes a proof of purchase receipt and can be used in a refund process.

In addition to the event presenter being responsible for delivering the advertised product, the ticket holder deserves the opportunity to "see and enjoy" the presentation. Enjoyment in this sense has little to do with approving or liking the performance but more with being able to see and hear the presentation in an environment free from unreasonable distractions.

If the facility fails in delivering these promises, the ticket holder may have the right to compensation that can include a partial or full refund of the ticket price or a ticket to a future performance. In some instances, the ticket holder might be relocated to an area within the facility that enables the promise to be kept. For example, patrons who buy a ticket to watch a baseball game have the right to complain if they were not informed that the assigned seat location is such that they are unable to see all of the playing field. In cases of this nature, the facility's or promoter's representative would either relocate the patron to a seat with an unobstructed view or if none were available then refund the price of the ticket.

Often when extremely popular attractions are being promoted, seating that is obstructed or offers a limited view of the event is made available to the public but only once the purchaser has been informed of the seat's problem. Tickets for these seats should be clearly marked *limited view* or *obstructed view*. In rare cases, seats that only provide the purchaser with a camera-projected view of the event, rather than a live view, have been sold and are referred to as "no live view" seats.

Some public assembly facilities are allowed to sell "standing room only" tickets to otherwise sold-out performances as long as the standing room only ticket holders do not block exits, entrances, aisles or the view of seated patrons. Since issuing more tickets than the facility has seats might violate the facility's occupancy rating, pre-approval from the local fire marshal is usually required before the box office manager can announce the sale of standing room only tickets. Of course, a specified number of standing room only tickets might be included in the occupancy rating.

A ticket is a revocable permit that the facility manager may, for a number of reasons, rescind, thereby disallowing admission to the holder. Typically, revoking the permit will initiate a refund of the ticket's price. Depending on the situation, a guest whose disorderly behavior becomes a distraction to others may have his/her ticket revoked and be escorted from the facility. A uniformed police officer might give an unruly patron the option of ejection or arrest. In cases involving disorderly behavior, a refund of the ticket's price is usually not a consideration.

Generally, printed on the face of the ticket is the name of the attraction, the date and time of the performance, name of the public assembly facility, and price paid for the ticket. This information becomes part of the ticket's guarantee obligating the presenter to produce what the ticket promises at the date, time, and place printed on the ticket.

Substituting one attraction for another and/or changing the time and place of the performance gives the holder the right to request a refund. If a ticket promises two entertainers and one does not perform, the ticket holder might have the right to a partial refund, if not a full one. In such cases, promoters typically announce prior to the start of the show which entertainer will not be performing, who the replacement will be, if any, and extend the availability of refunds to dissatisfied patrons.

Another refund situation might arise when an entertainer delivers an abbreviated performance. Generally, the headliner is expected to perform for at least 50 minutes. While the 50-minute guideline is not a law, it has evolved over the years to become an unwritten industry standard. If the entertainer fails to perform for at least 50 minutes, the audience might be due a refund.

BRITNEY SPEARS WALKS OFF STAGE AFTER POWER FAILURE

Britney Spears wasn't two songs into her June 14th, 2002 concert at the United Spirit Arena in Lubbock, Texas, [when] a transformer blew and the show was canceled. A member of Spears' management, along with the singer, came onstage after the second song to inform the crowd that the show had to be canceled. Basic arena power and lighting were unaffected, but stage power had been lost. Spears' show, which includes pyrotechnic effects and explosions, was apparently too much for the power supply. "I've learned more about transformers in the past three days than I've ever really wanted to know about," [the] venue [General Manager] told POLLSTAR.

"When [performers] bring up their cyberlights and their laser lights and everything else, it can shorten the life of a transformer," he said. "I never knew that." The audience reportedly booed once it realized the cancellation announcement was not part of the show.

[The General Manager] said he was hoping to get Spears to return rather than issue a refund even though it would cost the venue more money. Spears' tour ends July 22nd in Dallas. "Because most of the people we were dealing with were kids, they don't care about the money," he said. "They want to see Britney Spears. ... I know, obviously, the routing plays into it and I know she's awful busy, but boy, if we can work anything out, we're willing to do whatever we can."

The venue was informed June 19th there would be no return appearance. [The promoter] cited her touring schedule as the reason. Refunds were issued for the 13,351 ticket holders at Lubbock's Select-A-Seat main office.

Reprinted with permission by POLLSTAR magazine.

FIGURE 5-2

However, one of the most dangerous situations that can occur is when the main act of a high-energy event does not appear at all and the show is cancelled after the audience has been admitted to the facility. It is even possible the preliminary acts/artists have performed.

The main issues facing the promoter and the facility manager are when do you announce the situation and what do you announce? Is the show being postponed (because the artist became ill or was unable to get to the facility due to a mishap or some other delay) or is the show actually being cancelled?

If the answer is a postponement, the announcement should include the new show date, if known, and the audience should be told to keep and use their tickets for the new show date and that further information will be available as soon as possible. If the answer is a cancellation, the announcement must be carefully crafted since the possibility of crowd misbehavior is significantly increased. The announcement should include a reason for the cancellation and when and where refunds will be available. (See Figure 5-2 with an article about a concert being cancelled and the refund process).

Whether a postponement or cancellation, the facility should have in place a pre-recorded announcement for the existing audience that re-enforces the "on stage" announcement. The facility's staff needs to have received training in assisting the exit. The information distribution system to staff must be quick, precise, and understood. The major and most critical task is to exit the audience quickly and efficiently from the facility and surrounding area. If at all possible, the box office should be closed and its lights turned off prior to the announcement. An attempt to refund tickets for the exiting crowd can be a recipe for disaster. The history and image of the facility as being fair in protecting the rights of its guests can be an important element in the willingness of the audience to accept the negative situation, knowing it will be resolved soon.

When disagreements between presenters and ticket holders over the substitution of headliners and/or a change in venue or starting time leads to litigation, the courts tend to side with the ticket holders. Such litigation should be avoided as it is expensive and produces nothing but negative public relations for the public assembly facility and its management.

As with any contract, either party (in this case the ticket holder or the presenter) may alter the conditions of the contract so long as permission to do so is granted by the other party(ies). A presenter may substitute one act for another and/or change the time and place of the presentation as long as the ticket holder agrees. Tickets to collegiate sporting events, particularly basketball and football games, frequently are carrying a warning that the "Starting Time is Subject to Change." Understanding that many television broadcast decisions, especially collegiate, are made during the course of the season, season ticket holders have become conditioned to verify the starting time for each event. Some collegiate tickets carry the statement "Time To Be Announced."

In many states, each ticket must show in print the price paid. Printing the paid price protects the box office in case a refund is necessary. Since *complimentary* and *trade tickets* have no printed price, they are not eligible for a refund. If the public assembly facility uses preprinted tickets that include the printed price, trade and complimentary tickets are usually punched or stamped "complimentary" thereby eliminating them from any potential refund.

There is also the issue of tickets sold at less than full price. This may occur for several reasons. It may be the ticket is discounted from full price because it is a child's ticket, it is part of a group sale, it is part of an advertising coupon promotion, etc. If it is a hard ticket, some form of identification is needed on the ticket such as a stamp, punch, or cut. In instances where the only discount is for a child's ticket, there might be additional perforated stubs on the ticket, one being the "child's stub" that is removed at the time of the sale, thus signifying it is a reduced price ticket and informing the ticket taker to admit only a child. The other stub refers to an *audit stub*. This stub would be part of a hard ticket that is retained by the ticket seller. It is an inventory control device and accounting tool identifying at any given time how many tickets were sold and at what price. It provides a basis for estimating expected attendance at the event. Audit stubs are more likely to be used for multiple performance events or when several different events are on sale at the same time.

Of course, all of the above tasks can be achieved by computerized ticketing when the ticket is printed at the time and point of sale. The applicable distinctions are printed on the face of the ticket.

SAMPLE MUNICIPAL ORDINANCE

An ordinance adding to the City Municipal Code section 3-4.17 prohibiting the bringing into any public place where a sporting event or exhibition is being held any canned goods or bottled beverages; adding to the City Municipal Code section 3-4.18 prohibiting throwing, kicking or otherwise placing in motion any object except by authorized personnel; and amending section 6-3.19 of the City municipal code which prohibits sale of merchandise in certain public places except as authorized by appropriate authority by adding "County Coliseum Complex and Adjacent Public Parking Lots," as amended be it ordained by the council of the City as follows:

Section 1. Sections 3-4.17 and 3-4.18 are hereby added to the City Municipal Code to read as follows:

Sec. 3-4.17 CANNED GOODS OR BOTTLED BEVERAGES PROHIBITED AT SPORTING EVENTS.
No person shall bring into any public place wherein a regularly scheduled sporting event or exhibition is being held any canned goods or bottled beverages other than any vacuum bottle, canteen or other similar reusable container, except such persons be the suppliers of, or the agents or servants of such suppliers or the agents or servants of the person or corporation allowed by the department or agency in charge of said public facility to sell or otherwise make use of, the aforesaid articles in said public facility.

Sec. 3-4.18 THROWING OR KICKING OBJECTS IN PUBLIC PLACES.
(a) No person shall throw, kick or cause to be thrown or kicked or otherwise placed in motion any ice, liquid, paper, can, bottle, container or other object in any public place wherein a regularly scheduled sporting event or exhibition is being held.

(b) The prohibition of subsection (a) herein shall not apply to employees of the City, to employees of the public facility, and to employees or persons or corporations presenting said sporting event or exhibition, who are regularly engaged in the performance of their duties under direction of appropriate authority.

FIGURE 5-3

TICKETING AS A MEANS OF COMMUNICATION

In addition to event-related information, the ticket is an effective and efficient device for communicating venue-specific information directly to the customer, particularly policies relating to weapons, food and beverages, backpacks, cameras, umbrellas, banners and signs, and noisemakers. Baseball parks typically use the ticket to warn customers about foul balls. Ice hockey arenas use the ticket to warn about flying pucks and to explain the importance of keeping an eye on the puck during play. Performing arts centers might benefit by stating their late arrival seating policies on the ticket. When informed in advance, most customers will not hesitate to comply with the public assembly facility's policies and they will appreciate the notice. (See Figure 5-3 for an example of a municipal ordinance).

Of course, the printing of specific warnings is also very important from a legal perspective. All public assembly facility entrance restrictions must be clearly communicated to patrons, who purchase tickets in advance, before they arrive for an event. Not being informed of entrance restrictions until arriving at the gate generally results in an angry patron and the creation of a negative impression about the public assembly facility's management. Those guests purchasing tickets at the "gate" should be informed of the restrictions before purchasing the ticket. Appropriate signage at the ticket sale location can accomplish this task.

TICKETING AS A MEANS OF FINANCIAL ACCOUNTING AND INVENTORY CONTROL

The ticketing process allows the public assembly facility's management to communicate with customers in a way that contributes to marketing the facility and assisting with crowd management. Yet, the ticketing process probably originated as a financial accounting and inventory control tool. Once public assembly facilities began controlling their ticket sales activities and admissions into their facility, promoters and entertainers began to demand an accurate accounting of gate receipts. Consequently, ticketing, in whatever form it took, quickly became an extremely important facet of the accounting process. Tickets, although sold at the box office, were presented by the bearer and accepted at the entrance to the public assembly facility. It was a simple process to compare money collected at the box office with ticket stubs collected at the door. The introduction of turnstiles provided an even more efficient and effective means for managers to reconcile the amount of money collected at the box office against the number of customers passing through the gate.

The comparison of the ticket sales report, ticket stubs count, and turnstile counts serves as a positive auditing system. The final ticket sales reconciliation is accomplished through the use of the box office statement that shows the beginning ticket inventory for each price category. The calculated income from sales for each price category including complimentary and unsold (deadwood) is displayed and then combined for a total gross sales figure. The resulting figure is then compared with the total amount of money on hand from ticket sales. Those figures are compared with the *drop count* (ticket stubs total) and the *turnstile count*. The modern bar coded ticket can be "read" at turnstiles so equipped. The information collected can be used in a number of ways other than just verifying attendance. A look at the database generated by the bar code information (as well as other data collection formats) can provide critical information related to individual and group attendance and purchasing patterns. Use of these data is important in the development of direct mail campaigns and future advertising that may have a direct impact on attendance at upcoming events. This data may also be the catalyst for development of a new or revised marketing plan for the facility.

OCCUPANCY AND SEATING CONFIGURATIONS

Space available for the assembly of the public is assigned an occupancy rating by the local fire marshal. Each rating is based on the maximum number of people the space can safely accommodate based on a number of variables — primarily square footage, specific activity use, ingress and egress routes, and available exits. Typically, occupancy ratings are calculated and established during the facility's construction phase and prior to the public having access to the facility.

The public assembly facility manager must understand there will be times when meeting planners and promoters will ask for permission to exceed the maximum occupancy rating. Since only the local fire marshal has the authority to waive the established occupancy limit, it becomes the facility manager's responsibility to facilitate communications between the meeting planner and the fire marshal.

It is also the facility manager's responsibility to understand that the fire marshal's decision to waive the occupancy ratings, particularly in marginal cases, has a great deal to do with the fire marshal's confidence in the facility manager. Thus, it is prudent for public assembly facility managers to cultivate a healthy, trusting, working relationship with the fire marshal in their community.

Ticketing is the generally agreed upon method, inexpensive and defendable, to keep assembly space occupancy ratings from being violated. Specific seating formats are determined by a number of considerations, including event type, facility architecture, and the anticipated audience. Three common seating formats are

- **reserved** - Reserved seating establishes a separate ticket for every seat, fixed or portable, sold on a section, row and seat basis for an event.
- **general admission** - General admission seating is the seating format in which all seats are available on a first-come, first-served basis and is generally considered an opposite option to reserved seating. The general admission format can be also used when the house is scaled by identifying individual seating sections that are sold at different prices, but seating within each seating section is still on a first-come, first-served basis.
- **festival seating** - Festival seating is a form of general admission accommodation. Often the area directly in front of the stage or platform has no seating, other than a floor or ground surface, which provides the audience/spectators to gather to observe a performance. Festival seating in an amphitheater is more often at the back of the seating area and most often the audience is seated on the lawn to observe a performance.

Establishing a separate ticket for every seat, fixed or portable, in the facility is commonly referred to as reserved seating. Offering a reserved seat ticket not only promises the purchaser admission to the facility to experience the performance, it also promises permission to sit in the exact section, row, and seat number described on the face of the ticket. Should the public assembly facility fail to deliver a seat in the location promised, the patron is due relief which might be in the form of a seat relocation, refund of the ticket price, or tickets to another performance.

There are advantages and disadvantages to each type of seating. Selling an attraction as a reserved seat event eliminates the need for ticket holders to line up early in order to get a desired seat. It also reduces the potential of people being injured due to ticket holders hurrying to get through the facility's entrances once the doors are opened.

The issuance of reserved seat tickets completely eliminates the practice of attendees "holding seats" for later arrivals since each seat is individually assigned. Arguments and physical altercations can erupt when a ticket holder attempts to hold seats for individuals who have yet to arrive while others present wish to have the same seats. Reserved seat ticketing allows ticket holders to leave their seat at anytime in order to use the rest room or make purchases from the novelty and concessions stands. These same patrons might be afraid to leave their non-reserved seat vacant for fear someone would claim it. The freedom to leave and return to the same seat increases the probability that the patron will have a positive experience at the event and also increases the probability of the patron making additional purchases thereby adding to the facility's revenues.

Reserved seat ticketing also makes it easier for the public assembly facility manager to assist patrons who have lost their tickets or have had them stolen. In some cases, reserved seat ticketing allows the facility's management to locate a patron during the performance if an emergency situation arises that needs to be brought to the ticket holder's attention.

While popular, reserved seat ticketing has some disadvantages. Since every ticket transaction between a ticket seller and a ticket buyer involves some level of conversation concerning ticket availability and exact location, it takes more time to sell a reserved seat event than a non-reserved seat event. The cumulative effect of these necessary individual conversations can result in longer ticket lines and the need for additional security measures and ticket sellers. Ultimately, the need for additional staffing creates a more expensive ticketing process. Selling reserved seat tickets might necessitate having ushers at each seating section to assist ticket holders in locating their seat. This increased front-of-house staffing requirement adds to the cost of presenting the event.

General admission seating, which allows guests to select whatever seat they wish, may eliminate some of the problems associated with reserved seating but raises another level of public safety and patron comfort issues. General admission seating refers to guests actually being seated as opposed to festival seating. In a general admission environment, the public assembly facility's management, in concert with the local fire marshal, determines the maximum number of seats the facility can accommodate. The maximum number is then communicated to the box office manager along with specific event information such as the name of the event, ticket price, date and time for the event, place in which the event will be held, name of the promoter, names of sponsors, etc. If ticketing is computerized, the box office manager builds the event. If preprinted tickets are used, the box office manager contacts the facility's ticket vendor to order the tickets. In either case, the ticket must clearly inform the buyer that the event is a general admission event.

Some public assembly facilities are prohibited from scheduling general admission events because they can produce more complex crowd management problems. Since the issue of who gets to sit in the prime seating areas is determined simply by who gets to the seat first, crowds can arrive early at the public assembly and, when the facility's doors are opened, ticket holders might rush to be the first through. Public assembly facility managers must be cognizant of the nature of the events permitted to have general admission ticketing.

General admission events can cause increased pressure on the ticket sales process as well. Because there is no seating advantage gained by purchasing tickets in advance for a general admission event, patrons tend to wait until the day-of-show to acquire their ticket assuming the event will not sell out in advance. Providing an appropriate number of ticket sellers and security personnel can become a more difficult staffing issue when a general admission event is not sold out in advance because the number of attendees is not known.

Consequently, staffing decisions must be made in advance based on whatever information is available regarding the event's attendance based on ticket sales patterns for previous performances. Suffice to say, the decisions made might result in overstaffing and needless expenses or understaffing which could lead to longer ticket lines and the potential of not being able to provide security at the level required to protect the patrons, performers, and the facility's personnel. The experienced, knowledgeable box office manager's ability to accurately predict attendance is a valuable asset.

General admission ticketing does have advantages. Even though most of the ticket purchases might occur right before the event, the ticketing transactions are similar. Generally, ticket sellers can sell as fast as they can make change. It is also easier for the box office manager to build a general admission event than a reserved seat event since seat location is not an issue. In addition, it can be less expensive to staff the front-of-house if fewer ushers are used in a general admission format.

Technically, festival seating is general admission without chairs. However, festival seating can include elements of both reserved and general admission seating. Whether indoors or outdoors, festival seating creates a unique configuration where permanent or portable seats can be sold on either a general admission or reserved-seat basis and the area in front of the performance area in an arena or stadium is left open without seats. In an amphitheatre, the seating is normally located in front of the open area that is typically grass. Guests who want to sit in a seat section have the opportunity to do so as do those who wish to stand on the floor in front of the stage in order to experience an atmosphere that may involve high-energy movement and dancing. As in all seating and capacity decisions, festival seating requires the approval of the fire marshal. After the public assembly facility's management demonstrates the ability to secure and limit access to the floor from the permanent and portable seating sections, the fire marshal determines the maximum number of attendees the floor can safely accommodate using a formula that takes into consideration available square footage and exits. The box office can sell no more floor tickets than the fire marshal allows.

✳THE TICKETING PROCESS

So how does the ticketing process actually work? The promoter and the facility representative or box office manager work in concert to determine the maximum number of seats that can be made available for the event. Using a *production rider* (a document detailing the event's specific requirements in terms of stage location and size; sound and lighting equipment, and mixer location, and other pertinent information), and a seating chart for the facility (a seating diagram drawn to scale showing event equipment in place, floor space, and permanent and portable seating), the number of seats that will be available for sale is determined. Once the number of seats available has been decided, the information is transmitted to the promoter who decides ticket pricing. One option is to have all tickets priced the same. A second option is to *scale-the-house* whereby prices vary depending on seat location. It is not uncommon for family shows like the circus to have three or four scaled price breaks. (See Appendix A, Figure 5-4 for a seating diagram illustrating the concept of "scaling the house" with different ticket prices for different seating sections).

It must be understood that all three types of seating arrangements (reserved, general admission, and festival) can involve scaling-the-house. In a reserved seat scale, individual seat locations are identified. In a general admission scale, individual seating sections can be identified and sold at different prices. In festival seating arrangements, the floor may be priced differently than the seated areas. The latter could be either reserved or general admission, or a combination of both.

In scaling-the-house, the event's promoter makes ticket price break decisions based on the demographics of the anticipated audience, past history of the event at that particular venue, and the location of each seat in relationship to the stage. Of prime consideration are the variables of proximity, sightlines, and acoustics. As each of the noted variables improves, so does the value of the affected seats and vice versa. Thus the promoter will place the highest ticket price on those seats closest to the stage with the best sightlines and acoustical positioning. The promoter must then decide how many premium seats might be sold and at what price using the anticipated audience demographics and historical data as guidelines. Once that determination is made, the same decision-making process is employed to identify the number of seats to be included in the second and subsequent pricing tiers. Scaling is an art rather than a science, and the more experienced promoters tend to make the best judgments.

Generally, it is the box office manager's responsibility to determine the maximum number of tickets available for a performance. However, arriving at this determination can be complicated. Ticketing a single performance event using permanent seats and reserved seat ticketing, such as a concert in a performing arts center, is rather straightforward. Ticketing events in facilities with both permanent and portable seating can be more difficult. When ticketing events not requiring seating, such as trade shows, exhibitions, and outdoor and indoor festivals, the ticket manager must avoid overcrowding the facility and violating the safe occupancy regulations.

Some managers selling tickets to events such as popular traveling art exhibits solve the overcrowding problems by adding an entrance time to the ticket so that patrons may only be admitted at the time stated on their ticket. This allows for a continuous flow of patrons into the exhibit area while respecting the maximum occupancy figure established for the facility.

Regardless of the facility and event type, the ticketing process has some common dynamics. For a concert environment in a stadium, arena, or auditorium, the box office manager is typically prepared to make available one ticket for each seat in the facility deemed useable, if seats are being used, or a predetermined number of tickets calculated on available space if seating is not used. These tickets can be in the form of preprinted tickets (hard tickets), sequentially numbered tickets on rolls (roll tickets), or tickets to be printed at the point and time of purchase (computer tickets). In each instance, occupancy rules and regulations must be followed.

The operating principles of ticketing are the same for all productions apart from their type or size. Seating formats and occupancy limits must be determined, manifests developed, pricing established, seats held, pulled and killed, sale dates established, tickets sold, settlements conducted and revenues distributed. Understanding these processes and the sequence in which they occur enables the box office manager to assign appropriate space and personnel for maximum operating efficiency.

Agreement on the ticket inventory leads to the creation of a *ticket manifest*. The ticket manifest is one of the pillars of ticket accountability because it establishes the initial ticket inventory for an event. Assigning a universal price or scaled prices to individual tickets in the inventory is part of the process of creating the manifest. Following the assignment of prices, the box office manager can calculate the event's potential gross income, which is the total amount of money collected if all available tickets are sold at full price (face value).

Before the on-sale date, the box office manager, at the promoter's request, will remove (pull) an agreed upon number of tickets from the initial inventory. These tickets will not be sold. Instead they will be used in the promoter's promotional activities (e.g., trade tickets) or as complimentary tickets. Also, another agreed upon number of tickets (trouble seats) will be pulled from the inventory in order to accommodate guests requesting relocation because of a seat problem before the start or during the performance. However, relocation tickets not used by the early part of the event may be returned to the inventory and released by the ticket office for purchase even though the performance may have already begun.

In the United States, the Americans with Disabilities Act (ADA) requires facilities to provide reasonable accommodations to customers with disabilities such as appropriate signage, seat armrests that raise or no armrests at all, hearing assist devices, etc. (See Appendix A, Figure 5-5 for sample information sheets the facility should provide the promoter in the initial packet to ensure the seats are put aside for sale to individuals who meet qualifications specified under the ADA).

Therefore, before tickets are made available to the general public, the event coordinator and the box office manager must identify seating for customers with disabilities. Since the advent of ADA, most facilities have made physical modifications resulting in permanent seating locations for the disabled. These locations can be scattered in both the permanent fixed and portable seating areas, so long as they provide the accommodations required by the ADA. Many other nations, in addition to the United States, have laws and regulations similar to ADA pertaining to the accommodation of individuals with disabilities.

Tickets pulled for the disabled must be taken from each price whenever the house has been scaled for reserved or general admission. Once those seats are identified they are taken out of the general inventory, either by setting aside or by computer code, and held specifically for customers with disabilities. Because these set-aside tickets are not always sold, some public assembly facilities have adopted a policy whereby disabled seating not sold by a specific time prior to the event date, usually 24-48 hours, will be added to the inventory and made available for sale to the general public.

Since complimentary and trade tickets are not for sale, they are printed without a price if they are computer-printed at the time of sale. If the tickets are preprinted hard tickets, they are generally marked in some fashion so they may be readily identified as trade or complimentary tickets. Likewise, discounted tickets are printed or marked to identify the discount amount. In some instances, the purchase price of a ticket may be greater than its printed value due to surcharges imposed for processing and handling fees, special taxes, etc. There are also occasions when individuals or groups may sell tickets in return for a rebate (usually a percentage of the ticket price) for each ticket sold thereby reducing the actual value of the ticket purchase for the venue/event. The box office manager and the promoter agree on the revised ticket manifest and an adjusted potential gross is then calculated.

At the end of the ticket sale period, the amount of money owed the promoter by the box office for the sale of tickets is an amount equal to the value of original ticket manifest minus complimentary/trade tickets, discounted ticket's value, and the deadwood accounted for on the box office statement. The actual amount paid to the promoter is determined in the event settlement. In effect, the ticket sales receipts are treated as a credit in that calculation. Before the availability of computers and point-of-sales printing, all tickets were preprinted and shipped to the box office manager with a certified ticket manifest document. The box office manager would verify the ticket count and sign-off on the manifest document. (See Appendix A, Figure 5-6 for a sample Box Office Statement).

The manager of a computerized box office mirrors this same process with a post-event computer audit report that shows original inventory, complimentary and trade tickets, tickets sold, seats held (useable tickets), seats killed (unusable tickets), and unsold tickets. The same operating principle remains in effect regarding unaccounted-for tickets no matter which ticketing process is used: if a ticket cannot be accounted for, it is assumed to have been sold at full price.

TICKETING AS THE PUBLIC CUSTODIAN AND THE TAX COLLECTOR

Most performance contracts between the act's agency and the promoter require the promoter to pay a deposit, often half the agreed upon performance pay or guarantee, at the signing of the performance contract. The remaining half of the guarantee, and anything else owed the performer, is to be paid no later than the day of the event before the start of the performance.

It is not uncommon for a promoter to pay the initial deposit and then either ask for an advance from the box office to cover the other half of the guarantee or convince the entertainer that as quickly as the act is completed, the box office receipts will be available to meet their obligations to the entertainer. The facility manager and the box office manager must always keep in mind that the law in some jurisdictions requires box office ticket sales receipts to be held or placed in an escrow account in order to safeguard the public's money until such time that refunding is no longer an issue.

If refunds or partial refunds are in order, the box office must manage the refund process. If for some reason the box office has advanced ticket receipts to the promoter and the show cancels, the facility's box office may still be responsible for refunding tickets. Consequently, a wise manager addresses the promoter's access to advance box office receipts early in the development of the facility-promoter relationship. It is also prudent to include in the facility lease agreement specifics related to *box office advances*. One industry definition of a former box office manager is "one who authorized box office advances."

Despite their best efforts, public assembly facility manages can get caught in situations in which a performer refuses to go on stage before being paid, the promoter has no money, and a house full of anxious customers are seated for a performance. Given an appropriate time allowance, the manager could require the promoter to provide a certified check (or some other form of guaranteed financial instrument) in exchange for a box office advance. Unfortunately, there is rarely sufficient time available to make arrangements of this nature. The best resolution is assuring the entertainer that the money exists and it will be distributed following conclusion of the performance if the promoter provides the facility with an irrevocable letter directing the facility to pay if the act performs. Sometimes the only solution is to cancel the event and issue refunds to all ticket holders. When this occurs, the performer, the promoter, the public assembly facility, and the ticket holders all lose.

The box office may be required to add taxes (whether it is a sales tax, seat tax, or both) to the price of the ticket, collect the tax at the time of sale and remit the collected revenue to the local tax authority. It is not uncommon for facilities to remit due tax revenue on a monthly basis. In many government jurisdictions, uncollected admission and sales taxes become the responsibility of the facility that failed to collect and remit them. Since the ticket sale is not final until the contract is fulfilled (i.e., the event/performance occurs) the ticket sales proceeds, including the tax, are held by the box office. Once the contract is fulfilled, the various payments are made, including remitting the tax.

DESIGNING AND STAFFING THE WORKPLACE

Early in a public assembly facility's design phase, the box office must be recognized as central to the public's image of the facility since most customers will have some level of association with the ticketing operation. It is from these encounters that most individuals will form their opinion of the facility and its personnel. Thus, it is critical that the box office be designed, appointed, and staffed with more in mind than simply providing a place to sell and distribute tickets. Aspects that are important to a successful box office operation and the facility's image include an area protecting the customers from the weather, security (personnel, cameras, etc) and access to nearby adequate parking.

The box office manager is presented with a unique challenge in staffing the ticketing operation. Although the primary purpose of the box office is to sell and distribute tickets, customer service is also a function that must never be overlooked. The box office staff should be prepared not only for the volume of ticketing business it receives but also cognizant of the fact that the customer's impression of the public assembly facility and its management is often based on their interactions with the box office personnel.

Since encounters with front-line employees greatly affect the customer's impression of the facility, it is important for the prudent manager to empower for quality customer service. Creating a knowledgeable, customer-friendly box office staff is more difficult because most front-line ticket sellers are usually part-time employees. For this reason, it is extremely important for the box office manager to understand that customer service training must be provided for part-time and full-time employees alike.

The availability of attractive and informative signage, informed and helpful staff, and quick, accurate service are critical facets of a successful ticket office operation. The architectural design of the public assembly facility is also important in that, ideally, it must provide the box office with adequate work space, secure areas for handling and storing cash, appropriate storage space for equipment and supplies, and space separated from the busy work areas where the box office manager can meet privately with clients and customers.

TICKET DISTRIBUTION

Early box offices were charged with the responsibility of booking the boxes in the theatre, hence one theory as to the origin of the name. The box office might also have acquired its name because at one time the accepted method for keeping up with ticket information for individual performances was through the careful use of a physical container (boxes) for each performance. (Imagine a performing arts theatre putting a series of performances on sale where the ticket seller had to manage a box of tickets for each of the show's performances.) The name might also have come from traveling attractions like the circus where the ticket office was literally nothing more than a booth or large box housing boxes of tickets.

As promoters and facility managers came to realize, the crowd management and advance revenue advantages gained from selling reserved seats for performances quickly led to the obsolescence of the traditional roll ticket, especially in the larger facilities. Subsequently, specialized printing companies took up the challenge to provide individual preprinted or hard tickets based on seating charts provided by the public assembly facility. The ticket manager would coordinate specific seating chart information, event name, time, date, and location information to the printing company. The company would then print a ticket for each available seat and deliver the tickets to the facility along with a ticket manifest and their billing invoice. Prior to the on-sale date, the box office manager would verify the seating format and the ticket count and prepare the hard tickets for distribution.

In increasing numbers, public assembly facilities' tickets are computer generated and printed at the point of sale. High-speed data circuits carry information gathered at the point of the sale to a central computer that maintains the electronic ticket inventory. If a requested ticket is available, the computer releases it from the inventory and orders it printed on a printer at the point of sale.

Prior to the availability of computers, hard tickets were sometimes consigned to community/regional retail businesses. Creating these ticket outlets provided the retail businesses with extra walk-in traffic and additional advertising. These agencies also provided a customer friendly aspect to the ticket purchasing process by not requiring the buyer to go to the public assembly facility to secure the ticket. It also reduced the pressure experienced by the main box office when ticketing for popular attractions. Sometimes the public assembly facility's box office and the retail ticket outlets were connected by telephone which enabled the store employee to take the ticket order and collect the cash while a box office employee pulled the requested tickets. The sold tickets were then held at the box office (will call) under some sort of voucher number thereby enabling the purchaser to pick them up at the event by presenting the voucher. Although this ticketing system is still employed on a limited basis, computerized ticketing has rendered most voucher and consignment operations obsolete.

However, even major computerized ticketing companies must use vouchers (sometimes presented in a list of purchasers). This occurs when the ticket company accepts telephone orders the day of the event and the facility has no on-site advance sale box office operation. The downside of any voucher or voucher-type system is the need to then staff the will call area where the purchasers will pick up their tickets, usually when they come to the event. Few facilities, of those who have a will call operation, will accept unpaid will call. Since all of the tickets in will call, except complimentary, are paid for, they are held until the end of the show and cannot be sold. Any will call tickets that are not picked up, including complimentary tickets, should be noted on the box office statement and made available for the promoter's review.

Today, many box offices make their tickets available over the Internet, collect payment via credit card, pull the tickets from the computer's electronic inventory, and allow a facsimile to be printed from the purchaser's home printer. The ticket facsimile carries a bar code. When the ticket holder seeks entry to the event, the ticket is run through a reader to verify its legitimacy. This process offers the purchaser an immediate physical ticket without the box office having to provide ticket stock. It also presents the public assembly facility with some additional unique marketing opportunities. Turnstiles equipped to read bar codes are also available.

Stand-alone, unstaffed, computer-supported kiosks have emerged as a viable ticket distribution vehicle. Like the automatic teller machine is to banking, the kiosk concept offers a virtual box office at a convenient site. Some kiosks are equipped to allow the ticket purchasers a virtual view of the performance stage from the seat they consider buying. The opportunity to market compact discs and novelties associated with the event, to market restaurants and hotels near the venue, and to enable customers to make on-the-spot reservations are some of the advantages associated with the kiosk concept. Kiosk ticketing is one-stop-shopping at its finest. It also has a downside: the amount of time each potential purchaser in line might use reviewing ticketing, restaurant, and other options.

FINANCING THE TICKETING OPERATION

Aside from being one of the more traditional and fundamental activities in the public assembly facility industry, ticketing is costly. Computer equipment, data lines, equipment maintenance contracts, area licenses if the facility manages its own ticketing service, or contract/management fees if it uses a national service, credit and bank card expenses, ticket stock, utilities, insurance, and labor and management salaries/benefits are expenses that have to be supported. How then does the facility amortize the cost of such an important procedure?

The ticketing operation may be subsidized and/or may be a line item expense covered in the public assembly facility's operating budget. Depending on the type of business the public assembly facility does, it might be impossible for the ticketing operation to generate sufficient revenue to cover its own expenses. However, there are ways that ancillary revenue may be raised in order to help offset costs.

The box office might attract local sponsors and sell general advertising on the back of the ticket and on their ticket envelopes. In this age of electronic ticketing, the box office may add a convenience or service charge to the price of each ticket, particularly on tickets sold at outlets, through the Internet, or by mail or telephone. An additional computer fee charge is often added to cover some of the expense associated with computerized ticketing. Service or convenience charges were originally added to the ticket price and passed on to the ticket buyer to cover the cost of offering tickets outside the traditional box office point of purchase; the original service charge was probably a handling charge placed on mail order tickets to cover the cost of labor, envelopes, and stamps. As facilities installed computerized ticketing systems, these charges increased to cover rising expenses and to generate additional profits. The service charge concept has become so effective and financially lucrative that some facilities only provide day-of-show box office service.

In promoter lease arrangements, the public assembly facility might charge the promoter a percentage of ticket sale revenues in return for managing the ticketing activities associated with the show. There are also other ways a box office might charge an operator. Charging on a per-day rate or a time and labor rate are two possibilities. In many cases, the box office can earn interest on money deposited from ticket sales. Since 30, 60, or even 90 days may pass between the on-sale date and the performance date, it's possible for the box office to put that money into safe, interest-bearing accounts.

The box office also might be positioned to sell tickets for events outside the facility through Internet, outlet, mail, or telephone sales. Calculating the cost of offering each of these ticketing services and recommending an acceptable profit level for each of these services is the box office manager's responsibility.

⋆ TICKETING ISSUES: SCALPING AND COUNTERFEITING

Ticket scalping, or selling tickets for more than face value, is illegal in many states or legal jurisdictions. Scalping is fueled by the dynamics of supply and demand or by introducing, either intentionally or unintentionally, an undervalued product into the market-place. For example, a $25 ticket to a sold-out music concert might be worth ten times its face value to a ticket-less rabid fan, while a $500 front row ticket to a championship heavyweight boxing match might be worth $5,000 if offered to the right person.

While ticket prices for popular attractions may seem very expensive to the average person, the event's promoter establishes the price based on the number of tickets available for sale and the projected ticket demand, assuming the cost of producing the show, including a profit, doesn't exceed the potential revenue. Scalpers work on the supply and demand principle. Whenever scalpers determine the ticket supply is not sufficient to meet the ticket demand for a specific event, they then purchase tickets for face value or sometimes even more or less. The scalper then attempts to sell the ticket at a substantially higher price to a consumer willing to pay that price. What the scalper gets for a ticket simply depends on the intensity of the demand and the willingness of the consumer to pay a premium price. The value of a ticket declines rapidly and dramatically once the event begins. It is not unusual that a scalper might "eat" a quantity of tickets. Scalpers view their activity as a business and as such they believe they are no different than any other business person who purchases a product for one price and then resells it for a profit. However, despite their protestations, scalpers usually are not considered to be legitimate business persons. They likely have no regular place of business where they can be found, no business license, no federal or state tax identification number, no business insurance, etc. When a ticket is scalped for a price greater than its printed value, the facility does not get its share of the increased ticket sale price nor do the taxing agencies, including the Federal Internal Revenue Service, get their additional share. In effect, scalpers are business competitors with little or no overhead.

Interestingly, in the early days of rock and roll (1950s-1960s) most concert tickets were sold as one-price-for-all and were usually undervalued. Most shows were in small public assembly facilities seating only several hundred people. Concerts of that era were primarily staged to promote record sales, thus maximizing box office receipts was far less important than drawing large crowds. The costs for the acts and stage productions were relatively small. Scalpers quickly surfaced to take advantage of these products, devising ways to buy as many tickets as possible and then reselling them at "market" values.

This scalping process sometimes resulted in potential attendees only having access to prime concert tickets if purchased from scalpers. These individuals directed complaints to lawmakers expressing their belief that the practice of scalping produced a negative effect on audiences as well as lost tax revenue to communities and states. Subsequently, most states and many local jurisdictions have enacted anti-scalping laws prohibiting the resale of event tickets for more than the price printed on the ticket itself or restricting the resale to a specific amount above the original price. For example, some legal jurisdictions allow tickets to be sold for no more than $1 above the printed price. Thus, a $10 ticket could be sold for $11 while a $200 ticket could be sold for no more that $201. However, the scalping laws for each jurisdiction are not necessarily the same and public assembly facility managers, box office managers and security personnel need to be conversant with the specifics of the laws that prevail in the jurisdiction in which their public assembly facility is located.

Ticket brokering resembles ticket scalping in that both involve buying undervalued tickets and selling them at market value. *Ticket brokers*, however, operate in locales where selling a ticket for more than face value is legal under specified conditions.

Unlike the scalper, the ticket brokering firms are legitimate businesses and are regulated as such. In many cases, these brokers work in concert with the box office manager and provide an excellent service. Tickets unsold by a specified date are made available to the broker who in turn sells them, sometimes at a reduced price in return for an established percentage or fee, the same as would a major computerized ticketing agency. In so doing, the box office manager is able to generate ticket revenues that might have been totally lost as well as additional ancillary purchase revenues.

In addition, ticket brokers provide a service to individuals who discover, for whatever circumstances, that they will not be able to attend an event for which they have already purchased a ticket. In the past, persons in such circumstances would have to sell the ticket themselves (thus becoming a scalper) or lose their investment. With the advent of ticket brokers, this same individual may now sell their ticket to the broker, usually at a reduced price, and salvage a portion of their investment. The broker will then make that ticket available for public consumption at a price higher than what they paid for it. It is at this point that the line between brokering and scalping becomes blurred. Ticket brokers also charge service fees, similar to those of some public assembly facility box offices, to generate even greater revenues for their business. Internet-based ticket brokering is a growing trend.

Color photocopiers and color computer printers have made ticket counterfeiting easier than in the past, and as ticket prices escalate counterfeiting has become more prevalent. However, using technology, methods have been developed for combating ticket counterfeiting. Current methods used to validate ticket authenticity include bar coding, black light sensitive markings, imprinted holograms, smart card access and special paper stock. As the use of these and other emerging methods becomes more widespread, counterfeiting should become less of a problem in the future. Nonetheless, all public assembly facilities need to maintain their vigilance in order to ensure that all tickets to their events are legitimate.

✕ YIELD MANAGEMENT

✕ The practice of yield or revenue management involves the manipulation of prices in order to price events, seating, space, or services differently for different customers. Unlike retail goods that are priced the same for all customers, some products or services related to public assembly facilities lend themselves to multiple pricing plans constructed using yield management techniques.

✳ Yield management is a process that encourages facility managers to maximize the potential financial yield on rooms, seats, and/or space they manage by progressively and systematically discounting or increasing the price to the customer based on demand analysis in order to maximize yield.

✕ Five characteristics of products or services that make good markets for using yield management pricing techniques are:

- Fixed capacity (number of seats, display areas, etc., in a particular configuration is fixed).
- Customer demand can be identified and separated into distinct market segments based on willingness to pay (those willing to pay for better seats, locations, service, etc., can be separated from those customers unwilling to pay for premium prices).
- Product or service is perishable (when event begins, marketing opportunity is over).
- Product sold in advance of consumption (event has advance ticket sales).
- Consumer demand fluctuates (weekend, mid-week, or seasonal demand for the event).

The hotel and airlines industries appear to be successfully marketing their inventory by either increasing prices or discounting the prices, based on unsold inventory, as the product expiration dates draw near. When the expiration date is very close, both airlines and hotels put their product out to bid to other outlets in the belief that getting half the original price is better than nothing. Additional benefits to yield management can include a positive impact on ancillary revenue streams (greater ticket sales result in greater concession sales), strengthened consumer buying patterns, and brand loyalty enhancement. Like the hotel and airline industries, the inventory of services and products offered by public assembly facilities are dramatically affected by time. An unsold seat to a performance or event might have a $100 value minutes before the starting time but actually becomes worthless once the performance or event has commenced.

✕ Public assembly facility managers could benefit from studying the yield management models used for many years by many live theatres and subsequently devise an appropriate application for their various ventures. Located in close proximity to the theatre districts in London, New York City, and other major cities worldwide are ticket outlets that sell day-of-performance tickets at discounted prices. Although the theatre does not gain full ticket value, the discounted revenues are better than none and by filling the seat the probability of gaining additional income from ancillary sales is increased.

One example of how using yield management increased revenues relates to a struggling auditorium housing a summer entertainment series. The facility's manager noticed that ticket demand was highest on weekends and lowest Monday through Thursday. Tickets were priced the same ($30) for all performances. However, demand for weekend tickets was twice that of the facility's seating capacity while only one-fourth of available tickets for the mid-week performances were sold.

Through the use of yield management techniques, the facility manager increased revenues by changing two pricing policies. First, the price for weekend performances was increased to $45 to capture those willing to pay the higher price in order to attend the weekend performances. Second, the price for weekday performances was reduced to $20, thus attracting larger audiences, including those unable to get weekend tickets but willing to attend a weekday performance rather than not attending at all. In this case, new revenue was generated from the higher prices on weekends without affecting demand, and new revenue was generated from weekday performances due to the reduced price that produced an increase in ticket sales. The new pricing rules evolved from management's ability to divide the total market into segments based on demand and the consumer's willingness to pay.

Many sport teams (amateur, collegiate, and professional) that use stadiums and arenas are in the early stages of transforming their standard full-price ticket into a discounted ticket in two ways. One is to charge a premium price for weekend games, as in baseball. The second is to charge a premium price for specific events against teams such as current world champions, traditional rivals, etc.

It can be argued the concept of yield management is not new, but has simply evolved into its current form. It has long been "usual" for some event types to charge one price for advance sale purchases and a higher price day-of-event sales rather than reducing the price as expiration time nears. The strategy behind this yield management pricing format is to encourage advance purchase sales.

At times, however, the application of the yield management approach could result in stimulating day-of-event sales as opposed to advance sales. If this were to occur, it might result in making a decision not to book a second show (or third or more) because of the poor advance ticket sales when, in fact, a demand actually exists for additional shows. The end result would be too little supply for the actual demand and the creation of an ideal market for scalpers.

✳ SUMMARY

Ticketing for events held at public assembly facilities has been traced back to at least the ancient Romans. The issuance of a ticket constitutes a legal contract between the purchaser and event/venue. Every effort must be made to honor the contract. Whenever contractual obligations cannot be met, appropriate recompense must be made to the ticket purchaser.

The number of tickets sold, whether they are for reserved, general admission, or festival seating, depends upon the configuration of the seating arrangement and the occupancy limit established by the fire marshal. Tickets provide an excellent method for communicating event/venue information to the purchaser. In addition, tickets provide a mechanism for controlling crowd numbers and they serve as a financial accounting tool. Event promoters must establish ticket prices and, if scaling-the-house, determine and identify the location and number of seats to be included in each price break.

Every public assembly facility in the United States, and other countries with similar statutes, must adhere to the ADA's rules and regulations pertaining to patrons with disabilities. Providing appropriate signage, appropriate number of seats in each price category, making seats accessible via elevators and ramps, having hearing assistance devices available, and providing wheelchair spaces, and seats with lifting armrests or no armrests are but some requirements of ADA.

Box office ticketing must follow the laws of the local jurisdiction that pertain to the collection and safekeeping of ticket money and the remission of collected taxes. The box office is central to the public's perception of the public assembly facility. Every effort must be made to provide for the consuming public.

The Internet and computerization of ticketing distribution is revolutionizing the operation of the box office. Consumers want the convenience of shopping for tickets and seating locations on the Internet, as well as printing tickets from home.

Vending of tickets at higher than face value is becoming more commercialized and widespread thereby forcing facility management, as well as many promoters, including sports teams, to reconsider their ticket pricing and the possibilities of variable pricing.

The ticketing operation and process deserves the intense attention of the facility manager; it traditionally has been and continues to be a primary source of cash and revenue for the facility. Proper management of the box office operation and the distribution and settlement of box office proceeds is a critical function of the public assembly facility.

REFERENCES AND ADDITIONAL READINGS

Baugus, R.V. 2004. "Taking Inventory: Teaming Up to Move Tickets." *Facility Manager* (February/March): 20-23. Coppell, TX: International Association of Assembly Managers, Inc.

Herrick, Julie. 2001. "Selling Tickets at the Speed of Light." *Facility Manager* (July/August): 22-26. Coppell, TX: International Association of Assembly Managers, Inc.

6

BUSINESS AND FINANCIAL MANAGEMENT

INTRODUCTION

At the very center of each public assembly facility is the pervasive influence of fiscal accountability, without which business as usual would cease to exist. Business and finance are simply the measuring stick that drives decisions and their final outcomes. This chapter will attempt to address the fundamental business and finance concepts and principles that commonly pertain to the public assembly facility management industry. The successful management of public assembly facilities not only hinges upon, but begins with understanding these principles and converting them into sound financial leadership practices.

Irrespective of size, type, mission, or ownership, there are many common business dynamics associated with operating all public assembly facilities. The business and finance activities of a small, college-owned performing arts facility are surprisingly similar to those of a convention center, stadium, or arena. These activities usually involve:

- Developing the facility's budget.
- Providing information for budget presentations.
- Monitoring the facility's operating budget.
- Developing the capital expenditure budget.
- Developing financial reports.
- Developing rate and pricing schedules.
- Monitoring, and in some cases managing, the facility's risk management program.
- Monitoring and developing contracts.
- Monitoring and managing the facility's human resources (HR).
- Debt collection (accounts receivable).
- Payment of bills (accounts payable).
- Payroll, benefits, and retirement.
- Monitoring and managing ancillary and non-ancillary revenue streams.
- Managing cash flow and investments.
- Managing internal audits.
- Purchasing.
- Event settlement.
- Audit controls for parking, concession, catering, merchandising and box office operations.

If the facility has a business manager (by whatever name), that individual usually reports to the facility manager and is responsible for gathering, interpreting, and providing the financial information that enables management to make accurate and timely business and financial decisions. The typical business manager holds at least a bachelor's degree in business administration. Many have more extensive educational backgrounds in accounting, finance, marketing, management, human resources, etc. However, it is also important for the business manager to be knowledgeable about all financial aspects of public assembly facility management due to the unique manner in which these facilities are funded and managed.

THE OPERATING BUDGET

The operating budgets (money allocated to cover the operating expenses of the facility) for different facility types are more alike than they are different. Each facility type has similar expenses such as management salaries and benefits, permanent and temporary salaries and benefits, utilities, janitorial and maintenance supplies, and a variety of general and administrative expenses. In addition, there may be identifiable expenses associated with the revenue streams noted below. The operating budget identifies these anticipated annual operating expenses, identifies the resources allocated to fund them, and provides the facility's management team with a monthly report and analysis of current and year-to-date (YTD) revenue and expenses as compared to the actual budget. Exactly how a particular operating budget is developed and managed is ultimately the responsibility of the facility manager.

Profit after expenses from food and beverage, parking, and catering operations (whether managed in-house or contracted), along with those generated by facility rental, corporate sponsorships, naming rights payments, specialty seating, suite leases, co-promoted and promoted activities, ticket convenience fees or surcharges, advertising, novelty sales, etc. may contribute to funding the facility's operating expenses. However, in many instances the facility's revenue production is not sufficient to cover its general operating expenses, debt service (interest owed on monies borrowed to construct or refinance the facility), and set-aside cash reserves for future capital improvements. Thus, whenever an income shortfall occurs, some sort of subsidy is required to cover the overall operating deficit.

Publicly owned facilities, especially those constructed with an expectation of increased tourism, usually look toward the hospitality industry (hotels, motels, restaurants, vehicle rentals, etc.) for assistance in covering operating deficits. In most instances, assistance is provided in the form of dedicated taxes. These may be in the form of surcharges placed on general sales, food and beverage sales, lodging, vehicle rentals, amusements admissions and entertainment charges. College-owned arenas and stadiums generally gain revenue through assessing mandatory student athletic and/or activity fees. Performing arts centers frequently solicit endowments that are invested, and only the interest generated is used to cover operating shortfalls and sometimes physical enhancements. The principal remains intact. Performing art centers might also establish foundations and some or all of the donations may be used to supplement the operating budget. Whatever supplemental funding mechanism is selected, the facility's business manager needs to be involved in the decision-making process.

The operating budget, in addition to providing the basis for the narrative and quantitative financial plan, provides management with a pro-forma for a specified period of time that is expressed in detailed quantitative terms. Calendar year budgets begin on January 1 and run through December 31. Fiscal year (FY) budgets may commence on any date and conclude twelve months later. Many municipal entities operate on a FY budget that commences on July 1 and runs through June 30 the following year. Because FY budgets transcend years, they are commonly referred to by those years. Thus, a FY budget commencing on July 1, 2005, and concluding on June 30, 2006, would be referred to as the FY 2005-2006 budget. There are times when a public assembly facility's budget year may not coincide with that of the owner's budget year. In such cases, appropriate adjustments need to be taken to bring them in line. This process is often referred to as periodicity.

The budgeting process requires facility management personnel to plan in advance and develop and present their recommendations to their governing body. Once the operating budget is completed and approved, it provides management with an ongoing vehicle for communicating their financial plans and objectives to other decision makers within the organization. The development of an operating budget represents one of those unique management processes that allow managers to communicate both up and down the organization's hierarchy.

BUDGET PREPARATION

The budgetary process usually flows through four developmental stages: preparation, presentation, adoption, and execution. Careful preparation and effective presentation of the budget proposal is extremely important to the success of the public assembly facility. The budgeting process can be complicated since it involves accumulating and organizing historical revenue and expense data related to the facility's operation, assessing and projecting the facility's position in current and future markets, establishing goals and objectives that are consistent with the facility's mission statement, and understanding the overall economic and political environment in which the facility exists.

In most cases, the public assembly facility's operating budget is the result of the budgeting process selected by the governing body. A variety of budgeting formats exist. However, there are five that merit attention: line item budgeting, incremental budgeting, performance-based budgeting, planned program budgeting systems, and zero-based budgeting. (See definitions below)

LINE ITEM BUDGETING

Probably the most commonly used format, this is a systematic, accounting-oriented method of recording expenditures against various classification categories such as salaries, services, supplies, equipment, etc. The line-item budget process allows the business manager detailed control over facility expenses. This process works well for discussions of budgeting control, but not for resolving the broader questions of priorities and effectiveness.

INCREMENTAL BUDGETING

Sometimes referred to as the fair share approach, this is typically used by organizations employing a top-down style of management. Using this approach, all budget items (occasionally there are exceptions) are either increased or decreased by a prescribed percentage of the previous budget. Positive attributes of this budgeting format are that it is based on a previous year, does allow for line item analysis, and is easy to implement and administer. On the negative side, basic goals are not part of the analysis and the question of program priority is not addressed.

PERFORMANCE BUDGETING

This focuses on efficiency. Performance measures are used as the basis for budgeting and comparison of efficiency in production. Measuring efficiency requires quantitative indicators of both input and output. Since budgets are documents that present inputs in detail, it is a starting place for assessing the efficiency of the facility's operation. In a performance budget, the focus is on activities of the operation rather than objects. The performance approach stresses efficiency through relating money requests to organizational output. However, this format does not encourage discussion of effectiveness. This form of budgeting is based primarily on the input-output concept, and therefore is, generally, not considered an appropriate system for public assembly facilities.

PLANNED PROGRAM BUDGETING SYSTEM (PPBS)

This is an attempt to evaluate the programs in which the operation engages so as to choose the programs most appropriate to the facility's goals and objectives. Program budgets are characterized by the following similarities: expenditures are listed and attached to specific programs, a detailed narrative and multi-year timeline exists to explain each program, each program requires annual justification for funding, and quantitative program alternatives are listed. Attempting to institutionalize analysis in the executive decision-making process, PPBS stresses effectiveness through relating expenditures and revenues to goals. This process allows comparison and prioritizing of programs based on the public assembly facility's mission, goals, and objectives, financial realities and its physical limitations. This system can be effective for public assembly facilities that have two or more prime tenants. For example, the Boston Celtics (NBA) and the Boston Bruins (NHL) are the Fleet Center's prime tenants. Using PPBS, the Fleet Center's management can determine, in a fairly precise manner, the actual amount of time, space (including common space), and resources each tenant consumes. This information will enable the facility's management to include these costs in the lease contract for each entity.

ZERO-BASED BUDGETING (ZBB)

This blends concern for both efficiency and improved policy-making by requiring that operations organize current and proposed activities into decision packages and rank the packages according to importance relative to all other decision packages. This process evaluates existing programs alongside new programs and requires yearly funding justification for each. Using zero-based budgeting allows management to deal efficiently with programs that have outlived their usefulness or that are simply not producing desired results related to program objectives. A down side to this system is the potential for business managers to expend all funds in each budget category based on a fear that failing to do so will result in the next FY budget being reduced accordingly.

FINANCIAL STATEMENTS

A critical aspect of the financial management system is the creation of accurate and timely financial statements necessary for the overall effective management of the facility. Four very useful financial management tools that can be created by the business office are an income statement, a balance sheet, a detailed operating cash flow statement, and a capital expenditures statement. (See Appendix A, Figures 6-1 through 6-3 for sample statements).

The income statement is designed to report the financial performance of the business entity for a specific period of time such as a month, quarter, or year. Net income represents the difference between operation revenues and operating expenses for the specified period. The income statement presents the results of operations, that is, it reports for a specific period of time those items that provide the total revenue, those items that represent the total expenses, and the resulting net income or loss. Facilities often include this information both on a current basis (such as this month) and YTD.

Whereas the income statement reports financial activity for a specific period of time, the purpose of the balance sheet is to report the public assembly facility's financial status for a particular point in time. The balance sheet specifically addresses the facility's current financial status and provides information relative to the sources and uses of funds statement (cash flow).

The first task in preparing the cash flow statement is to calculate the various changes that have taken place in the asset and liability accounts. The net change in each account is then classified and sorted according to whether it is a source or a use of funds.

The sources of funds are:

- Net income.
- Depreciation.
- Assets.
- Liabilities (bonds, loans, etc).

The detailed operating statement shows income and expense by category and allows the tracking of each item of revenue and expense to its source. Using the detailed operating statement in tandem with the current budget allows the business manager to determine whether the facility is performing better or worse than expected based on variances from the budgeted figures to the actual figures. The business manager should be able to explain these variances.

A final important report in facility financial management is the capital expenditures report. Policies vary, but typically capital expenditures are purchases of equipment costing more than $5,000 and with a life of five years or more. Often, facility management will present to owners a five-year capital expenditure forecast, which is updated annually. Each year of the five-year budget is included, in sequence, in the annual business plan. Competent capital expenditure forecasting and budgeting is essential to the operation of a well-maintained facility.

Since it is the responsibility of the business office, under the direction of the facility's business manager, to determine the financial health of the facility and its various activities, the business manager must have command of a systematic process to make that determination. One of those systems or processes is called *cost accounting*. By identifying and isolating every facility activity and determining the associated costs, the business manager is able to produce a multi-dimensional picture of the facility's financial status.

Effective facility managers need to understand precisely how accountants view and measure costs. Conversely, business managers must be able to look at their facility through the eyes of the public assembly facility manager. The objective of a properly implemented and managed accounting process is to provide management personnel with a valuable tool to assist them in the decision-making process.

Determining the price of a soft drink sold from a concession stand should demand a thorough investigation of its actual cost to the facility, which would include the cost of product, storage/inventory, taxes, labor, housekeeping, paper products, spoilage, capital costs, depreciation, etc. Determining the rent structure for the facility's prime tenant should follow the same process.

The business manager should have the ability to identify costs associated with the tenant and the tenant's activities and arrange that information in such a way that it is understandable to the facility manager. The real object of cost accounting is to create a management tool that will:

- Measure the activities of the operation in terms of the local currency.
- Assist management in looking at general business decisions.
- Justify the need for increased, or decreased, funding or reimbursement.

The allocation or distribution of costs is an inescapable challenge in nearly every public assembly facility operation. How the cost of shared services are allocated, how *fixed overhead* is allocated, and how *variable expenses* are applied are difficult questions. The answers are not always clearly right or wrong.

Cost allocation, in a general sense, is the assignment of costs to one or more cost objectives. A cost objective is any activity in which a separate measurement of cost is desired. Public assembly facility event management, by its very nature, requires a separate measurement of cost concerning each event activity.

Since the nature of the various costs may differ, they must be defined in a separate manner. Cost allocation encompasses the assignment of expenses incurred from direct and indirect cost categories. Direct costs are expense items that can be identified specifically with a single cost item such as insurance, basic utility charges, and management salaries. Indirect costs are expense items that cannot be identified specifically with a single cost item such as general administration, utility usage, and overtime wages not related to a specific event.

Labor is a common expense for all facilities and all events. Direct labor represents wages paid or owed as a direct consequence of an event or activity. Indirect labor represents wages paid or owed as an indirect consequence of an activity, such as general administration, equipment repairs, specialized employee training, consultant fees, etc. These labor expenses are usually reported as general overhead.

Public assembly facility overhead represents costs not specifically identified that benefit the facility in varying proportions and are allocated in some form of a percentage or specific local currency amount to the facility or specific departments. Overhead is applied to products and services because of management's desire to account for and recover all costs. Overhead is not generally a directly identifiable expense, but it will become a part of the service or product cost and will funnel into the expense stream when the overhead costs are added to the cost of goods or services sold. It is essential to recognize and understand the important role that overhead cost plays in the ultimate cost of goods and services. Each aspect of overhead behaves differently with respect to the level of activity and must be analyzed thoroughly.

Some overhead costs are fixed, some are variable, and some are mixed. Fixed costs such as debt service, service contracts, and professional services are constant. Variable costs, such as indirect labor and supplies, change in proportion to the activity. Mixed costs or semi-variable costs contain both fixed and variable elements such as an employee who is paid for a 40-hour work week and then earns overtime pay for additional hours. Calculating a facility's overhead ratios typically includes associating a common denominator to factor each result; fixed overhead totals using a factor of operating event days or operating hours, while variable overhead totals use a factor of occupancy loads to determine the cost per patron.

In addition to implementing and managing the processes that allow for the monitoring of facility costs and revenue streams, the facility's business manager might be responsible for a number of day-to-day financial activities such as cash management, inventory, *fixed assets*, labor, utilities, contracts, and risk management.

CASH MANAGEMENT

Common to almost every public assembly facility is the issue of dealing with an accumulation of cash, whether it is derived from box office ticket sales, rent deposits, parking collections, concession sales, catering sales or novelty sales. Cash-on-hand is an ever-present issue in the public assembly facility management industry. Presented below are some of the generally accepted principles concerning the handling of cash.

- Bond all employees who have access to cash. Bonding is a type of insurance that protects the facility from loss brought about by employee theft. The bond premium becomes a cost to the facility. Typically, business managers, box office managers, accountants, concession managers, and those employees whose every day work involves the handling of cash are bonded. The premium for this protection is so expensive that it usually requires the acceptance of a very high deductible in order to make the premium affordable. For this reason, many municipalities forgo bonding and simply accept the risk (self insuring).

- Where the process allows, the use of cash registers is advised. This can improve the efficiency of the reconciliation of cash draws and cash on hand at the end of every shift. Having a cash-out cashier on hand to reconcile cash draws and sales in the presence of the seller is desired. Leaving large amounts of cash in the building overnight presents serious risks that must be addressed with personnel and physical/equipment solutions. These might include a night watchman, controlled access, and a substantial fireproof vault. When possible, routine bank deposits with a security escort is desirable.

- Unannounced cash audits are strongly recommended. Periodic, but formal, cash audits create a healthy tension in cash management. Cash audits of the box office, or any cash operation, should include validating the amount due against ticket/product sales. In the box office, this is determined by tickets originally available, less tickets on hand (deadwood) equals tickets distributed. A break down of how distributed tickets were sold will result in the amount of cash required to balance. For purposes of the sold number, this would include tickets sold at full price, discounted prices, traded, and complimentary. This format is valid for both hard tickets and those sold from a computer. While not physically present, tickets remaining in the computer's inventory would be classified as "available" and thus considered as deadwood.

- The facility's checking account must be safeguarded. All checks should be preprinted and consecutively numbered. Checks in excess of a specific dollar amount should require two authorized signatures. The facility's bank accounts must be reconciled monthly in order to verify deposits, balances, and withdrawals.

- A facet of the business finance function often abused is *petty cash*. The facility should not maintain a petty cash fund larger than needed. Strict procedures should be established concerning the use of the petty cash account and it should be reconciled regularly. It should be firmly established that without prior authorization and the presentation of purchase receipts, petty cash should not be part of the purchasing process.

- If the facility has a history of generating excess cash, even short-term excesses, investment of that cash in interest-bearing accounts or certificates of deposit might be in order. Significant interest income can be earned through careful management of cash from the time of collection until the time of payout to promoters by placing it into short-term sweep accounts. In many instances, owners (such as other municipal departments) will manage and monitor the investment of excess cash. When this occurs, the public assembly facility manager should lobby to credit the facility's operating account with a portion, if not all, of the interest income generated from the facility's excess cash.

ACCOUNTS PAYABLE AND RECEIVABLE

Two additional common financial functions are the billing and collecting for products and/or services and making payments for services and products received. A procedure for dealing with accounts receivable should be established and strictly followed. All receivable accounts should be frequently reviewed to verify payment. Delinquent accounts should be notified. Registered letters should be sent to non-responding delinquent accounts. If the debt is still not paid, the debt should be removed from the facility's accounts receivable and the burden assumed by the owner or a collection agency. If the debt continues to remain unpaid, it should be declared uncollectible and written off. Each step in this process should be undertaken in a timely manner and documented.

Accounts payable (accounts to which the facility owes payment) should be managed as diligently as accounts receivable. However, given the fact that the public assembly facility gains by keeping its money in interest-bearing investments for as long as possible, it is prudent for the facility to delay making payments for as long as good business practices will permit. This can be called "aging" the bill.

The public assembly facility's business office will be involved in the managing of the facility's inventory of supplies and equipment. Insisting that supplies be stored in a secure area and that a check-in/check-out system be in place and enforced will lessen the potential for supplies being misappropriated. Unscheduled audits of stored inventory and holding supervisors responsible for maintaining and accounting for these items will help reduce shrinkage, especially with respect to consumable products such as housekeeping and general maintenance supplies.

Timely submission of supply orders prevents the need to deal with rush orders which tend to be much more expensive. When needed products/services must go to bid, adherence to the established bid process will speed the process and reduce administrative costs. All received purchases should be recorded and the specifics of the order verified to ensure that the correct items have been delivered and in the quantity ordered. Generally, supplies should be inventoried and stored in a manner that allows for the issuance of items on a last-in, last-out basis. This is especially true for perishable items and those with a short shelf life.

AUDITS

Unscheduled *internal and external audits* that focus on the handling of the facility's finances coupled with audits that focus on the facility's adherence to policies and procedures are necessary in maintaining a healthy business environment. In applying the audit process, generally, one of the public assembly facility's events, such as a concert, trade show, exhibition, etc, will be randomly selected. The various transactions associated with that event will be reviewed from the start of the event until its conclusion. The audit process might include a review of contracts, advertising agreements, box office receipts, settlement document, payments to vendors, clients and customers, and payroll documents. Special attention must be given to those charged with conducting the internal audits to ensure that no favoritism or collusion occurs. And although departments may be selected for audit by random, a mechanism must be in place to ensure that all departments are audited within a specified timeframe.

A thorough investigation of a randomly selected business activity should give the auditor a sense of how the facility is being managed. Without some sort of "annual physical," facility managers might grow myopic and lose focus on the overall goals and objectives. The audit process can provide an unbiased observation of the facility's finances and the way the facility is operated and managed. In most instances, the public assembly facility manager is provided a draft of the audit report and given a period of time to deal with or at least debate any negative issues brought to light by the audit before the report is released to the governing body. Although the audit process may at times be stressful for the facility's management and may require significant demands upon their time, the audit process and the subsequent report should be viewed by the facility's management team and its governing body as an excellent opportunity to evaluate performance.

SETTLEMENTS

The settlement process which represents the formal accounting and distribution of funds related to facility events, is a somewhat unique activity associated with the public assembly facility. The process itself is not so unique as is the timing of the activity. In most businesses, billing and collection activities occur "after the fact" or after the transactions have taken place. Bills are issued and payments are normally made at the end of the month or within thirty days. The settlement process in a public assembly facility, however, usually takes place the same day or night of the event and occasionally while the event is literally taking place. For example, a stadium concert that has generated a million dollars in ticket sales might be settled while the headliner is still on stage. This may include presentation and payment of bills for labor, transportation, rent, and catering; reconciliation of tickets and ticket receipts; and, writing checks and/or making bank wire transfers. The settlement process has evolved as a way for the event promoter to receive money collected through box office ticket sales in order to pay accumulated bills for their engagement prior to moving on to their next engagement. The process also allows/provides the public assembly facility manager an additional way to monitor box office receipts. (See Appendix A, Figure 6-4 for a sample event settlement statement).

Representation at settlement depends on the structure of the event. For example, a settlement for a traveling theatrical event promoted or presented by the performing arts center will require a representative from the facility who is authorized to issue checks and a representative from the theatre company who is often the tour's accountant. Present at the settlement for a commercially presented concert will usually be a representative from the public assembly facility's management, the tour's accountant, and a representative from the promoter's operation. Typical documents needed at the settlement include:

- A box office statement detailing tickets distributed, sold, and not sold.
- Invoices from the facility documenting production, security, and contracted or house labor required by the event and provided by the facility.
- Invoices concerning equipment owned or secured by the facility but used by the event.
- Catering bills.
- Advertising bills with back-up materials.
- Invoices for anything else asked for by the event and provided by the facility.

It is essential for the facility manager to have a copy of the artist's contract available if the public assembly facility is the promoter or a copy of the facility's lease agreement if a commercial promoter is simply renting the facility.

The settlement process has evolved to allow the public assembly facility to withhold from box office receipts an amount equal to the promoter's or the attraction's financial obligation to the facility and for the facility's representative to ask the promoter or the tour's accountant how the remaining revenue should be distributed. Promoters who need cash on the night of the show are obligated to inform the facility in advance so the correct amount of cash is available. At one point in time, most events were settled in cash but that's no longer the case. Today, most settlements are concluded through the issuance of a check by the public assembly facility or by remitted funds using a bank wire transfer.

NEGOTIATING THE CONTRACT

The negotiating phase of the contracting process in most facilities is headed by the facility manager. In facilities with a business manager, that individual might also be involved in implementing and monitoring the financial terms of the contract; a sales and marketing manager also may have responsibility for contract negotiations, especially in convention centers. Contracts exist between agencies and acts, agencies and promoters, promoters or agencies and facilities, facilities and contractors, and facilities and patrons.

A contract is an agreement between two or more parties based upon sufficient consideration to do or to refrain from doing some lawful activity. A contract must create an obligation. In addition, a contract must have the following four aspects:

- Mutual assent.
- Capable parties.
- Fair consideration.
- Terms.

A common contract is the lease agreement that allows the public assembly facility, or a portion of it, to be rented for a specific period of time for some specific lawful activity. The facility usually receives an agreed upon amount of money (rent) from the promoter for the use of the facility. The rental payment may be either a flat fee or a percentage of the total ticket sales revenue.

If the public assembly facility's management acts as the promoter, as is often the case with performing arts centers, the management contracts directly with the artist's agency. Much of stadium, convention center, exhibit hall, and arena business is rental business whereby management allows the facility to be leased by a promoter in consideration for rent. In the case of lease/rental arrangements, the promoter usually reimburses the venue for expenses such as front-of-house staffing, stagehands, and ticket expenses in addition to paying rent. Sometimes the estimated cost of all these items is combined with the rental fee in an all-inclusive flat payment for rent and services.

Due to the large number of contracts used in most public assembly facilities, it is very important for the manager to understand negotiating philosophies, strategies, tactics and techniques. Unlike with some contract negotiations, facility managers frequently negotiate a series of contracts with the same party. Consequently, the astute facility manager will keep in mind the need to develop and nurture relationships along with trying to negotiate a satisfactory deal. Many successful facility managers ascribe to the "win-win" school of negotiating philosophy, understanding that the deal has to be good for both parties if a long and mutually beneficial relationship is to occur.

HUMAN RESOURCES

Since one of the largest expenses for any facility is labor, direct and indirect, public assembly facility management should be skilled in identifying, recruiting, hiring, training, and paying employees. An effective manager will mandate the development of procedures for the hiring of full- and part-time employees. In addition, management should normally specify procurement procedures concerning subcontracted labor. The facility's responsibilities include:

- Being aware of and understanding the laws concerning Immigration and Naturalization Service (INS) documentation in hiring (INS is part of the United State's Department of Homeland Security) or the appropriate agency in other countries.
- Monitoring facility hiring and firing activities in light of employee rights and responsibilities.
- Managing the payroll process and being knowledgeable about rates of pay, payroll dates, workers' compensation insurance, withholding taxes, and overtime.

The typical public assembly facility employs a relatively small staff of full-time employees while maintaining a large pool of workers willing and able to work on a part-time event-related basis.

Its type, volume, and kind of business it attracts generally dictate the size of the public assembly facility's full-time staff. Small facilities might have a general manager, a business manager, an operations manager and/or building superintendent/engineer. On the other hand, a large facility might also employ managers and support staff for security, advertising and marketing, catering, concessions, box office, event coordination, house-keeping, etc. Full-time hourly employees might work 37.5-40 hours a week and may be eligible for overtime pay for any additional hours worked. However, it should be noted some jurisdictions allow for the employment of hourly employees who are not eligible for overtime compensation. Management will specify which job categories qualify for over-time payment and those that do not. Management will also decide whether to use time cards and they may dictate the guidelines used to determine overtime.

HUMAN RESOURCES GUIDELINES

Normally, a public assembly facility develops and implements human resource guide-lines that mirror those of other agencies under management's supervision. Although the public assembly facility management business can be very different from other "public works" activities, the organization of human resources services information is quite simi-lar. Typically, most facilities/agencies under a municipal or public university ownership will use similar processes in developing job descriptions, announcements and applica-tions, advertising openings, collecting and processing applications, interviewing and selecting employees, and evaluating performance. Agencies and/or facilities generally fol-low common guidelines for employee promotions and dismissals.

A carefully constructed and accurate job description should be established for each job title. The job description should include at least:

- A title that accurately describes the job.
- Description of the nature of the work.
- Examples of work assignments.
- Supervision received and provided.
- Skill-level and physical requirements associated with the job.
- Required experience.
- Minimum educational requirements.

The job description is crucial to the human resources process because it provides the basis for the formal relationship between employee and employer. The objective of those responsible for recruiting and hiring employees is basically twofold: to attract applicants who meet established job qualifications; and, to identify and hire people who will perform their assignments at the level and in an appropriate manner required by the position.

The first part of the recruitment process involves announcing position openings and then identifying and hiring people with adequate skills, training, and abilities to do the job described. A careful assessment of the job applications which evaluates the merits of each candidate can accomplish most of this process. Education levels, accumulated skills, work history, etc. can and should be verified. Depending on the position, credit checks and security background checks may also be required.

The second part of the recruitment process involves screening the applicants. Identifying and hiring employees whose personalities and work habits mesh with the existing employees in the work group and whose personalities and work ethics contribute to, rather than detract from, the facility's ability to achieve its goals and objectives can prove much more difficult. The key to successful hiring is having an individual responsible for the human resources process who completely understands the job position to be filled, knows the necessary interactions required with other facility employees, and is cognizant of the facility's mission statement. Employing a carefully structured interview for all candidates, requiring candidates to provide writing samples when appropriate, and including current employees on the interview team will generally provide important insights relative to the compatibility of the candidate.

If the initial applications are thoroughly screened in order to identify candidates to interview, then each candidate interviewed should have the necessary skills and abilities to perform the job. Thus the ultimate goal of the interview process is to identify whether the candidate possesses the personality, temperament, and work ethic that should enable him/her to work in harmony and be productive with other members of the workforce.

The "matching game," placing employees in positions in which the employee's qualifications and the position's requirements best fit, is more art than science. Generally, facility managers in the United States may hire whomever they desire as long as positions are: properly posted and advertised; the candidate meets the qualifications stated in the job description; the decision to hire is in accord with the requirements of the Equal Employment Opportunity Commission and the Americans with Disabilities Act; and, there has been no discrimination on the basis of certain protected characteristics such as age, national origin, gender, race, or religion.

EMPLOYEE ORIENTATION

Orientation is the process of introducing new employees to the workplace. The orientation program should also be structured to assist the new employee in understanding the facility's overall goals and objectives and the employee's role in that process. Training is the process of instructing and guiding the development of the new employee in the workplace. To be successful, the training program should guide the employee through a series of exercises or experiences that teach how to respond to specific requirements of the job. While orientation is normally a one-time activity, training should be an ongoing part of the employee development process.

The public assembly facility's manager is responsible for determining the most effective and efficient employee training programs for the operation and these programs should be aligned with the facility's overall goals and objectives. The public assembly facility's manager should document and keep verifying records for each employee successfully completing the orientation program and all other successfully completed training programs.

COMMUNICATIONS

Communication is another critical element in human resources management. In addition to the employee policy and procedures manual that outlines the rights and responsibilities of the employee, there are other excellent communication vehicles available such as:

- Written materials provided during orientation and training sessions.
- Bulletin boards.
- Employee newsletters.
- Scheduled staff meetings.
- Job specific employee manuals.

Employee evaluation is another important communication tool for supervisors to communicate job expectations. All employees deserve to hear how they are doing. Formal annual reviews of all employees are typical, though continuous coaching and evaluation is advisable in many supervisory situations. Although this process can be an arduous one, it is a desired practice that benefits management and employees alike. An employee evaluation and development plan can contribute equally to the professional and personal goals mutually shared by the employer and employee.

Managing Part-time and Casual Labor

One major difference in public assembly facilities and that of most other businesses is the large number of part-time or casual employees that are hired to work events. Consequently, a very important task of the facility's HR is the orderly record keeping of this segment of the labor force.

Many public assembly facility managers use the terms part-time and casual labor interchangeably or use casual labor to encompass both. However, it must be noted that a difference may exist between casual and part-time labor, even though casual labor works only part-time. The difference may be one of how the employee's schedule is driven/determined. A casual employee's schedule can be one that is, most always, event driven; no event, no work.

An employee who is considered part-time is more likely to be scheduled to work a specific number of hours on a continuing basis. This might include a position such as a clerk-receptionist who works four hours X number of days each week. Some public bodies term this "regular part-time" to differentiate from individuals who are hired for part-time tasks, not event driven, but for a short-period of time (e.g. an annual maintenance function requiring extra bodies).

The distinction between these part-time and casual employees is murky. The distinction of regular part-time individuals is more clearly recognized.

An ironic situation exists in that a regular part-time employee may not be scheduled to work enough hours in a year to receive fringe benefits while casual employees may. For example, in California the number of hours required to receive fringe benefits in jurisdictions that are part of the Public Employees Retirement System (PERS) is 1,000. Employees reaching that level then receive the fringe benefits retroactive to their first hour of employment. At the same time, casual employees such as ushers, ticket takers, and other "event" personnel may qualify for fringe benefits by a union contract, on a monthly basis, simply by working a certain number of hours, such as eighty.

Few if any public assembly facilities, regardless of size, type or business volume, can afford to maintain a full-time event staff such as ushers, ticket takers, ticket sellers, security guards, peer security, runners, etc. Nonetheless, these personnel are essential for the proper operation of facility events and activities. Traveling attractions, concerts, trade shows, performing artists, meetings, assemblies, and conventions pay for casual labor but they depend on the public assembly facility to supply and manage these employees.

There are a couple of ways that a facility can accomplish the task of providing this work force. Under an in-house operation, the facility may assume the responsibility for identifying potential employees; recruiting, hiring, and organizing their paperwork; and, training, managing, insuring, and paying them. Another way would be for the facility to subcontract the labor, turn the process over to a local union, or use a combination of in-house and subcontracting or local union. Each procedure has its advantages and disadvantages and each decision should be based on the availability of the labor pool, payroll, skill requirement, available training programs, employment statutes and regulations, the political climate, and other related factors. Traveling theatrical productions and musical attractions often have a union stage crew with the show.

As mentioned earlier, many public assembly facilities depend on subcontracted labor to staff housekeeping and some front-of-house positions. Labor positions requiring only minimal training and experience but direct and sometimes intense supervision, might also be subcontracted to labor providers. Some labor providers specialize in certain areas such as housekeeping personnel, general construction workers, general uniformed security guards, peer (T-shirt) security guards, ushers, and supervisors. They also may be able to provide experienced and well-trained first-aid personnel.

In many publicly owned facilities, contracting for these services must go through a bid process. Once the bid is let, a single provider usually supplies all the required casual labor called for in the contract. When labor is subcontracted, the public assembly facility typically initiates the labor call, the provider supplies the labor, and the facility is then billed for the personnel and the provider's administrative expenses. In some instances these expenses may be recharged to facility users. Allowing a subcontracted provider to supply casual labor not only eliminates the expense of recruiting, training, and insurance, it also eliminates the cost of producing and managing the payroll.

Another potential source of labor is the independent contractor. Independent contractors are individuals hired to do specific tasks such as repair telescopic risers, dismantle and repair message and scoreboards, etc. By definition, independent contractors are unsupervised, set their own work hours, are paid at the completion of the task, and are self-insured. Before independent contractors are allowed to work, depending upon the job, they should be required to provide their certificate of insurance and endorsement naming the facility, its officers, employees, and agents as additional insured. Some public facility managers believe part-time labor associated with events meet the definition of an independent contractor thus excusing the facility from wage and hour considerations and insurance. However, most event personnel must perform tasks in ways specified by the hiring body/facility, during specified hours and specified locations. Consequently, they do not meet the United States Internal Revenue Service's criteria as independent contractors.

Volunteers are unpaid employees who represent yet another labor category. It's not unusual for most, if not all, of the entire front-of-house staff at performing arts centers to be volunteers. Many universities use students as ushers and find the practice both efficient and effective. If the public assembly facility were situated in an environment where ready and able volunteers are available from colleges and universities, senior citizen centers, civic and fraternal organizations, and booster clubs, it would benefit the public assembly facility financially, politically, and from a public relations stand point to utilize their services. The facility manager must keep in mind that although volunteers are unpaid, their personal safety is still the responsibility of the facility; therefore, they need to be protected by the facility's general liability insurance policy. The facility manager must also remember that volunteers require training and work incentives to motivate them just as do paid workers.

RISK MANAGEMENT

In every activity in which the public assembly facility participates, there is an element of risk (potential for harm) and liability (responsibility). Typically, the public assembly facility's management is involved in monitoring, if not directly managing, the facility's activities concerning *risk management*. The facility management team must understand that risk is omnipresent and that potential individual and/or facility liability exists at all times. Thus, it becomes the responsibility of the public assembly facility's management to design a plan for dealing with risk management and the attendant liability issues.

The public assembly facility manager is responsible for communicating to all full- and part-time employees the importance of understanding that potential risks are associated with every activity held in the facility and on its grounds. They need to understand the concept that every employee is a member of the risk management team and that they must be constantly vigilant in recognizing, reporting, and eliminating all potential risks. The team must understand that any risk left unmanaged may become a threat to the facility as well as to their jobs. Potential risks must be identified and either isolated, repaired, replaced, or completely eliminated.

Whether dealing with a common attendee slip-and-fall or a catastrophic structural failure, risk and liability are the two most important considerations. For virtually every accident that ends up in litigation, the common questions that will certainly be asked of the facility management are: "Should you have anticipated the accident? If so, what was done to prevent it?" An appropriate risk management program will provide the facility's management with the information required to properly respond to these critical questions.

There are five basic ways for dealing with risk: avoid, assume, prevent, reduce and transfer.

1. **Risk avoidance**. Sometimes the very best method of dealing with an exposure to loss is to try to avoid all possibility of the loss occurring. A striking example is the decision to not schedule heavy metal concerts to avoid the associated high risk liabilities. Some risks are not avoidable and, in such case, the exposure to loss for this type or risk can often be reduced but not entirely eliminated. For other exposures, avoidance is the only reasonable alternative, especially for those risks when the chance of loss is high and loss severity is also high.

2. **Risk assumption.** Risk assumption means assuming the consequence of a loss will be borne by the party exposed to the chance of loss. Often risk assumption is a deliberated, planned risk management decision. This is, the assumption of the risk is undertaken with the full understanding of the consequence of a potential loss, and with the full understanding the consequences will be borne by the one assuming the risk. Many risks are assumed because the consequences of a specific loss would not be costly enough to justify using any other risk management tool. Sometimes risks must be assumed such as deductible provisions in an insurance policy. In summary, deliberate risk assumption is a desirable alternative when the maximum severity of loss is relatively low and the chance of loss is also low.

3. **Loss prevention.** Loss prevention activities are utilized to lower the chance of loss and to make the occurrence of loss less frequent. There is a close connection between loss prevention activities and insurance premiums. The more effective the loss prevention, the lower should be the insurance premiums. Whenever the frequency of loss is high, loss prevention activities should be applied. However, loss prevention is feasible only if the benefits realized from few occurrences of loss are greater than the cost of the loss prevention measures.

4. **Loss reduction.** Loss reduction activities are designed to reduce the severity of losses that do occur. Regardless of all the preventive steps taken, some losses will and do occur. Loss reduction activities aim at minimizing the impact of the losses. Examples would be the installation of an automatic fire sprinkler system which is not designed to prevent fires but to stop the fire from spreading, fire walls or silent alarms. In general, when the severity of the loss is great and when the loss cannot be avoided or transferred, loss reduction activities are appropriate — provided the cost of said activities does not exceed the benefits gained.

5. **Risk transfer.** Risk transfer means the original party exposed to a loss is able to obtain another party to bear the risk. The usual way to transfer risk is to obtain insurance coverage whereby contractually the element of risk is given to the insurance provider. Insurance is an especially appropriate risk management tool when the chance of loss is low and the severity of a potential loss is high. Beyond the usual way of transferring risk through the use of insurance, there are non-insurance risk transfer methods that can be utilized as well. The hold harmless and indemnification clauses in facility user contracts have been an effective method of public assembly facility managers in transferring risk to the facility users. In addition, when managers contract out services (e.g., security, ticketing, concessions, etc.), they also transfer the risks associated with those specific areas of operations to the contractor.

FREQUENCY OF LOSS		
	LOW	**HIGH**
LOW	**RISK ASSUMPTION** Also, loss prevention & reduction if costs justify the benefits.	**LOSS PREVENTION** Also, loss reduction if costs can be justified. Assume risk if cost of prevention or reduction can't be justified.
HIGH	**RISK TRANSFER** Insurance. **LOSS REDUCTION** Take preventive measures if loss can't be transferred.	**RISK AVOIDANCE** Also, loss prevention & loss reduction if possible.

SEVERITY OF LOSS (vertical label at left)

There may be times when the facility's booking manager will be requested to book an activity for which the potential for accidents is so great that it would not be in the facility's best interest to enter into a contract. As noted in Chapter 3 — Scheduling Facilities and Booking Events, one reason not to book an event is when it is apparent "based on historical data" that the event poses a danger to those in attendance. In such cases, the facility's response to the booking request would be one of avoidance. It is not uncommon for facilities to avoid activities that have both a high frequency of risk as well as a high potential for risk . But, in all instances, the practice of avoidance must be justified.

Just as some events justify avoidance, there are also events and activities with such a low risk factor that the facility itself may be willing to assume the associated risk. For example, the facility manager may be willing to rent the space for a small meeting without requiring the planner to purchase additional insurance. However, public assembly facilities are less likely to take on the assumption of risk due to the extremely high number of suits arising out of basically insignificant incidents. The litigious nature of society has forced public assembly facility managers to protect their facilities and their employees at all times.

Regardless of the risk management philosophy, the public assembly facility's plan should direct the facility manager to seek and implement ways of reducing and managing anticipated risk. This may be accomplished by understanding the nature of the event, its anticipated audience, and the facility itself relative to potential accidents. Armed with this knowledge, the facility's risk management team may be able to identify and isolate potential accidents and implement measures that may totally eliminate them or at least minimize the possibility of occurrence.

Another common method for dealing with risk is simply to transfer it to someone else. The transference process involves "holding harmless" the public assembly facility and its employees. When this occurs, the facility and its employees are sheltered from any liability or financial responsibility associated with injury or loss of property due to negligence. Facility managers who elect to deal with risk by transference will require clients leasing the facility to include indemnification clauses in their contracts that hold the facility and its employees harmless. In essence, the client assumes responsibility for any and all negative occurrences during the rental period.

The most common method for transferring risk, however, is through the purchase of insurance. Requiring both insurance and a hold harmless clause is also a possibility. Public assembly facilities normally have a general liability insurance umbrella policy that protects its property, employees, guests, and invitees. It is normal procedure for a public assembly facility manager to require event promoters to properly insure themselves as well as their attraction, agents and all employees associated with the event. Further, the promoter will be required to name the public assembly facility as an additional insured for a pre-determined amount of coverage and provide both a certificate of insurance and a valid endorsement. The purpose of this process is to give the public assembly facility two layers of coverage — its own general umbrella policy and the additional coverage provided by the promoter.

Some facilities use what is called a "Master Users" policy, either a stand-alone arranged by the facility or a part of the facility's public liability/property damage policy. This approach allows the user to have the required coverage under the umbrella of the facility's policy. There is often a charge to the user for this coverage.

The cost of insurance premiums for public assembly facilities and attractions has escalated to the point where insurance coverage is sometimes simply not affordable. The reasons for the escalation include the frequency of accidents and the severity of injuries, the number of suits and high cost of defending and paying judgments, and a general increase in crowd misbehavior. At one time, concert promoters could insure themselves, the attraction and its employees, and the facility and its guests and employees with a million dollars in coverage at a cost of less than twenty-five cents (US) per person attending the event. Unfortunately, current insurance costs have significantly impacted the total operating expenses of attractions and facilities alike.

SUMMARY

There are many similar business operating dynamics associated with all public assembly facilities. Each facility has its own operating budget. However, for some facilities the cost of operating is greater than the income they can generate. Consequently, these facilities must seek supplemental funding in order to cover their operating deficits.

Fiscal year budgets are more common than calendar year budgets. There are several budgeting systems from which public assembly facility governing bodies may select. The more commonly used systems include line item budgeting, incremental budgeting, performance budgeting, and zero-based budgeting. The budgeting process usually flows through four developmental stages: preparation, presentation, adoption, and execution.

The issuance of financial statements is critical to any financial management system.

Income statements are designed to report the financial performance for a specific period of time such as a month, quarter, or year. Balance sheets report the financial status for a particular point in time and provide essential cash flow information. Operating statements show income and expenses by category and allow the tracing of each item of revenue and expense to its source.

Cost allocation, in a general sense, is the assignment of costs to one or more cost objectives. A cost objective is any activity in which a separate measurement of cost is desired. Public assembly facility management, by its very nature, requires a separate measurement of cost concerning each event activity.

Direct and indirect labor costs are common expenses for all facilities and all events. Direct labor represents wages paid or owed as a direct consequence of an event or activity. Indirect labor represents wages paid or owed as an indirect consequence of an activity or event such as equipment repairs, consultant fees, etc.

Public assembly facility overhead represents variable costs or those not specifically identified that benefit the facility in varying proportions and are allocated in some form of a percentage or specific local currency amount to the facility or specific department. Overhead costs might be re-charged to users based on a formula included in the contract.

The public assembly facility business manager might also be responsible for day-to-day activities such as cash management, inventory, fixed assets, labor, utilities, contracts, and risk. Safeguards must be implemented to protect the facility's checking account. Preprinted and consecutively numbered checks should always be used, and checks above a specified amount should require two authorized signatures. All bank accounts should be reconciled monthly, and strict policies regarding the use of petty cash should be adopted in an effort to avoid abuse. Unscheduled internal and external audits focusing on the handling of the facility's finances and adherence to its policies and procedures are highly recommended.

Managing accounts receivable and accounts payable are two additional responsibilities of the business manager. When practical, public assembly facilities should follow the practice of maximizing the time funds are in an interest bearing accounts by "aging" the bills.

The settlement process employed by public assembly facilities is not in and of itself unique, but it is unique with respect to the timing of the activity because it typically occurs the same day or night of the event. In fact, it sometimes occurs while the event is taking place.

Labor, both full- and part-time, is a major expense for public assembly facilities. Managers must be knowledgeable of laws and regulations related to the recruitment, hiring, and termination of employees as well as those related to the payroll process. Carefully constructed and accurate job descriptions should be established for each job title. Depending on the position, credit checks and security background checks may be necessary prior to hiring an applicant.

The key to successful hiring is having an individual responsible for the human resources process who understands the job position to be filled, knows the necessary interactions required with other facility employees, and is cognizant of the facility's mission statement.

Some public assembly facilities subcontract for their part-time event staff and thereby eliminate the expense of recruiting, training, insuring, producing, and managing the payroll for these employees. For certain tasks, the services of an independent contractor may be engaged. Before commencing any work, depending on the job, the independent contractor should be required to present a certificate of insurance that names the public assembly facility, its officers, employees and agents as additional insured. In turn, the public assembly facility should add the independent contractor's name to its "named additional insured" section within the facility's umbrella policy.

Volunteers represent another labor category. Although not paid, their safety becomes the responsibility of the public assembly facility. Facility managers must remember that volunteers, just like paid workers, require training, supervision, and work incentives to motivate them.

Basically, there are five ways to deal with risk: avoidance, assumption, prevention, reduction and transference. Risk management must be stressed with all employees because of the many factors that may potentially threaten the facility, its patrons, and its employees.

REFERENCES AND ADDITIONAL READINGS

Cotts, David G. and Edmund P. Rondeau. 2003. *The Facility Manager's Guide to Finance and Budgeting*. New York: AMACOM.

Dropkin, Murray and Bill LaTouche. 1998. *The Budget-Building Book for Nonprofits: A Step-by-Step Guide for Managers and Boards*. San Francisco: Jossey-Bass.

Dropkin, Murray and Allyson Hayden. 2001. *The Cash Flow Management Book for Nonprofits: A Step-by-Step Guide for Managers and Boards*. San Francisco: Jossey-Bass.

Fried, Gil, Steven Shapiro, and Timothy DeSchriver. 2003. *Sport Finance*. Champaign, IL: Human Kinetics.

Livingston, John Leslie. 2001. *The Portable MBA in Finance and Accounting*. Hoboken, NJ: John Wiley & Sons, Inc

Madden, Turner D. 1998. *Public Assembly Facility Law: A Guide for Managers of Arenas, Auditoriums, Convention Centers, Performing Arts Centers, Race Tracks and Stadiums*. Coppell, TX: International Association of Assembly Managers, Inc.

Ruppel, Warren. 2002. *Not-for-Profit Accounting Made Easy*. Hoboken, NJ: John Wiley & Sons, Inc.

Skinner, Bruce E. and Vladimir Rukavina. 2002. *Event Sponsorship*. Hoboken, NJ: John Wiley & Sons, Inc.

7

ANCILLARY SERVICES AS REVENUE GENERATORS

CHAPTER OUTLINE

⼊ INTRODUCTION

Impressions are powerful and lasting influences on human behavior and experiences, whether good or bad, will shape the frame of reference someone has of a given environment. The public assembly facility has the same challenge that all retail businesses have — of attracting guests with discretionary time and income and maximizing sales. Creating product demand and repetitive patronage for entertainment-based, niche commodities requires an uncanny ability to focus on establishing a trust relationship with the guests. Ultimately, the target audience must get more than they bargained for — meeting and exceeding expectations whenever and wherever possible. To accomplish this, each guest should be afforded a "value added" experience. This chapter will focus on some of the more prominent ancillary programs that help the public assembly facility manager create an inviting environment laced with positive experiences that tend to draw guests and generate additional revenue.

All public assembly facilities share a common thread in their mission statement: to fill, not necessarily sell, all available seats (or floor space for convention centers and trade shows) as frequently as possible. Why not sell all the seats or floor space? Some public assembly facilities may have financial profit as their primary focus while others may concentrate more on providing programming that best serves the community's needs. Regardless of their mission statement's emphasis, the success of any public assembly facility is contingent on its ability to attract clients and guests.

The concept of selling all seats may be literally applied to arenas, stadiums, performing arts theatres, and amphitheatres. With respect to convention centers that normally do not have traditional seating, it should be interpreted to mean attracting conventions, multi-day meetings, trade shows, and conferences that bring large numbers of out-of-town attendees who spend "new" money in the community thereby stimulating the local economy. Of course it must be recognized that other types of public assembly facilities also attract out-of-town audiences (out of the taxing jurisdiction) who also spend "new" money.

One challenge may be the filling of seats while a greater challenge is providing a level of service that will leave each guest and event promoter with a very satisfied feeling as a result of having attended or promoted an event in the public assembly facility. The experience of attending an event is much more than buying a ticket and sitting in a seat. There are a host of other variables associated with attendance. For example, were there any traffic problems encountered while traveling to the facility? Was parking available and easily accessible? Were the parking area and the walkways to the facility viewed as a safe environment? The experience continues when the guest enters the public assembly facility. Did the quality of the food and beverage service meet expectations? Were the rest rooms clean and quickly accessible? Was the event or activity entertaining? There are a myriad of dimensions to the guest's experience, and each must be tended to with great care.

The wide variety of facilities in terms of size/capacity, design, and purpose results in differences in their interest or ability to offer some programs. Consequently, it is important for the management of public assembly facilities to inform and educate prospective attendees and event promoters as to what they should expect. For example, many small theatres, auditoriums, arenas, civic/community centers present events for which no tickets are issued, no food and beverage service is available, and no programs or novelties are sold.

✗ Event components (such as parking, food and beverage, novelty items, etc.) not only serve to enhance the guest's experience, but provide additional income streams for the public assembly facility's operating budget. In this sense, they may be referred to as *ancillary services*. Basically, ancillary services and revenue sources are the same thing. The primary revenue sources for a public assembly facility are renting space in the facility and presenting events. All other revenue sources are referred to as ancillary.

Some public assembly facilities may have a wide variety of ancillary services available to tenants/users such as equipment rentals, providing information technology resources including wireless computer applications and up- and down-links for teleconferences, freight handling (drayage), box office, general labor, utility charges, set-up labor, decorating services, sight origination fees, promotions, and event advertising. In addition, services provided directly to attendees, such as automatic teller machines and computer cafes, can also be excellent revenue generators. The public assembly facility manager needs to pay close attention to all possible ancillary services and their potential for generating additional revenue through purchases, fees, and surcharges.

In most facilities, the numbers of seats or possible attendance capacities are basically fixed. The revenue from admission or space sales is relatively consistent for the type of event involved. While these prices increase over time, it can be argued the better opportunities for increasing total revenue are from ancillary services, particularly those that are creative and new to the facility. To achieve these goals, the manager needs to be certain the highest standards of quality are maintained with respect to service, product and presentation. Constant feedback from users of the services, and/or purchasers of products, is essential. Focus groups of attendees such as season ticket holders plus random interview or questionnaire sampling of attendees and multiple event producers are all possible follow-up evaluation approaches to soliciting feedback.

The scope and number of possible ancillary services, and consequently revenue generators, are very broad. This chapter will focus primarily on food and beverage, merchandise and novelties, and parking as ancillary activities that are significant revenue generators. The basic issues and requirements for success in these areas are applicable to other possible ancillary areas. Some revenue generating activities are also discussed in Chapter 4 — Sales and Marketing.

✗ FOOD AND BEVERAGE: WHY IS IT SO IMPORTANT?

Throughout history, the greatest pastime when members of the human race gather is eating. There is something special about the dynamics of "breaking of bread together" that people enjoy. When you add to this mix the combination of sport and entertainment, you have a powerful experience. For many public assembly facilities (especially those larger in size, with greater numbers of seats/space, and presenting more commercial programs than a community center, small theatre, or auditorium) the food and beverage service may represent the most important ancillary service provided. Many events are scheduled during mealtime and business hours. As a result guests expect to have food and beverage available. Such expectations represent an opportunity to generate substantial additional revenue. Scheduling during these times also enhances the value of hospitality rooms, entertainment suites and VIP areas in which food and beverages are available. The presence of these facilities can be used as a "hook" in attracting upscale guests.

Convention centers without food and beverage service and dining facilities may have a more difficult task in attracting multi-day meetings, conventions, conferences, or trade shows. In much the same way, stadiums prohibited from selling beer are not as attractive to professional sport attendees. At the same time, it is usually expected alcohol will not be sold at high school or collegiate events, although more and more universities are selling alcohol. While individual tastes may vary, food and beverage operations seek to provide an array of universally popular items as well as those popular within the geographic region. Having these items available tends to enhance the guest's overall event experience. Some would categorize this as providing group hospitality.

Over the years, the number of available events/acts/shows has declined whereas the number of public assembly facilities has increased. The net result is a much more competitive marketplace. Public assembly facility managers must employ aggressive sales and marketing techniques to attract more events to their facility in order to generate necessary operating revenues. Once an event is booked, providing food and beverage concession items appropriate to the event can create excellent revenue streams.

✄ In-House vs. Contract - The Great Debate

Food and beverage service operations have grown exponentially in terms of sales and profits. A public assembly facility's food and beverage service operation may range from the traditional concession stand and basic catering to fine dining and banquet facilities. Older public assembly facilities may still only offer the traditional concession stand operations. However, new and refurbished food and beverage service facilities are designed to enable the concessions manager to offer an expanded menu, one that frequently includes items from well-known restaurants and gourmet selections. Guest demands for these offerings are generally accompanied by higher expectation levels. Some of the newer public assembly facilities also feature fine dining restaurants located on the premises and which are open to the general public as well as facility guests. The presence of premium seating areas, such as luxury boxes, provides another avenue for providing upscale/fine dining food and beverage service. Depending upon the event, an increase in the availability of specialized services, golden circle suites and VIP areas may be warranted.

With there being little doubt about the potential for gaining significant profits from a properly managed food and beverage operation, prudent public assembly facility managers must give this operation their utmost attention. This then gives rise to the question of who should be managing the facility's food and beverage operation. A public assembly facility manager has the option of managing the food and beverage service in-house or awarding a private company a contract to operate the concession. Numerous public assembly facilities have privatized their food and beverage service operations. (See Figure 7-1 for advantages of both in-house and contract).

IN-HOUSE -VS- CONTRACT	
SELF OPERATION	**PRIVATE CONTRACTOR**
■ Ability to retain control	■ Capital investment management
■ Ability to retain flexibility	■ Use of proven systems
■ Ability to retain all financial control	■ Provides liability protection from operations, especially alcohol

FIGURE 7-1

How does a public assembly facility manager decide whether or not to privatize the facility's food and beverage service? The manager should assess the infrastructure of the facility to determine whether self-operation or privatization would be most lucrative financially. Included in these considerations would be an analysis of the available labor pool, level of staff skills, staff training requirements, labor laws, financial resources, capital equipment, and the manager's time and ability to effectively oversee such an operation. While each public assembly facility exists in a different situation, there are distinct advantages to both self-operated and privatized food and beverage service management.

Simply stated, if the food and beverage service is self-operated, the public assembly facility's management maintains total control of labor, products, services and profits. When allowed to function in a for-profit mode, some public assembly facilities, both large and small, have generated substantial profits from their self-operated food and beverage service. However, the public assembly facility must also assume all of the risks associated with the operation. This operating format works best when the principles and policies governing the public assembly facility's operation allow the manager to function in a for-profit mode. Unfortunately, restrictive bureaucratic measures can, at times, complicate this structure and could potentially have an effect on product quality.

If contracting, the facility manager will want to use the *request for proposal* (RFP) and/or a *request for qualifications* (RFQ) in order to select best overall contractor. There is an important distinction between the RFP and the RFQ. The purpose of the RFQ is to pre-qualify firms by ascertaining they have the experience, financial ability, knowledge, etc. to provide the nature, level of service, and quality of product desired and identified by the facility. RFPs are then sent to only those firms that have been deemed qualified.

In any case, however, it is important that the selection process be a proposal for professional services rather than a bid, otherwise some municipalities may require you to only select the company proposing the highest commission without regard to the equally important issues of management ability, quality of investment, company's financial standing as well as their operational experience and reputation in comparable venues.

When a public assembly facility contracts its food and beverage operations to a private company, the facility's manager is able to spend more time overseeing other aspects of the facility's operation. Depending on the type of contract, the private company might assume the responsibility for labor, health and alcohol laws compliance, food/product costs, all liability and often the cost of providing and amortizing the furniture, fixtures and equipment (FF&E) and even the food and beverage physical build-out costs. The most common contract form is a commission agreement whereby the concessionaire pays the facility a percentage of gross sales. If it is a management-fee-based contract, the concessionaire receives its management fee and likely an incentive bonus. The bonus can be based on various combinations of achieving pre-determined goals. These can include a percentage of *gross revenue*, a percentage of net revenue, or a reduction in cost or subsidy.

With the advent of so much construction utilizing tax exempt bonds over the last several years, however, more and more venues are required under IRS rules to have another form of management fee contract structured with the concessionaire earning a lump sum fee and incentive based on any criteria other than profits. There are many technicalities to this type of agreement and the facility manager should contact their bond counsel for a complete understanding of the rules.

There can be other permutations of these basic formulas. There are instances in which there is also a disincentive clause in the contract that requires a rebate of a part of the base fee if certain targets are not met. If it is a profit-percentage-based contract, the concessionaire simply receives an agreed upon percentage of the profits. Incentive bonuses may be included in the contract whereby the concessionaire's percentage of the profit increases once established amounts of profit are achieved.

Sometimes when a private company manages the food and beverage operation, tensions may build between the facility manager and the concessionaire over issues such as event bookings and staffing requirements. The wise facility manager will learn to quickly resolve any differences and to create a positive working environment for all parties.

Whether concessions are operated in-house or through a private contractor, the facility manager is still responsible for ensuring that the food and beverage service operation functions in the most efficient way possible. Regardless of the type of food and beverage contract, the public assembly facility manager must reserve the right to approve product quality, menu selections, and product pricing. It is also critical that facility management retain the right to approve the hiring and/or removal of the food/beverage manager.

Bigelow points out that too many managers believe that when a private contractor is involved, there is little they can do to enhance the food and beverage service operation. (Bigelow, 2003). Yet, just because the contractor appears to be performing efficiently does not relieve facility managers of their responsibility for periodically assessing the quality of service being delivered and to ensure it meets or exceeds agreed upon standards and objectives. In the same manner, public assembly facility managers operating in-house food and beverage service should be constantly examining their operations in order to maintain high standards while maximizing efficiency. Given the importance of food and beverage service as an ancillary profit center and the role it plays in producing guest satisfaction, the public assembly facility manager has a responsibility to efficiently manage and promote exemplary food service to all guests.

⚘ PHYSICAL LAYOUT AND DESIGN

When new public assembly facilities are being planned, from a day-to-day operating perspective, careful consideration should be given to convenient parking access, adequate and conveniently located rest rooms, cleaning and maintenance, food and beverage service operations including portable concession services, and the overall presentation quality of the facility. Of particular concern is the size and design of food and beverage service areas. In all public assembly facilities that offer food and beverages, these areas may include concession stands, kiosks, *commissaries*, food preparation and storage, loading docks, and waste disposal areas. Arenas and stadiums with luxury suites and clubs especially require skilled design for food and beverage facilities.

In all cases, the owner and builder should examine the public assembly facility's purpose carefully along with the functions and events the facility is expected to accommodate. This form of examination will help determine the type of food and beverage areas required and their number, location, layout, and size. Financial and capital resources also must be taken into consideration when shaping this determination. The elimination of potential flaws during the design stage will serve to minimize operational problems and allow for maximizing profits once the project is completed. The proper placement of concession stands requires careful planning.

It should always be remembered that concession stands generate significant revenues if positioned in optimal locations. Products will be more easily marketed when traffic flow, ingress and egress, and the positioning of concession stands are planned as a package. (See Figure 7-2 for some design flaws within concession operations).

SOME DESIGN FLAWS WITHIN CONCESSION OPERATIONS:

DESIGN FLAWS WITHIN CONCESSION OPERATIONS:

- Inadequate number of concession stands relative to seating capacity.
- Inadequate kitchen location and space.
- No installation of floor drains in kitchen and stand areas.
- No provision for hawking (selling food, beverage, or novelty products in the audience area) or vending operation (selling food, beverage, or novelty products from stands or kiosks.)
- Service elevators inadequately located relative to storage facilities.
- Inadequate size and location of loading docks and storerooms.
- Inadequate ventilation for cooking capabilities.
- Insufficient water and energy availability.
- Insufficient concourse areas to accommodate traffic flow.
- Access and location of support services.

Courtesy of Russo (1980)

FIGURE 7-2

An important consideration is the availability of support facilities such as kitchens that are ample in size and convenient in location. This is of particular importance to convention centers because they rely heavily on their ability to cater large meals and other social functions. Adequate refrigeration and dry storage space are necessary for a kitchen to properly function. The location of shipping and receiving areas and the proper location of service elevators, in multi-level facilities, can further maximize the productivity of food and beverage service employees.

Some public assembly facilities use a commissary to accommodate vendors and hawkers and to provide security for stored products. Hawking items in the seating areas is often very effective because many people are reluctant to leave their seats during a close contest or an entertaining performance. Others may not be physically able get to concession stands or wait in the lines that generally form at intermission and/or during sporting event breaks. Thus, making products available to these guests while they remain in their seats produces sales that otherwise might not occur. Failing to provide an area to accommodate the needs of these vendors and hawkers is poor design and planning. Management must overcome these shortcomings.

Managers of existing public assembly facilities who do not have carte blanche to create an optimal environment for their food and beverage service operation should still evaluate potential improvements that might assist in maximizing their operation's success. Questions to be asked include: Would the improvement costs be justified when compared to the additional revenues that might be generated (A classic ROI — return on investment — analysis)? Are the areas in which the food and beverage service operation function attractive to guests? If not, what would be the cost of making them more attractive? Would the makeover result in the generation of additional revenues? Of equal importance, would the physical improvements increase the ability to serve the event's guests and improve the quality of the experience in attending the event? In essence, managers should be aware of and ready to deal with the need to make changes on a continual basis.

✕ FOOD AND BEVERAGE MERCHANDISING

Food and beverage sales are enhanced through the implementation of shrewd and timely marketing and merchandising techniques. To effectively motivate purchases, great focus should be given to creating appeal by stimulating the guest's senses based upon recognition of their guest's wants and needs. From an attractive visual impact to enticing aromas wafting through the air, the concessionaire can expect the guest to make impulsive purchase decisions by creating an appealing environment. From the beginning, concessions operations should make sure food and beverage menus listing available items and their prices are prominently posted. Providing potential purchasers with a view of food in preparation, such as hamburgers and hot dogs on the grill, may stimulate their sense of smell and sight in a way that might persuade them to purchase the item. The same is true for displaying the various sizes of beverage, French fries, popcorn, and other products. Managers must be constantly aware of changing trends and prepared to make appropriate adjustments to their menus. (See Figure 7-3 for food service per capita spending).

To assist in the marketing of menu items, the manager should take great care to have adequate signage present throughout the facility, but especially in proximity to the concession stands, that depict the various menu items in a stimulating and graphic manner. In the same vein, many public assembly facilities contract with regional and national brand name companies to sell their products on an exclusive basis. When this occurs, the names of these products should be included in all product-related signage. Seeing the name of the known product may provide additional brand recognition thereby further inducing the guest to purchase that item.

Purchases from concession stands and kiosks, as well as visits to on-premise restaurants, are often spontaneous decisions. Public assembly facility food and beverage man-

FOODSERVICE PER CAPITA SPENDING

EVENT	LOW	HIGH
High School Sports	$0.25	$2.00
College Basketball	$1.25	$7.00
College Football	$1.50	$8.00
Minor League Baseball	$3.00	$10.00
NBA Basketball	$4.50	$15.00
NHL Hockey	$4.50	$15.00
MLB Baseball	$6.00	$15.00
NFL Football	$6.00	$20.00
Championship Games	$10.00	$40.00
Concerts	$1.25	$15.00
Family Shows	$1.50	$4.50
MLS Soccer	$3.00	$7.00

(Bigelow 2003)

FIGURE 7-3

agers seeking to create and maintain a successful operation must present and package their offerings in an enticing manner. They must create an appropriate menu and price it reasonably based on attendee expectations and industry standards for their geographic region. It is very important that all personnel are properly trained to be efficient, effective, and courteous at all times. The creative use of lighting technology contributes to the presentation of available food and beverage items. Enabling guests to continue to view the event via strategically located closed circuit television screens while making their food and beverage purchases will allay the fear of missing portions of the event.

✶ FOODSERVICE AS A MARKETING TOOL

Although food and beverage is considered an ancillary service, it has the potential to significantly enhance the public assembly facility's image. As an increasing number of public assembly facilities seek to generate additional revenues by renting space for private events, the availability and quality of the facility's food and beverage service operation become paramount. For instance, stadiums, arenas, and performing arts facilities with on-premise restaurants, or luxury suites and/or clubrooms may rent these areas on unscheduled event dates for private parties, weddings, and banquets. It is important to market the availability of facility space and ancillary services, including back-stage services, to potential clients in order to take full advantage of additional revenue-generating opportunities. Of course, this type of activity is common for convention and community centers.

Convention centers generally depend upon their in-house operation or concessionaire to provide for the food and beverage needs of groups meeting in its facility. Convention centers must strive to keep their costs in line with its competitors, such as hotels and other banquet facilities, in order to successfully compete for meeting and convention business and the attendant food and beverage service. In as much as convention centers host international, national, regional, and local meetings and conventions, the food and beverage service should be marketed in a manner that targets each of these diverse guest segments. In every instance, the same rules apply with respect to the high quality of the food and beverage service, its efficient and convenient delivery, and its appearance at presentation.

The ability of the convention center to attract international, national, and regional conventions and meetings is very important because their presence helps to fill hotel rooms and the attendees generate additional business for area restaurants and retail stores thereby contributing to the economic viability of the community. Hosting local meetings and conferences may not generate substantial "new" revenues but does allow the convention center to provide for community needs. At the same time, existing money in a community that is circulating has a positive impact on the economic vitality of that community.

TRENDS IN FOODSERVICE

To remain viable in a competitive environment, food and beverage service operations have experienced dramatic changes during recent years. In addition to the traditional concession stands, many public assembly facilities boast dining service with some featuring on-premise fine dining restaurants. Public assembly facilities that offer luxury suites are afforded an excellent opportunity to generate additional revenue by providing catering to the occupants during scheduled events and by providing for the catering needs when the suites are used for private parties, receptions, etc. Public assembly facility managers are also leasing facility space to local and/or national companies so they may sell their product at the facility's events. For example, one company might lease space to sell beverages while a second might sell specialty sandwiches and a third may provide the on-site catering.

Some trends in food and beverage service operations include:

- Food courts taken from the shopping mall concept where a variety of short order foods are available in a common seating area.
- Specialty carts strategically placed in high traffic areas selling such items as Espresso coffee, ice cream bars, gourmet hot dogs, etc.
- Internet ordering for suite holders.
- Decreased price sensitivity for quality product.
- Licensing agreements with brand name pizza chains, fast food restaurants, and local ethnic restaurants.
- Increased use of name brand products. Studies show sales increase 10-300 percent with brand name products because guests relate to quality and familiarity.
- Destination restaurants and lounges.
- Performing arts theatres' club seating.
- Use of charitable organizations to operate concessions booths, reducing labor costs and maintaining quality service.
- Credit, debit, ATM, and smart cards used for foodservice.

- In-seat ordering from a cellular phone.
- Exhibition cooking. Guests buy with their eyes and this proves freshness.
- Increased cooking capabilities for concessions. Charbroiling, grilling, and deep frying are replacing the boiled hot dog.
- Local, regional and ethnic foods - Italian, Mexican, barbecue, and Asian are all very popular.
- Celebrity chefs.
- Locally made/microbrewed beers.
- Brand extension (not just adding new items but improving and adding variety to core items).
(Bigelow, 2003)

Many food and beverage service options are available to the public assembly facility manager with respect to menu items, management alternatives, and branding opportunities. Prudent public assembly facility managers realize the impact the food and beverage service can have (both positive and negative) upon the satisfaction level experienced by their guests, their operating revenues, and the marketing potential for their facility. Wise managers will take appropriate action to maximize each of these opportunities. Appropriate use of logos and signage associated with the various products available for sale will not only assist in stimulating guest purchases, it also provides an opportunity to charge the product producers/distributors with a fee for their placement within the venue.

✗ HAWKING AND WAIT SERVICE

Depending on the type of event, many guests will make purchase decisions based upon the convenience of having merchandise, food, and drink brought to their seats. Hawking (i.e., selling concessions and novelties in the venue seating areas) is a typical way this is accomplished in many events that have applicable formats such as arena and stadium sporting events, and family shows. Some of the more creative ways to enhance hawking sales include utilizing local dignitaries or media personalities to participate, usually pushing a special cause or promoting endorsements. Suffice it to say, the entertainment value of an animated peanut salesman or program vendor in the stands can provide an exceptional experience to a baseball game audience while increasing the per caps (dollars per person) of sales.

In some facilities, especially those with box or club seats, wait service may be provided to enhance the guest experience. This service may include menu cards at each seat and an individual that periodically comes by, sometimes with an electronic recorder, to receive any orders. This exclusive service tends to be relegated to larger sporting complexes, but can be retrofitted into most any facility that desires to raise the level of guest satisfaction. In so doing, management is enhancing convenience and is providing the guest with value added service.

✗ BEER AND ALCOHOL SALES

As a significant revenue stream for public assembly facilities, beer and alcohol service has become a staple product that enhances the guest's experience while attending sport and entertainment events. Beer and alcohol service has become so established in the marketplace as an expected offering that its availability can be the deciding factor for the guest when making the decision to attend an event. If multiple venues are competing for patronage within the same market, the most often attended facility will most likely be the one serving alcohol.

Accompanying the consumption of beer and alcohol is the public assembly manager's responsibility for effective alcohol management. Training of servers and attendants is a necessary part of managing the alcohol service environment. Due to increasing fan violence and liability issues, concession and event managers are using techniques to qualify service standards prior to events. (See Figure 7-4 for guidelines from TEAM).

A risk analysis using any variety of criteria can assist management in evaluating the potential risks and need to employ alcohol management techniques, such as limiting size of containers, number of cups that can be sold per person, and early cutoff of sales. Age demographics, seating configurations, and guest service ratios may be applied to determine whether the event will have a restricted, limited, or full service environment. (See Appendix A, Figure 7-5 for sample documents on determining the sale of alcohol).

ALCOHOL SELLER/SERVER INFORMATION

ID GUIDELINES
Serving alcohol to underage people is illegal in every state. Use the three ID Guidelines to help avoid problems.

1. Ask for positive ID - don't guess.
2. Ask for more proof if you have any doubts.
3. Know where the alcohol is going.

CUT OFF GUIDELINES
Sometimes it becomes necessary to refuse a sale and inform a guest that he or she will not be given any more alcohol. Follow these guidelines to help diffuse the situation.

1. Say "No" and move on. Keep the line moving.
2. Give clear reasons and don't judge the guest. Never say "You're drunk."
3. Call for backup if the guest makes trouble.

SAFE-DRINKING GUIDELINES
Keep your guests safe and having a good time while they're drinking by following these guidelines.

1. Buy time. At an outlet, limit the number of drinks a guest can buy. In the stands, limit the number of times you walk by people who may be misusing alcohol.
2. Offer alternatives to alcohol. Suggest food and non-alcohol beverages to impaired guests.
3. Use the personal touch. Make eye contact and some friendly conversation with every customer as often as you can.

✗

This information was excerpted from the TEAMS Training Manual. TEAM (Techniques for Effective Alcohol Management) Coalition is a non profit organization promoting responsible drinking and positive fan behavior at sports and entertainment facilities.

FIGURE 7-4

Beer and alcohol companies enjoy the benefits of a captured audience and often are great advertisers and sponsors of sporting and public events. This provides a unique opportunity for the public assembly facility in several ways. Although all related elements are usually wrapped together, spin-off revenue benefits usually include pouring right deals, product prices, promotional products, prominent advertising exposure, and presenting sponsorships, to name a few.

✴MERCHANDISING

The selling of merchandise and novelty items is another ancillary service that has proven popular with guests. The terms merchandise and novelty items refers to tangible non-perishable souvenir products. These souvenirs are also referred to as "product."

Some of the earliest novelty items such as pennants, programs, and buttons were sold at carnivals, circuses, and sporting events. In later years, popular music concerts, aimed at increasing the sale of favorite artist records, introduced new types of novelty items, especially recordings of the artist. Elvis Presley was one of the original musical artists to produce a full-line of merchandise and novelty items for fan purchase.

The sale of event merchandise and novelty items has in the past been a major income source for public assembly facilities. While facility profits from merchandise has been shrinking over the last several years, it is still a viable source for ancillary income. These opportunities come from tenant sport teams and artists who perform concerts in the facility. Touring events such as professional wrestling, ice-skating shows, and even Broadway productions also represent excellent opportunities for the sale of merchandise and novelty items. "Branded" items, with the team or touring show's logo, are extremely popular items as are event-specific items memorializing the fact that the purchaser "was there."

Known by some in the merchandise sales business as the blowout — the moment when everyone in attendance leaves the premise — it is very often one of the best times to sell merchandise. Capturing the moment of elation from a grand finale or the exuberant high of a competitive victory can extend the sales market exponentially. Special attention and emphasis should be given to capture this unique opportunity

Public assembly facility managers have several merchandise operating formats from which to choose. Similar to the food and beverage service, public facility managers may elect to operate their merchandising in-house or to contract the operation to a private company. In most instances, the event itself travels with its own novelty and merchandise operation including product and staff. The decision is best determined after conducting an analysis of the local/regional business climate and taking into consideration factors such as the public assembly facility's type and mission; the size, training, skill level, and availability of its staff; and, its event schedule. What might be the correct decision for one public assembly facility might not be appropriate for another. Important decisions of this nature should be made only after all facets of the issue have been thoroughly considered. It must be understood at all times that the potential to generate large revenues also generally carries with it the necessity to accept significant risks. These determinations should be part and parcel of the booking, scheduling, and contracting process.

✕ TYPES OF MERCHANDISING CONTRACTS

Basically three kinds of merchandising contracts prevail among public assembly facilities: flat-rate fee, per-person fee, and percentage-of-sales fee. Bigelow offers the following descriptions of these arrangements:

The *flat-rate fee* is often used when volume is expected to be low or in smaller buildings. In this instance, the facility manager receives a one-time fee for granting the right to sell merchandise. This is not the best option in terms of maximizing revenue from merchandise.

The *per-person fee* is based upon assessing a certain amount for each guest in attendance. It is effective if researched carefully in terms of per-capita spending but will not be effective if these data are unavailable.

The *percentage-of-sales* is by far the most popular method. The merchandiser splits gross sales with the retailer/facility. Although more revenue can be earned by the facility under this arrangement, it requires more financial and personnel controls to be in place. (Bigelow, 2003).

Both the flat-rate fee and the per-person fee provide income to the facility with little or no involvement for equipment or labor. The facility also has no reporting requirements for payment of wages, product, etc. The percentage-of-sales approach is more labor intensive on the part of the facility management, especially in exercising inventory controls of the products being sold. The prime issue in collecting a percentage of sales is "what is the total sales figure?" Because merchandise sales are more often cash sales at multiple locations, the financial/audit controls are more likely to be a result of inventory controls at a central location.

While there is no absolute formula for any arrangement, it is common for the artist/attraction to receive approximately 70 percent of the profits and the public assembly facility to receive the remaining 30 percent. The facility must then deduct its cost of sales, labor and maintenance of the point-of-sale. These costs tend to range from 8 to 12 percent. Thus the public assembly facility's net commission will fall in the 18 to 22 percent range. However, this distribution percentage may vary depending on the state of the industry.

The final amount the facility receives from any of the contract arrangements can also be impacted if a middle-man/concessionaire has been given the rights to the merchandise operation. In that instance, the concessionaire would contract with the event promoter, provide the services involved, and pay the facility an amount of the concession contract. It is likely this would be less than had the facility directly handled the merchandise operation but the facility has transferred risk and responsibility to a third party. Bigelow notes a declining supply of available events has resulted in some public assembly facility managers lowering their percentage take of the merchandising profits in an effort to attract events to their facility. (Bigelow, 2003).

In all financial arrangements, the division of the revenue/cost of doing business is ultimately determined by the risks, responsibilities, and contributions (labor, product, equipment, selling rights, etc.) each party assumes or brings to the table. The more a party is involved and at risk, the greater its expectations when sharing revenue.

As with other facility functions, the public assembly facility manager should be knowledgeable of the current merchandising environment in order to maximize profit regardless of the fee structure elected. Although fans and guests may request a myriad of novelty and merchandise products, items offered for sale at a particular event should be selected based on the anticipated audience, their historical purchasing data, and the profit margin the item offers. An attractive and clearly visible display of available merchandise and novelty items combined with an efficient sales system and staff will produce the most successful financial results. Merchandise and novelty points-of-sale should be adequately staffed to assist the guest in making their purchases. Forms of payment including cash, credit, debit, and smart cards should be accepted. Sales personnel should be uniformly dressed, knowledgeable about each item offered, and trained to be courteous and professional at all times.

Merchandising can be an added income source if properly managed. As with other public assembly facility functions, the manager must be aware of the various management alternatives in addition to being conversant with the current status of the merchandising business. To protect the interests of the public assembly facility, the manager must take the required steps to ensure that all parties to the merchandising operation are held accountable for fulfilling their responsibilities and obligations.

Precautions must also be taken to prevent the sale of stolen products, non-licensed products, and any item that infringes on copyrighted logos or marks. Security personnel should be responsible for the protection of all money in addition to ensuring only authorized persons sell merchandise and novelty items on the facility's premises. Enforcement of security measures may include the seizure of "bootlegged" merchandise. It is very important the facility obtain legal advice in setting its rules and regulations and enact procedures consistent with laws pertaining to these issues. Local authorities should be requested to enforce laws and regulations governing unlicensed vendors selling food and beverages or merchandise and novelty items on public or private property in proximity to the public assembly facility.

GUEST PARKING AND VALET SERVICE

Parking is another ancillary service revenue stream that is often not maximized. Although most parking operations charge guests a flat fee to park while attending an event, people are willing to pay additional sums for added conveniences. Depending on the number and location of available parking spaces, the public assembly facility manager may construct a stratified fee schedule charging higher prices for parking located closer or more convenient to the public assembly facility. (Larson, 2003).

Selling parking passes to frequent users of the public assembly facility, making daytime parking available to the general public during non-event days, leasing parking spaces on a monthly or annual basis to individuals who work in proximity to the facility, and making valet parking service available during scheduled events are examples of how a parking operation might generate additional profits. The facility manager should carefully assess the parking inventory (parking locations and spaces available); staff available for assignment to the parking operation, and the facility's event schedule in order to determine what types of parking services might be appropriate and profitable. The service might vary from event to event.

Most guests pay for their parking in cash. Therefore, an accounting system with appropriate audit controls must be adopted to discourage employee theft. Employees allowing guests to park free or who pocket a portion of the collected fees represent two forms of theft that may occur if proper supervisory and accountability measures are not implemented and enforced. Some public assembly facility managers separate their cashiers from other parking employees in an effort to reduce the number of individuals handling the money. Other theft deterrent measures include the issuance of numbered tickets that must be displayed on the front windshield of each vehicle entering the parking area, physically counting the number of parked vehicles shortly after the event has commenced, and using advanced technology by installing electronic devices (often buried) that provide a count of the vehicles passing through the parking entrance. The same appropriate security procedures should be employed with respect to concession and novelty sales.

Whenever a public assembly facility provides parking for its guests, the facility must be prepared to assume the risk involved in this operation. It matters not whether a fee is charged or the parking is free; the facility must provide a safe environment for both the guests and their vehicles. To accomplish this, the parking areas should be well lit; surfaces free from debris, snow, ice, and other hazards; and, the surface must be kept in good repair. Parking personnel should be present in the parking areas before, during, and after the event in order to deter potential property thefts or physical assaults. Parking lots and garages must provide for the safety of pedestrians leaving and returning to their vehicles. Guests also expect assistance will be available in the event problems are encountered with starting a vehicle and when requesting directions about exit routes to particular areas. Parking personnel need to be trained and properly equipped to meet these expectations.

Parking for many public assembly facilities can be a very complex issue. For both new facility development and planning and existing facilities alike, parking has become a critical issue with respect to the location and design of parking lots/garages, allocation and location of sufficient identified "handicapped" parking spaces in order to comply with ADA's handicapped parking requirements, and providing for the safety of pedestrians within the parking lot or garage. In planning for parking, traffic surveys should be designed and conducted. Planners should work in close consort with the various community services departments, especially the police traffic control department.

Parking lots/garages should to be designed to allow for controlled and efficient entry and speedy exit of the vehicles. Sufficient personnel should be available to collect parking fees or check pre-paid tags. Entering vehicles should be directed to park in specific areas based on a parking plan. At the conclusion of an event, parking personnel should be available to direct vehicles out of the lot/garage. As many exits as possible should be opened to facilitate the surge of vehicles departing at the same time. Local police departments should be consulted and advised of anticipated event attendance. The police should be requested to provide appropriate personnel to direct traffic to and from the facility. Based on previous knowledge, all "choke points," "bottlenecks," or "gridlock" areas should receive special attention by traffic personnel. Depending on the size of the anticipated crowd, some streets might be restricted to one-way traffic both before and after the event, in order to better move the volume of vehicles.

Often sufficient parking is not available in close proximity to the public assembly facility. Available resolutions generally require the assistance of other agencies. One method is for the public facility manager and the director of public transportation to develop a plan that expands the number of buses or other modes of transportation that service the facility prior to and following a scheduled event. Another is to establish one or more remote parking areas within the community and to provide either municipal or private contracted bus service from those sites to the facility. The cost of this bus service might be borne by the user or billed to the event.

TAILGATING AND RV PARKING

Other periodic opportunities exist whenever attendees demonstrate an interest in congregating in advance at the site of an event. One tradition at many sporting events is the tailgating party. Facility management may provide logistical support for these events but must also exercise control. Parking lots, especially those with parking spaces designed to accommodate RV's and motor homes, can capitalize on this demand and the additional profit it will generate. In the same vein, other formats exist for large expanses of parking lots with concepts for use such as flea markets, outdoor trade shows, etc. Some public facilities have installed water/waste, electricity, and even data connections in some lots in order to attract touring RV caravans and/or their convention, fair or exhibition business.

SUMMARY

Ancillary services contribute to the achievement of guest satisfaction, and the revenues they generate are essential to the financial success of the public assembly facility. Of the many ways to generate ancillary revenue, the food and beverage operation is extremely important to all public assembly facilities. Some other ancillary services include parking, novelty sales, catering, automatic teller machines, computer cafes, providing box office services to other organizations, rental of in-house equipment, arranging for satellite teleconferences, etc.

A major decision faced by all public assembly facility managers is who should manage the food and beverage operation and the sale of novelty items. Should it be managed in-house or contracted out to a service provider? And, if contracted out, what type of contract — management fee-based, percentage gross sales or percentage of net sales — would be most beneficial to the facility? Regardless of how these services (and all other ancillary services) are provided, the facility manager must maintain control over product/service quality, menu selections and product/service pricing.

The quality of the food and beverage operation can affect the reputation of the public assembly facility both positively and negatively. It is the responsibility of the facility manager to monitor the quality level of both product and service rendered to the facility's guests. Efficient operation of the food and beverage service is directly related to the kitchen and food preparation facilities available. Also important are the location and quality of the point-of-sale facilities. Appropriate display of signage listing menu items and their prices is most important. And, operating in a highly competitive marketplace, the facility manager must keep abreast of industry trends related to products/services offered and the mode of delivery. Armed with this information, the manager needs to make those adjustments, if any, deemed appropriate.

The merchandising of event-related products can also be a revenue generator. Public assembly facility managers must make appropriate contractual agreements with the suppliers and/or vendors of these products. Event parking is another major revenue source. The parking location must be in close proximity to the facility, it must be clean and safe, and its employees must be user friendly. Due to the amount of money generated by parking, usually cash, appropriate measures must be employed to ensure payment from each entering vehicle is received and that all collected fees are accounted for and deposited with the business office.

The opportunities to generate ancillary revenue are restricted only by the vision and creativity of the facility management team. The wise and successful public assembly manager will solicit and investigate all suggestions for additional ancillary services and will make every effort to implement all that are appropriate.

REFERENCES AND ADDITIONAL READINGS

Bigelow, Chris. 2003. *Foodservice Management,* unpublished manuscript. Coppell, TX: International Association of Assembly Managers, Inc.

Cotino, Richard M.1996. *Handbook of Equipment Leasing,* 2nd ed. New York, NY: AMACOM.

Larson, Ann. 2003. *Revenue Sources,* unpublished manuscript. Coppell, TX: International Association of Assembly Managers, Inc.

Russo, Frank. 1985. "Event Management" in *Successful Sport Management.* Ed. Guy Lewis and Herb Appenzeller. Charlottesville, VA: Michie Co.

Shock, Patti J. and John M. Stefanelli. 2000. *On Premise Catering: Hotels, Convention Centers, and Clubs.* Hoboken, NJ: John Wiley & Sons, Inc.

EVENT MANAGEMENT

8

CHAPTER OUTLINE

⋊ INTRODUCTION

Before the entrance doors open, the lights dim, the puck is dropped, or the curtains rise, the *event management* process has been well under way. Event management is one of many important functions for which a public assembly facility manager must assume responsibility. This chapter focuses upon the public assembly facility management's relationship to each and every event or activity that takes place in the facility and details the preparation and planning required.

Although public assembly facilities may vary in terms of mission and configuration, they are each designed to produce events such as trade shows, conventions, meetings, conferences, concerts, athletic events, or performing arts productions. Producing events serves many purposes including the generation of revenue, fulfilling the community's programming needs, and enhancing the quality of life for those residing within the community and surrounding areas. To successfully produce these events requires extensive planning and attention to detail on the part of the public assembly facility's management staff.

The commitment of the public assembly facility's time and space for a specific purpose through contracts, agreements, or leases is ultimately the beginning of the event management process in a public assembly facility. The most critical aspects of the event management process are (1) the communication of pertinent details (dissemination of information) and (2) the resulting coordination of those activities. The role and responsibility of event management is that of integrating the necessary resources at the right time and location to effectively deliver the experience. In short, the event manager, regardless of venue type, is responsible for bringing about the tangible deliverables that are promised or committed. To accomplish this outcome, this chapter will focus on a number of specific steps and the associated tools needed for event management. Among the more salient points to be covered are the production rider and production requirements, event documentation, patron service staffing, safety, security and *crowd management, emergency preparedness,* and *crisis management.*

In the production of every event, public assembly facility managers or their staffs interact with all of the involved parties such as the performer, the agency, the promoter/presenter/producer/planner (hereinafter called *promoter*), and the audience. Ultimately, the public assembly facility manager is the central figure charged with balancing the relationships among these parties as they work collectively toward producing the event. In some instances, one or more of these parties may work independently with the facility manager and only when the event occurs do all of the stakeholders come together at one place and time.

⋊ EVENT MANAGEMENT EMPLOYEE DESCRIPTIONS

Typical titles for employees who are the promoter's contact point and deal with event-related issues include event services manager, event supervisor, and event coordinator. Although not always, these positions are typically a part of the facility services and

SELECTED EVENT MANAGEMENT POSITIONS

EVENT SERVICES MANAGER
The event services manager reports to and works under the direction of the operations manager. This person controls and monitors the customer contacts aspect of the public assembly facility operations by planning, monitoring, directing, delegating, controlling, and managing the event's coordination, wardrobing, security, crowd management, telephone, and outside contractor service function; performs related responsibilities as required.

SENIOR EVENT COORDINATOR
The senior event coordinator is responsible for planning, organizing, and controlling events within the facility as assigned and assists the event services manager in supervising the day-to-day activities of event services, to include but not limited to supervising event coordinators, preparing event outlines and scaled drawings of event areas, coordinating equipment distribution, event billing, monitoring event assigned, and such other functions and duties as required by the event services manager.

EVENT SUPERVISOR
Performs professional and supervisory work assisting in the utilization of entertainment, recreational, and convention facilities. Duties are varied and require some independent action as well as a thorough knowledge of facility's rules in assisting with the supervision of the day-to-day activities. Employee has regular contact with inside and outside sources related to the planning for and providing of services needed by facility's users.

EVENT COORDINATOR
The event coordinator is responsible for organizing and controlling events within the facility as assigned and monitors the logistical interfacing of these events, to include but not limited to the preparing of event outlines and scaled drawings of event areas and coordinating equipment distribution and event billing. The duties will include all event coordination tasks after events are booked through their conclusion. Ensures tenant requirements are met and facility rules, regulations and policies are adhered to by serving as a liaison between the facility and the tenants; assists tenants in the planning of their own events; and performs related responsibilities as required. Position reports directly to the senior event coordinator.

FIGURE 8-1

operations department, and the role of those holding these positions is to facilitate the event planning and implementation processes. Again, each of these positions may be filled by a single individual or through a collaborative effort depending on the public assembly facility, the specific event, and the volume of events booked.

Regardless of how the positions are filled, promoters expect the role of the event manager to be assumed by a knowledgeable person or persons employed by the public assembly facility. If the facility's size or event volume does not justify assigning a dedicated employee to coordinate the event-related information and to make appropriate decisions, then others must accomplish these tasks such as the booking manager, the operations manager or, at times, the facility manager. In every instance, someone must assume the responsibilities for coordinating activities and disseminating information to the promoter from the facility as well as coordinating and relaying information from the promoter back to the appropriate facility personnel.

Job descriptions for the management positions noted in Figure 8-1 are presented in the *IAAM's Position Description Handbook* (IAAM, 1994) that address these event management positions. The positions are not necessarily presented in hierarchical order. Any particular facility may have all or none of these positions.

Regardless of the type of public assembly facility or the nature of the event, there are similarities in the way facility managers initially approach the event. Once an event is booked, the management staff it is assigned to depends on the type and size of the public assembly facility, the number of staff available, and the nature of the event. In a university setting, for example, events scheduled for the sports arena may be assigned to one staff member while events to be held in the institution's performing arts center may be assigned to someone else. Some public assembly facilities may have staff dedicated to event coordination while others may require their employees to function in various roles, one being that of event coordinator.

Event-day surprise issues can be frustrating and perplexing. For example, imagine discovering the day of a concert or play that the show has a new set which is much larger than the one you built, thereby forcing you to remove seats that were already sold. Or planning for 1,000 people to attend a women's basketball game only to have 12,000 people seeking admission. A concerted effort to minimize problems is the clear theme and objective of effective event management. A sound planning process will eliminate chances of details falling through the cracks. Management staff, particularly seasoned personnel, can often anticipate event problems and forewarn the public assembly facility manager. Facility management is able to more easily communicate and discuss these concerns with the event promoter if they share a positive rather than a neutral or negative relationship. Structuring a forum for these kinds of discussions is a serious and sometimes difficult management task because it is time-consuming and takes the department managers away from their primary responsibilities. Some managers, even the talented and more experienced ones, struggle with being able to view event presentation from an overall, global perspective. It is the public assembly facility manager's responsibility to create a management team rather than just a group of independent department managers. Left to operate in relative vacuums, individual management departments, such as security, business office, facility operations, box office, marketing, and so forth, may adopt objectives that are beneficial to their particular unit but detrimental to the overall economic viability of the facility, or they may fail to disseminate information critical to the successful operation of the other units. Effective management requires a cooperative, positive effort and communication between all units of the organization.

ELIMINATING THE DISTRACTIONS

While the planning process may vary from facility to facility, the objective for every event should be to plan and prepare in a way that both the performer and the audience are focused upon each other and are not subjected to distractions when they come together. (See Figure 8-2 for an example of a hidden distraction). If this objective is achieved, the performance will be successful; thereby enhancing the public assembly facility manager's potential to gain future business from both the guests and the promoter. However, if planning is overlooked or goes awry and distractions occur, the manager's relationship with guests and promoter is diminished along with the potential for future business. Guest distractions contribute to a negative experience and may include poorly lit parking lots, rude event personnel, unclean restrooms, long concession lines, poor acoustics, and

---

EVENT DAY DISTRACTIONS

A well-known comedian talked about playing to two identical audiences in Las Vegas. He had contracted to present a Friday and Saturday evening performance in order to accommodate the delegates attending a very large convention. The first night was magic-every joke worked, his timing felt perfect, he had the audience in the palm of his hand. The next night-nothing! The audience was distant, uninvolved, lifeless, and miserable. The second show did not go as well. As he was leaving the backstage area, he noticed the stage manager's event document which indicated the temperature at show time on Friday was 78 degrees but on Saturday it was 67 degrees Fahrenheit. In visualizing the Saturday evening audience he recalled that at least half were women wearing sleeveless dresses. He concluded that women don't laugh when they are cold and neither do the men who brought them. From that point on, one of this entertainer's performance requirements was that the room temperature be at least 72 degrees.

FIGURE 8-2

uncomfortable temperatures. Likewise, distractions for promoters and artists may include not having the right equipment available when needed, unclean dressing rooms, poorly catered meals, and failure to accommodate special requests. Imagine a load-in for a large convention without the exhibit booths being properly located, *piped and draped*. What type of message does that convey to the convention coordinator? In an increasingly competitive marketplace, facility managers and their staff must consider every detail carefully. In other words, setting the stage for an event to be successful must not be left to chance but rather demands careful attention from conception to the event's completion. A sellout for one event may lead to future sellouts if the guests have had a good experience.

EVENT PLANNING AND PRODUCTION

Event planning and production begin once an event has been booked and contracted. Following booking, there are critical points where department managers, involved staff, and promoters need to discuss every aspect of the event in detail. In the course of these discussions, important issues and challenges specific to the event will be identified and addressed. Most problems are easier to deal with if identified early. As a rule, the later a problem is discovered, the harder it may become to resolve.

The public assembly facility management team has a number of event responsibilities that include:

- Providing both market and venue information/regulations/restrictions to the promoter in the event planning stage.
- Providing a qualified and motivated workforce as required — a "crew" for setting up, taking down, and operating equipment necessary for the presentation and a front-of-house staff to deal with the attending public.
- Providing, either partially or solely, safety and security for the event, the working staffs and crews, and the event attendees.
- Providing the promoter with a properly prepared facility and assisting him/her in developing an advertising and promotion campaign if necessary.

- Coordinating ancillary services for patrons (food and beverage, parking, etc.).
- Planning and preparing for building emergencies.

Before booking an event, the promoter should be provided with what many public assembly facility managers refer to as a *promoter packet*. This packet is designed for the promoter new to the facility and contains basic information such as:

- Line drawings of spaces available for rent.
- Seating diagrams.
- Layout of meeting rooms and breakout spaces.
- List of house-owned equipment and corresponding rental rates.
- List of available labor and corresponding rates.
- List of hotel locations.
- Maps.
- Names and addresses of service vendors.
- House/facility rules and regulations.

An important part of the packet is a description of the facility's operating philosophy along with specific information about available catering, parking arrangements, novelty and retail sales, tax collection, business license requirement, fire and safety codes, and any other restrictions or requirements particular to the facility. A well thought-out and designed information packet should answer many of the general questions promoters have when deciding whether or not to book the public assembly facility for their event.

In the past, some promoter packets were produced as fairly expensive brochures and pamphlets. Today, the marketing method of choice for many public assembly facilities in this phase of the information dissemination process is to include the necessary information on their Internet website. For the most part, web pages are less expensive to produce and update than printed pieces, generally easy to navigate, and are universally accessible. The Internet has transformed the way public assembly facilities do business. In this instance, for those promoters unfamiliar with a specific public assembly facility, viewing a facility's Internet website quite often takes the place of an onsite visit. The level of information provided through the website is only limited by the creativity of the facility's marketing department. Numerous websites not only provide the promoter with facility information, they also present links to other websites such as the visitors and convention bureau, local hotels, and event calendars. An important element of facility web sites is the ability for promoters and meeting planners to actually download venue floor plans in a variety of formats, including .pdf — Adobe Acrobat (probably the most common format); .dwg — AutoCAD (used by many entertainment show designers and professional decorating companies for exhibits, etc.); and .flp — Optimum Settings (a software program used by many meeting planners for room setups).

Event management and its planning is the act of organizing and coordinating multiple details, some concurrently and others in sequence, to produce a tangible experience for an audience. The more organized and detailed the planning process, the more likely the event's success with minimal problems for the event manager the day of the event.

Generally, the events that require the greatest coordination are touring shows, theatrical performances, conventions, and commercial music concerts. On the other hand, banquets, assemblies, and small group meetings may require less staffing, but may also require extensive coordination due the client's expectations.

From several perspectives, touring theater and concert productions are similar. Both tend to travel between performances, from site to site, using buses for the talent and supporting cast and trucks to haul their equipment and props. They will perform in a number of different public assembly facilities during the course of their tour, some for one-night stands, some others for multiple performances. Because of performance frequency while "on the road" and the expense of transportation, standard criteria for essential support services and products that are more common and generic, are specified and requested at each public assembly facility in which they will appear. Establishing these specifications helps the act maintain consistency in the quality of their performance.

These standards also provide for efficiency in the load-in and load-out process even though the process takes place in different locales, on different stages, and in different public assembly facilities. Some of the tasks included in the process are transporting show equipment; off-loading and assembling props and/or sets; preparing costumes; accommodating requests from performers, promoters, and crew members; installing sound and lighting units and reinforcement equipment; and positioning front-of-house staff. At the end of the performance, the process is reversed as the show's equipment, props, staging, and costumes are broken down, moved to the loading docks, and stowed on the trucks.

Staging a convention, *exhibition*, or large meeting demands much the same effort and coordination as that required for touring theater and concerts productions. Convention centers must have established policies and procedures relating to convention, exhibition, and meeting setups, advance delivery of equipment and materials from the organizers and exhibitors, provision of electrical service and audiovisual equipment, exhibit booth sizes, pipe and draping and furnishings, food and beverage service, meeting room capacities and configurations, exhibit breakdowns, and the movement of materials and equipment for shipping or pick up at the loading dock.

✳THE PRODUCTION RIDER

To make this detailed process work, a document is developed by the act/event explaining in detail each of the elements required by the production in order to produce a quality performance. This document is called the production rider (also referred to as the performance rider or contract rider) and is part of the performance *contract* signed between the promoter and the performer/agency. Once signed, the promoter is agreeing to provide everything stipulated within the production rider. While all events have, in fact, production riders, the theatrical, touring shows, concert production, and convention/exhibit riders are typically more complex. Riders may include the following:

- Labor requirements.
- Administration/production offices.
- Dressing room requirements.
- Staging requirements (stage, sound, lights, *rigging*, and special effects).
- Staff call times for both load in and load out.
- Parking access for equipment and trucks, artists, and other show personnel.
- Hotel accommodations, if required.
- Catering for crews and entertainers.
- Backstage security requirements.

Once the act/performer is contracted, the promoter becomes responsible for making sure the production rider requirements are met. If the promoter fails to provide what the production rider stipulates, the act/performer has the prerogative to cancel the performance and expect compensation from the promoter for breach of contract. Consequently, the promoter should always have knowledge of the production rider requirements prior to booking an event. By providing the public assembly facility with a copy of the rider and its requirements, the promoter further assures his/her ability to comply with the contract expectations.

The promoter relies on the public assembly facility manager to fulfill many of the conditions of the production rider. Therefore, it is critical that the promoter meets with facility management to ensure that the facility can actually fulfill each of the facility-related requirements stipulated in the production rider either independently or with assistance from external entities. Typically, this initial meeting could include the promoter, the facility manager, event manager, facility's operations manager, and departmental representatives from security, marketing/promotions, and the business office. A careful review of the production rider by the working staff should uncover any problems that must be solved or negotiated before the promoter signs the contract. It must be clearly understood that unless the contract between the promoter and the facility includes agreements as to what requirements of the artist's rider the facility agrees to fulfill, there is no legal obligation to do so. Anything in the artist's rider that the public assembly facility does not agree to fulfill still remains the responsibility of the promoter and the artist. Many, if not all, of the rider's requirements will have associated costs. The public assembly facility manager should be certain these costs are identified and agreed upon as to who should pay for each item. A key issue is who can agree to expenses. An Attachment to Contract is used to designate who is authorized by the promoter to make commitments, including charges by the facility. Having this in place as a part of the contract/lease allows for a clearer and more efficient operational relationship during the entire course of the event.

Occasionally, the promoter may want to complete the facility lease agreement and establish an on-sale date before the public assembly facility manager and/or operations manager has reviewed the production rider. To avoid such requests, the facility's operating policies, which should have been brought to the attention of the promoter in the event booking stage, should clearly state that tickets will not go on sale before a lease agreement is signed and the production rider reviewed and its conditions accepted. The promoter may challenge this posture since she/he ultimately shoulders the responsibility for ensuring that the production rider requirements are met. The fallacy of this argument is that there can be instances in which a rider requirement cannot be accomplished. For example, an agreement between the artist and promoter to use pyrotechnics during an indoor performance is explicitly prohibited and illegal in some jurisdictions. Nonetheless, any request to prematurely complete the lease agreement should be denied or at least tentatively agreed to "subject to...," because, whenever the requirements of the production rider are not fulfilled, it is the facility and its employees who are subjected to the reaction of the upset performers and production crews.

As stated earlier, while the production rider is generally specific to touring shows, theater, and concert productions, all events have some form of production criteria that the event depends upon, formal or informal, which serves the same or similar purpose. Convention centers generally use a *banquet event order* (BEO) to confirm catering reservations and room setup sheets to stipulate necessary seating arrangement, audiovisual equipment, floor plans, show booth locations and so forth. Every event should have a similar type of document stating exactly what the public assembly facility management and those producing the event have agreed upon with respect to room arrangements and necessary production equipment and who is responsible for providing what.

Particular attention must be paid to timing requirements for live televised events Whether a convention, trade show, athletic contest, a banquet, political speech, theatrical performance, Fourth of July celebration or an awards program, live televised events have their own particular timing demands. These events must start on time and often must be programmed to conclude at a specified time. If commercials are involved, they must be accommodated and accounted for within the time frame. Special effects must be ready for implementation upon demand signal. All associated with the event production must be organized in a manner that will insure that the timing requirements are met in order to facilitate a smooth presentation.

EQUIPMENT AND STAFFING NEEDS

While the following discussion focuses more on issues included in riders for touring shows, many of the requirements are applicable to all events, although they may be implemented differently. In effect, the rider spells out what is needed to produce the event such as labor, equipment, special effects, the artists' needs, and other unique requests. For example a BEO might include table decorations, servers' dress, service time, sound/lights for a program, plus other items. Just as it is not feasible for a traveling attraction to carry all the necessary production labor personnel with it (such as *stagehands, riggers*, loaders, drivers, *runners, followspot* operators, and so forth), it is also not feasible for it to carry all the equipment needed to produce the event. The production rider should outline in detail the specific type/kind of equipment and personnel that will have to be provided from local sources. Usually it becomes the responsibility of the facility's staff to procure that equipment and have it and the necessary operators available as needed.

Many full service public assembly facilities have their own fork lifts, spotlights, tables and chairs, crowd control barriers and/or bike rack barricades, performance stages, electrical hook-ups, water/gas/compressed air lines, telephones and jack lines, dressing room furniture, and A-frame ladders. Typically, equipment owned by the public assembly facility is available to the promoter on a separate rental basis, but may be included in the contract agreement. Rental and services expenses are documented on a separate equipment rental invoice and the total included on the *settlement sheet* for collection. Event promoters are provided with a rental rate card depicting cost of equipment and services as a part of the contract agreement process. Special equipment can usually be rented if the request is made within appropriate timelines. Unusual equipment requests will generally surface early in the discussions between the public assembly facility's operations manager and the event promoter.

While the production rider clearly determines the number of stagehands, riggers, loaders, equipment operators, etc., required by the event, there is no such document that definitively outlines the staffing needs for the front-of-house. The front-of-house staff is primarily composed of part-time employees who are recruited, trained, employed, and supervised by the public assembly facility's management. It is not unusual for some facilities including performing arts, small auditoriums/civic centers, university facilities, etc., to use volunteers. The actual number of front-of-house staff required for a particular event is determined by the public assembly facility management based on judgment as to the staffing level necessary to ensure the comfort and safety of the guests attending the event. Staffing levels are influenced by the type and size of the event and its past history, the facility's physical configuration, and also by the staffing history of the public assembly facility. The front-of-house staff includes ushers, ticket takers, medical or first aid staff, security personnel, ticket sellers, and custodians. In short, front-of-house staff personnel (event staff) are present only when there is an event.

EVENT PLANNING NEEDS OF LOCAL PRODUCTIONS

Smaller events, meetings, and theatre concerts, particularly those produced by local amateurs/non-professionals, often require special attention during the event planning stage. Providing the local promoter with an opportunity to meet with the public assembly facility's staff is the best way to avoid surprises on the day of the event. Simply providing the local promoter with the "promoter information packet" may not be sufficient if the local promoter is not a professional and lacks the background and experience necessary to understand all the aspects related to producing an event. It's not unusual for an amateur promoter to have contracted with an act and signed off on the production rider before signing a lease agreement with the public assembly facility.

Producing a concert, exhibition, trade show, athletic competition, and so on can be complicated and risky to the public assembly facility's image and financial standing. Most public assembly facility managers will concur that the more difficult events to manage are those produced by local good-hearted, non-professionals who simply do not understand the risks involved or the details, intricacies, and necessary planning associated with a well-orchestrated event. Therefore, the public assembly facility manager must create policies, procedures, and processes that guide and encourage promoters, whether professional or non-professional, to collaborate with the public assembly facility's department managers in achieving positive event outcomes.

DIAGRAM LAYOUTS AND FLOOR PLANS

Once the promoter, event manager, and the operations manager have made their initial decisions concerning space accommodations for the various aspects of the event, such as room sets, equipment needs, and parking, it becomes the responsibility of the facility to create a detailed diagram of the spaces committed, a listing of the equipment provided and the projected labor necessary to produce the event. (Figures 8-3 and 8-4 are sample diagrams). Computer software is available that enables the operations manager to produce scaled drawings of the space(s) the client has requested. When designing the floor plan, some additional factors that must be addressed include: room capacity (official capacity versus the number of people that can fit in a theater style configuration versus a classroom configuration or the number of tables that can be set for a buffet style banquet versus a banquet with wait service), fire code restrictions, and functionality (positioning the stage or head table at the opposite side of the entrance doors so latecomers will not interrupt the program).

Providing the operations staff with detailed space drawings and a list of required equipment and services provides a very useful tool when setting up for the event. The more scheduled event activity there is within the public assembly facility, the greater the need for detailed space drawings and lists. For example, if a public assembly facility has multiple events scheduled for the same time or day, particular care must be taken to verify that room times committed to each event do not overlap, that sufficient time is provided in order to changeover the room, and that there is sufficient equipment available to cover everyone's requests (such as not mistakenly committing four lapel microphones when the facility only has three).

Potential problems may be discovered in the event planning process during the design phase conducted by the operations department. Before proceeding with further planning, the client should be required to approve and sign off on the diagrams and accompanying details prescribed. Although this will not ensure against last-minute changes by the promoter, it will give the operations department a level of protection and the right to charge the client for any additional services requested and provided. If additional equipment/services are requested/added to the event, the clients should be required to authorize a written *change order* and a revised *cost estimate* should be issued to eliminate any financial surprises.

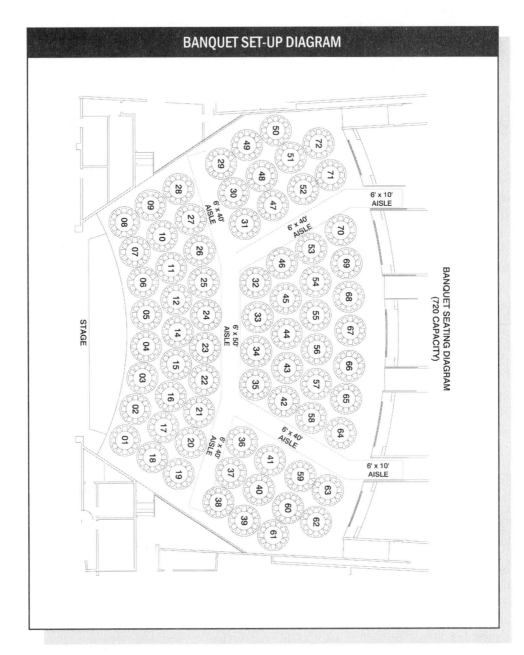

FIGURE 8-3

EXHIBIT SET-UP DIAGRAM

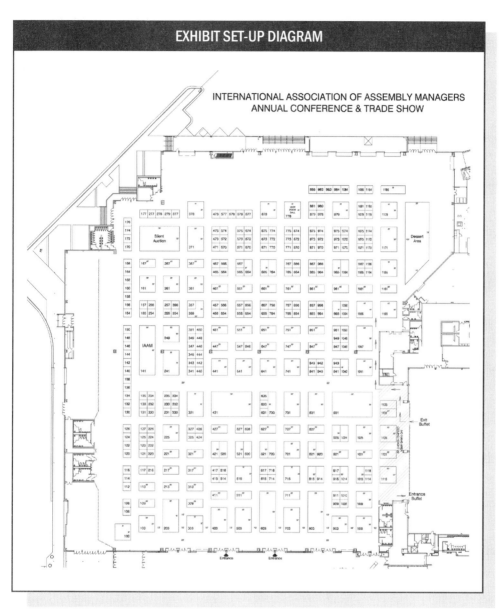

FIGURE 8-4

EVENT TIMELINE

EVENT TIMELINE

<u>May 28, 2003</u>
Doors @ **5:30**pm
Show @ **6:30**pm
End @ **10:30**

Single Scale Seating

Sections: **Floor &**
Bowl Seating

<u>$25.00</u>

Who	What	When	How
F	Conversion **IN**	5/23/03 **completed**	Event floor, All dashers set and removed, plugs in place
F	Locker,Catering,&Production rooms	5/23/03 **completed**	Remove materials, clean, vacuum, sanitize, set open,
SH	Stage set	5/27/03 **3:00am**	Sand Hollow will set a 40x60 stage. Positioning will be determined by BM.
P	Production Set	5/28/03 **8:00AM – 12:00PM**	Trim all from previous show - Dasher & coverage drape, prep lighting set, FOH prep, spots, headsets, com link, power, patches, Greenroom, Please cover all cables after placement. Prep 2 30' trusses for wings.
P	Dressing Room Set	5/28/03 **8am-11am**	Refresh all drapery, furniture, tables, chairs, analyze for secure and tight set
F	Load in prep	5/28/03 **8:30am**	Set out all forks, open roll up door, clear tunnel of refuse, set ramp for dasher dam lip, prep flagger & sign 7 cone set
F	Cones set	5/28/03 **8:45am**	Place cones on lane, set all signage, Flagger reports at this time for load in.
P, SH, E	Load In	5/28/03 **9-11am**	Sand Hollow will load in show, Electrician arrives @ 9:00, flagger on street and down below in garage.
F	Facility restore	5/28/03 **11-2pm**	Replace plug, set stairs, tighten all rails, set ready for show
P, SH, E	Lunch advantage	5/28/03 **12pm-2pm**	Try to grab a bite and take advantage of show production slow
P, F	Pre show checks	5/28/03 **3pm-4pm**	Check all technical aspects, trim drapery, stairwell check, bathrooms ready, stanchions set, door check, merch set. Set Floor entry signage outside
ALL F, P, ES, BO, M, EM GM	Arena Check	5/28/03 **4pm-4:30pm**	Check arena for show readiness, adjustments if necessary, setup front street entrance signs and prepare entry. All fluorescents in c-level tunnels out, breezeway & backstage tunnels lights out, all drapery adjusted and ready, all doors & seats secure & safe, concourse clear, backstage lights out up to red door,
ES, EM, GM	Event Briefing	5/28/03 **4:45pm**	Cover security requirements, last call, obstructed view seats, relocation areas & procedure, CMS, ES coord, GM, & EM *(staff posted on grove to usher people in line with floor tickets to go to front street entrance.)*
ALL	Doors	5/28/03 **5:30pm**	All staff in positions, doors to be called by MOD, house lights ready & on headset, custodial ready, Front street ready, merch ready.
ALL	Show	5/28/03 **6:30-10:30**	Show Duration
F	Cones set	5/28/03 **10:00pm**	Place cones on lane, set all signage, Flagger reports at this time for load out. if necessary assist truckers into position. A few cleanup crew members report at this time, along with a few conversion crew
ALL	Crowd Load out	5/28/03 **10:30 - 10:45**	Begin ushering crowd off the floor area
ALL	Load out	5/28/03 **10:45 – 1:00**	Load out begins, remove load in plug & dashers, remove entire house setup with the exception of needed setup for MMA
F	Post Event Cleanup	5/28/03 **11:00pm**	Remainder post event cleanup & conversion crew reports to restore facility
SH, F	Stage Out	5/29/03 **2:00am – 3:30am**	Stage to be removed

Notes: _____

_____
_____
_____
_____

FIGURE 8-5

ESTABLISHING EVENT TIMELINES

Another tool for event planning is the *event timeline*. (See Figure 8-5 for an example of an event timeline). A meeting to develop the event timeline will assist the event manager with scheduling issues and identifying potential problems. During this meeting, the *running schedule* will be outlined with an in-depth discussion of "what happens when." Depending on the specific issues and the size of the event, individuals representing the following areas could be involved:

- Food and beverage/novelties.
- Parking and traffic.
- Stagehands.
- Engineers.
- Box office.
- Management.
- Event personnel.
- Housekeeping.
- Promoter/producer.
- Local agencies such as police, fire, public transportation, etc.

(Note: Quite often for small and routine events, only the promoter and a liaison from the public assembly facility meet. The liaison then disseminates the information to others as needed.)

As the public assembly facility staff reviews the event's schedule on an hour-by-hour basis, issues and concerns may arise that will require clarification and discussion. Issues such as event staff parking, load-in and load-out schedules, meal and rest breaks, dress and decorum, and the event's start, intermission, and ending times all have different implications for the various groups that make up the work staff. Bringing the staff together and creating a timeline that accommodates the needs of each area will enable the staff to assess the event comprehensively and efficiently. In essence, the front-of-house must relate to the needs of the *back-of-house* and vice versa. Although simple in concept, the feedback gained from a meeting of this nature generally proves very useful in reducing distractions or surprises on the day of the event.

THE EVENT FILE (PRODUCTION MINUTES)

The event file is a valuable tool created by the event manager to document planning activity and track progress. The event manager might maintain a written diary or a running commentary to document events. This diary chronologically documents the event, starting with the booking memo and concluding with event debriefing meeting notes. The diary is a log of the interactions among the event manager, promoter, and the attraction. Upon conclusion of the event, the diary, along with the contract, production rider, settlement sheet (which includes labor, equipment, and other charges), *box office statement, certificates of insurance,* event drop counts, ticket stubs, *deadwood,* etc, becomes a part of the event file. These documents provide management with an understanding of the entire event process and factual information needed to respond to any questions. Having access to a detailed description of the last time the event played at the public assembly facility can provide valuable information to the facility's current staff as well as to the act or attraction itself.

PATRON SERVICES STAFFING

Event Personnel	Quantity	Hours	Rate	Payroll Tax		Total
Ushers and Ticket Takers	17	5.75	$6.50	$ 209.67	$	845.05
Early Arrival Usher for walk up	2	9.00	$6.50	$ 38.61	$	155.61
Usher Captains	3	5.75	$8.00	$ 45.54	$	183.54
Event Staff Supervisor	2	12.00	$11.00	$ 87.12	$	351.12
T-Shirt Security All Day	2	17.50	$11.50	-	$	402.50
T-Shirt Security	23	7.00	$11.50	-	$	1,851.50
T-Shirt Security Coordinator Fee	1	FLAT	$25.00		$	25.00
CMS - Security	3	5.75	$17.00	$ 96.77	$	390.02
CMS - Coordinator Fee	1	FLAT	$25.00	-	$	25.00
CMS - Supervisor	1	7.00	$20.00	$ 46.20	$	186.20
Uniformed officers	2	6.00	$37.50	-	$	450.00
Box Office On Sale Labor	1	2.00	$8.00	$ 5.28	$	21.28
Box Office Lead	1	3.75	$8.00	$ 9.90	$	39.90
Box Office Labor	1	2.75	$6.75	$ 6.13	$	24.69
Box Office Labor	1	4.75	$6.75	$ 10.58	$	42.64
Merchandise Labor	1	4.75	-	-	$	403.08
Custodial	1	5.00	$8.93	$ 14.73	$	59.38
Custodial	1	5.00	$8.50	$ 14.03	$	56.53
				TOTAL:	$	5,513.04

Setup and Post Event Personnel	Total	
Conversion	$	1,000.00
Post Event Cleanup	$	760.10
TOTAL:	$	1,760.10

Misc Expenses	Total	
Credit Card fee (2.60%)	Please Insert	
Floor Tape	$	25.00
Furniture Rental Insurance	$	12.50
Catering	$	4,967.85
TOTAL:	$	5,005.35

Production Personnel and Equip.	Total	
Stage Rental	$	1,500.00
Run of Show	$	95.76
Load In	$	233.08
Load Out	$	35.91
Sand Hollow - Production In	$	3,076.00
Sand Hollow - Show Call	$	700.00
Sand Hollow Production Out	$	1,780.00
Sand Hollow - 15% Admin Fee	$	833.40
ICM Fork Rental	$	55.73
TOTAL:	$	6,809.88

Payouts	Total	
Bravo Entertainment (cash)	$	-
TOTAL:	$	-

Show Revenue	Total	
SAS Gross ticket Sales	$	69,625.00
Suite Sales	$	-
TW Gross ticket sales	$	19,800.00
Concessions	$	4,349.14
Merchandise	$	3,721.11
TOTAL:	$	97,495.25

TOTAL SHOW EXPENSES: $ 19,088.38

TOTAL SHOW REVENUE: $ 97,495.25

Confidential

6/2/2003 10:50 AM

FIGURE 8-6

Another valuable management technique is for facility managers to have on their desks when arriving the following day at least these four reports: first aid log, general incidents (public contact) report, box office statement and settlement, and an event summary that includes traffic and parking.

BACK-OF-HOUSE SECURITY

Everything behind the stage such as dressing rooms, buses, trailer trucks, common catering areas, meet and greet areas, etc., are referred to as back-of-house. Security personnel, either in-house or subcontracted, normally provide protection for these areas. Decisions related to their number, positioning, and hours on location are usually outlined in the production rider. Even though the production rider spells out back-of-house requirements or if there is not a formal rider, public assembly facility managers must remember that ultimately they are responsible for the safety and security of the act, the audience, and the working staffs and therefore it must be made clear to all parties that the final decision-making authority resides with the facility's management.

FRONT-OF-HOUSE STAFFING

As stated, the front-of-house staff is a mixture of staffing positions ranging from ushers to armed, uniformed security/police when appropriate. The public assembly facility's event manager usually determines the components of the event staffing mix based on variables such as projected attendance, type of event, time of year, time of day, weather, community expectations, the event's history, community influences, facility restrictions, legal regulations, etc. Because the public assembly facility management has the responsibility for decisions that directly affect the promoter, such as front-of-house staffing decisions, it is wise to provide the promoter with an estimate of these associated costs, as well as other costs, prior to the start of the event. (Figure 8-6 is an example of the staffing schedule for an event).

Prior to event day(s), if promoters believe the event to be "overstaffed," there are ample opportunities for them and the event coordinator to look at an alternative staffing scheme. Staffing and cost estimates not only give the promoter an early awareness of one of the larger event expenses, they also provide the event coordinator some insight into the security manager's approach to ensuring the safety of the event. This process provides vital information to the decision makers at a time and manner that allows them to review, react, and adjust the staffing plan, if deemed necessary. Again, the reason for engaging in this process is to prevent event day surprises from occurring.

MANAGING RISKS IN THE EVENT ENVIRONMENT

Protecting the assets of the facility and reducing its liability are key roles of facility management and are often considered back-of-house functions; responsibilities are, more often than not, delegated to the facility services/operations department. Although risk management is a facility-wide discipline and may be implemented by management, many of the functions may be performed by operations due in part to oversight of the *physical plant.* In case of fire or other reasons for evacuation, procedures, processes, and communications are preplanned, established through training, and implemented, both internally and externally, with the appropriate local agencies.

In cooperation with the facility manager and facility services and operations department, the event manager plays a key role ensuring that the event is operated in a safe and secure manner. Responsibilities in risk management areas include:

- Event certificate of insurance.
- Proper contract management.
- *Risk assessment.*
- Security and crowd management planning, including planning to "harden" the facility against threats and provide effective screening and admission protocols.
- Emergency and crisis management planning.
- Alcohol management.
- Fire code and life safety planning.
- Staff training for risk management responsibilities.

While events designed to attract large numbers of guests to the facility are desirable from a business perspective, they also bring with them an increased degree of responsibility. During all such events, event managers literally hold the safety and well-being of the guests in their hands. Whether the audience is a small meeting group or 100,000 sport fans, the responsibilities and need for preparation remain the same. The satisfaction, well-being, and safety of guests, employees, performers, contractors, and all others depend upon the care taken by the public assembly facility manager and the management staff. The facility manager must convey this sense of responsibility to each and every employee. From the parking lot to the performance itself, the well being of everyone must be safeguarded.

Readiness for dealing with disastrous circumstances during a public event is critical to effective event management. The list of possible problem areas includes:

- Medical emergencies.
- Fire/fire alarm.
- Bomb threat/explosion.
- Mechanical/equipment/structure failure.
- Power failure.
- Natural disasters/severe weather.
- Civil disturbance/riots/other criminal acts.
- Hazardous material release.
- Terrorism.
- Building evacuation.
- Air conditioning contamination.
- Food poisoning.
- Suspicious mail/packages.

✳ SECURITY PLANNING

Through the 90s, facility and event "security staff" were focused on routine crowd management and policy enforcement roles; increasingly, security staff also was trained to provide quality customer service.

In the aftermath of the September 11, 2001 terrorist attacks, security planning has taken on new emphasis. For high profile events, large budgets are devoted to upgrading facilities' capabilities to deter and defend against terrorists attacks. Safety and security measures, though present in most venues, are now more overt in nature and extensive in options, but must repeatedly be reviewed and evaluated for circumstantial/situational conditions. Typical enhancements to security include perimeter protection measures such as installation of bollards and closing of streets; heightened admissions procedures, including the use of metal detectors; more rigorous employee screening and background checks; improved credentialing of employees, contractors and facility visitors; more extensive use of closed circuit television (CCTV) monitoring; and modification of HVAC air intakes to eliminate the possibility of introduction of biological or chemical agents by terrorists.

Most facilities and major events also use sophisticated programs to assess security risks and threats. A typical assessment model includes these elements:

- Asset assessment – Assets include the facility and its occupants. What are the core functions and processes of the facility? What are the critical building elements, including structural and informational? For each asset, what is its value, i.e., to what extent would its loss cause a debilitating impact on the facility?
- Threat assessment – Threats might be from terrorists/criminals, but also from natural disasters, civil disturbances, mechanical or power failures, etc.
- Vulnerability assessment – Given various threats and threat scenarios, facility vulnerability assessment might consider factors such as the facility's level of visibility, the facility's value to the community, the facility's value within the objectives of terrorists, potential for collateral damage, and the facility's "hardness" or "softness" in providing access by aggressors.
- Identification of countermeasures – Given various threat scenarios, how can the facility prepare preventive and response plans?

Using some type of quantitative rating system is helpful in establishing priorities. For instance, a staff brainstorming session on threats at a facility could yield hundreds of possibilities. By rating the likelihood of a particular threat, facility management can establish priorities and attempt to develop complete plans for only those threats of highest risk. (Figure 8-7 is an excerpt from one of the IAAM planning guides that show use of a decision tree.)

IAAM's "Best Practices Planning Guides for Safety, Security and Emergency Preparedness" assist the event manager in assessing risk factors and determining threat levels. Utilizing the decision tree checklist, event organizers are encouraged and directed to

DECISION TREE

Sample Decision Tree Questions:

■ Has the Office of Homeland Security issued a "Severe Condition" (Red) Warning?

   No   Yes —— Management should consider canceling the event.

   |

■ Has the event been classified as a Secret Service "Special Event" under the Office of Homeland Security?

   No   Yes —— Management should implement Level #4 measures.

   |

■ Is the event being broadcast nationally or internationally?

   No   Yes —— Have specific and credible threats been received by the event organizers or police?

        Yes —— Management should implement Level #3 measures.

   |

FIGURE 8-7

evaluate various environments that may exist and provides the accompanying response recommendations. (Figure 8-8 provides a list of resources available for safety and security planning.)

RESOURCE CENTER

IAAM has developed extensive planning guides and training materials for facility managers to use in designing and training for security, emergency planning, life safety and crowd management. Most of the informational material, including reference links and downloadable material can be found at IAAM's Center for Venue Management Studies at IAAM's web site at: http://www.iaam.org/CVMS/CVMSsafety.htm

Below are some resources that are available:

■ Safety and Security Best Practices Planning Guide for Theatres and Performing Arts Centers (member only download).
■ Safety and Security Best Practices Planning Guide for Arenas, Stadiums and Amphitheatres (member only download)
■ Safety and Security Best Practices Planning Guide for Convention Centers/Exhibit Halls (member only download)
■ Safety and Security Best Practices Planning Guide for Emergency Preparedness (member only download)

Emergency Planning Resources and Links

■ Homeland Security Advisory Vehicle Borne Improvised Explosive Devices
■ SSTF State Handgun Laws
■ SSTF Weapon Position Statement
■ Facility Pre-Employment Information and Verification: The First Level Of Security Defense
■ FBI Alert to Stadiums
■ Safeguarding Building Ventilation Systems

Also, see safety and security publications available for sale at: http://www.iaam.org/Products/catalogue.htm

FIGURE 8-8

EVENT SPACE AND STAFF CAN SHAPE CROWD BEHAVIOR

Design and use of space can exert subtle influences on a public assembly facility's guests. In fact, some of these influences are so subtle guests remain totally unaware of their behavior being modified by the facility's design. On the other hand, guests are very much aware of the feelings they experience as they interact with the facility's event staff. Much of the public assembly facility's public image, as previously stated, results from the guest's interactions with the front-of-house staff, including ushers, ticket takers, greeters, security guards, ticket sellers, and parking attendants. Guests also interact with food/beverage and merchandise workers. Therefore, each of these individuals becomes, by default, the caretaker of a facility's valuable asset, its public image. With this dynamic understood, the public assembly facility manager must recruit, hire, train, and monitor personnel accordingly.

In a sense, the question becomes what is customer service and where does crowd management begin? The two are inseparable. When staff controls ingress by taking tickets, monitoring *turnstiles* and doors, checking for prohibited items, enforcing building/event policies, and implementing the evacuation plan, if necessary, it is managing the crowd by providing customer services: guests are admitted efficiently and effectively, provided with directions to their seat or other locations and are able to enjoy their time at the facility in a safe environment.

✗ CROWD MANAGEMENT

Each audience has its own personality: country and western audiences are considerably different from those attending alternative rock and roll performances. Fans attending a sporting event at a stadium one weekend may be very different from those in attendance the following weekend. Security personnel should not allow themselves to be lulled into believing "an audience is an audience" and dealing with each in the same manner. Every audience is different. A thorough understanding of crowd management, as opposed to *crowd control*, can assist the security management team in understanding the differences in crowds and in making appropriate crowd management or crowd control decisions. (See Appendix A, Figure 8-9 for crowd management definitions and duties).

The exact number of security personnel placements, especially for the front-of-house, is determined by the event's potential for crowd management challenges. For example, a symphony orchestra performance will require less "visual uniform presence" than a hard rock show where alcoholic beverages are served. *A trade show* centered on home improvement products and projected to attract 20,000 attendees over the course of a weekend might require a security director, door guards at each entrance/exit area, and a first aid team. On the other hand, an alternative rock show projected to attract an audience of 8,000 may require the presence of uniformed security/police, door guards at each entrance/exit area, a first aid team, and a host of T-shirt security personnel.

Sometimes, crowd management problems that occur at events have virtually no connection with the event or the public assembly facility. The facility and the event simply become involved because the feuding elements, either by accident or design, decide to confront each other at that site and during that event. For example, there have been numerous incidents in which inner city youth gangs have caused violent disruptions at high school football and basketball games. In these instances, neither the competing teams nor the high school arena or stadium in which the contests were being held had anything to do with the conflicts.

After watching 10,000 college football fans rush onto the field and tear down the goal posts following a dramatic ending to a hotly contested game, it becomes crystal clear that once a large crowd decides to do something, there is very little the public assembly facility's security management team can do to stop them. As frightening as this may appear, it is equally unsettling to realize that if a fan were to sustain an injury in an incident of this nature, the public assembly facility's management team and/or its owners may potentially be held liable.

The public assembly facility's security manager is charged with the responsibility to assess each event and recommend the appropriate staffing requirements. The security manager assumes the role of liaison between outside law enforcement agencies and the facility's security personnel, including contract security if used. Creating and maintaining relationships with local law enforcement agencies is critical. Depending on the event, these agencies should be involved at the event planning stage so they will be knowledgeable of the event thereby enabling them to respond faster and more effectively if a crisis were to occur. Security managers should be collecting as much intelligence about upcoming events as possible.

Information may be obtained from networking with other public assembly facility security managers, following the reports of traveling attractions through the trade publications, observing ticket line crowd behavior when the event goes on sale, and visiting or talking with other public assembly facility's staff where the event is performing in order to understand the behavior to be expected of the act's fans. Each of these information sources is beneficial in keeping the security manager sharp and informed.

PATRON AND GUEST COMMUNICATION

Policies adopted by the public assembly facility that have a direct effect on guests should be prominently displayed and advertised. Some policies remain constant whereas the implementation of others may depend on the event. For example, constant policies would include prohibiting smoking or carrying weapons within the confines of the facility while policies related to the use of cameras and recording devices or the age limit for children being required to have (or not have) their own ticket may change depending on the event. In all instances, every effort should be made to inform guests in a timely manner of these policies.

USING VISUAL AND AUDIBLE MESSAGES

Graphics and/or signage are an important part of the crowd management program. Properly conceived and professionally produced, graphics often can better and more rapidly inform guests than can facility employees. Graphics may be permanently installed or posted only when needed. For example, signage posted in a very visible manner at the entrances to a facility displaying the facility's policy regarding prohibited items may save the guest from the embarrassment of having such an item confiscated during an event or from the inconvenience of finding a safe storage place for the item or having to discard it prior to gaining admission.

Public address systems and message boards provide two excellent means for immediately delivering communications to large numbers of guests. It is extremely important for the public assembly facility manager to provide the public address/message board operator with pre-recorded messages/instructions that are to be used in the event of emergencies. This same information should be provided to the event receptionist. This is especially true if a situation occurs that necessitates evacuating guests from the public assembly facility.

CROWD PROBLEMS AND PATRON ISSUES

While it is virtually impossible to develop detailed procedures covering every potential problem event staff may encounter, the event manager will have preplanned responses to predictable and repetitive problems. Dedicated event staff will tend to "do something" whenever a problem does occur. Unfortunately, without clearly written and understood procedures, these well-meaning staff members may initiate an action that does not meet with management approval or solve the problem.

A manual containing approved procedures for dealing with general activities such as traffic control, parking, opening the house for an event, resolving seating and ticketing problems, dealing with unruly guests, ejections from the premise, medical emergencies, demonstrations, and so forth should be provided to each employee and then reviewed and discussed on a routine basis. The manual should also address procedures and responsibilities for potential major incidents such as bomb threats, fires, riots, shootings, terrorist activities, etc. Special attention should be given to procedures related to the evacuation of guests from the facility and its grounds in emergency situations. In addition, the facility should provide all appropriate personnel specific policies and procedures applicable to each event; this can be accomplished verbally or in writing.

INCIDENT REPORTS

Whenever an incident occurs, facility personnel should be instructed to record all pertinent information relative to the incident on an *Incident Report Form*. (See Appendix A, Figure 8-10 for a sample form). These report forms should be kept on file for no less than the time period allowed by state law (or other legal jurisdictions) for filing a lawsuit by the party(ies) involved in the incident. Only authorized individuals should have access to these reports. Medical information related to those involved must be kept confidential and only shared with individuals or agencies authorized by law and/or those authorized by the specific individual's consent. Accountable staff members should be required to complete these reports following the event before their departure.

SETTING AND ADJUSTING EVENT STAFFING LEVELS

Often when a public assembly facility prepares for doors opening, the casual observer will note a huge ratio of event staff personnel per patron, frequently anywhere from one to 100-250. Depending on the event, the maximum number of employees on duty is at the time the doors open. Due to the sporadic "on-again/off-again" nature of the public event business, the majority of patron service and event staffing roles are filled by labor and part-time labor. Because these service providers are usually in front line roles, in direct contact with the public, extensive efforts need to be made by the public assembly facility management to develop customer friendly attitudes and programs.

ADMISSION CONTROL AND OCCUPANT INGRESS/EGRESS

Traditionally, event managers have been concerned with guest entry (*ingress*). They work diligently to provide the most efficient way of allowing ticketed guests to enter the facility. In the same vein, they must be equally or even more diligent in providing guests with the most efficient routes for exiting (*egress*) the facility. Public assembly facility entrance and exit points, as well as the concourse flow pattern, require special attention.

Access control takes place at all physical entrances to the various areas of the facility complex, including parking lots, loading docks, patron entrances, backstage and employee entrances, etc. During events when heightened security is required, a security perimeter may be established; an outside line perhaps coinciding with outside fencing of the facility and its parking areas. Examples of access control techniques from IAAM's "Safety and Security Planning Guide for Arenas, Stadiums and Amphitheaters" (IAAM, 2002) include:

- Inspect all bags, including equipment bags and other containers of persons entering the venue.
- Require each licensee, organizer, team, etc. to provide a pass list, certified by management, of all representatives who will enter the venue.

- Venue management and lessees will not issue credentials to non-essential personnel or other persons.
- All event employees, media, contractors, exhibitors, and vendors must wear IDs issued by management. All temporary employees, contractors, vendors, media, and visitors should be issued daily passes that correspond to the "color of the day." Passes should not be issued until verification from their point of contact within the venue has been established. All temporary passes should be returned to security upon exiting.
- Photo IDs must be worn at this level of heightened security.
- No persons other than authorized user personnel and guests should be permitted in the dressing rooms, i.e., players, performers, spouses, coaches, media, staff, cleaning, maintenance, catering, etc.
- Artists and team members should not bring guests, other than immediate family, a significant other, or friend into the back-of-the-house areas.

During periods of heightened security, access controls and search techniques combine to sanitize the event areas of the facility. Similar to what happens at airports when access controls are breached and airport terminals are evacuated, public assembly facilities also must have procedures for when facility security sanitation is not maintained. Entrance control requires that all exit/entry doors be checked to ensure that the *panic hardware* is functioning properly.

In the desire to control ingress, facility tenants will sometimes ask that panic hardware be disabled or take it upon themselves to disable these devices. Since the public assembly facility management is ultimately responsible for the safety of the attending public, it is clearly the event manager's responsibility to make sure the panic hardware installed on every marked exit door remains operable at all times. In most jurisdictions, disabling panic devices constitutes a serious criminal offense.

Historically, management personnel have been concerned with guest entry issues and, for the most part, have developed excellent resolutions. However, since the advent of worldwide terrorist activity, public assembly facility managers have to be concerned with controlling key locations against unlawful entry either onto the property or into the facility itself. This vigilance must be maintained on a twenty-four hour basis, every day of the year.

Regardless of when the facility was constructed, facility managers must determine whether sufficient barriers exist to prevent unauthorized entry onto the property and whether there are sufficient buffer areas or clear zones between those barriers and the facility. If deficiencies are detected, it becomes the manager's responsibility to initiate corrective measures to ensure as much as possible the safety of the public assembly facility and its guests.

EMERGENCY PLANNING AND CRISIS COMMUNICATIONS

Emergency planning is an ongoing activity that should involve every department within a facility. From the event manager's point of view, *emergency preparedness* takes on

---

ATF BOMB THREAT CHECKLIST

Exact time of call:
Exact words of caller:

QUESTIONS TO ASK
1. When is bomb going to explode?

2. Where is the bomb?

3. What does it look like?

4. What kind of bomb is it?

5. What will cause it to explode?

6. Did you place the bomb?

7. Why?

8. Where are you calling from?

9. What is your address?

10. What is your name?

CALLER'S VOICE (circle)

Calm	Slow	Crying	Slurred	Stutter	Deep	Loud	Broken	Giggling	Accent
Angry	Rapid	Stressed	Nasal	Lisp	Excited	Disguised	Sincere	Squeaky	Normal

If voice is familiar, whom did it sound like?
Were there any background noises?
Remarks:

Person receiving call:
Date:

Telephone number call received at:
Report call immediately to:
(Refer to bomb incident plan)

Bureau of Alcohol, Tobacco and Firearms (ATF), 2003   FIGURE 8-11

heightened importance during events because of the high stakes in a facility occupied by many people. The event manager must have the knowledge and competence to carry out emergency responses if necessary. Emergency response will include appropriate actions from a broad range of facility occupants, including event staff such as ushers and security personnel, medical staff, facility management, police, and fire officials. The emergency plan will include a chain of command protocol; one that includes an incident command system specifying who is in charge, during what times, and under what circumstances specific to the various types of potential emergencies. For instance, in many locales and emergency plans, the facility's general manager or her designee may have responsibility for ordering a building evacuation in circumstances where police or fire officials do not have obvious jurisdiction, such as in the case of a bomb threat. (Figure 8-11 is a sample bomb threat checklist). This is an extremely important aspect of public assembly facility management.

Emergency plans should be specific to the facility and its locale. For instance, some facilities, based on their geographic location may have need for hurricane preparedness, tornado preparedness, blizzard preparedness, earthquake preparedness, etc. Such plans need to be coordinated with local offices of emergency management and/or local police and fire departments.

In addition, it is important to know the location of fire and safety items and electrical controls in each area of a facility. When an emergency situation arises, having this information immediately available is critical. All appropriate personnel should be familiar with this information. Further, diagrams such as these should be posted in multiple locations in the areas involved and at a central location.

Another important element of emergency planning is crisis communications. In the event of an emergency, the event manager may have a role in managing not only internal communications, but also communications with other stakeholders such as families of facility occupants, public officials and facility owners, the press and media, vendors and suppliers. Each facility should have a crisis communications plan to manage these various activities.

TRAINING

Public assembly facilities deal with a variety of audiences, each with its own characteristics. With this in mind, the security, emergency, and crowd management plans must be developed in a way that allow management to account for the different needs and characteristics of each audience. In developing a crowd management training program for the front-of-house employee, most public assembly facility managers come to realize that often the best approach is to expose all staff to a broad-based facility orientation followed by training specifically related to the individual's area of assignment or possible assignment.

In all aspects of the training program, customer service and guest safety must be emphasized as the primary goals. For example, newly hired ushers should be required to attend an orientation session that acquaints them with the facility's physical layout and the location of areas such as concessions stands, restrooms, first aid stations, telephones, and seating sections. It is vitally important for these personnel to understand where these places are located because the majority of questions asked by guests relate to these locations.

They should also be required to attend a session that focuses on the specific role they play in the overall event presentation. For instance, ushers should be taught how to assist in solving seating, ticketing, and public safety issues. They also need to understand their role in the event of a necessary facility evacuation, and they must be provided guidelines to assist them in determining when to request assistance from a supervisor. All public assembly facility crowd management training should include components related to facility hardware, design, and use. Other components should include personnel training, a procedures manual, and graphics and audiovisual materials. Finally, all new employees should attend a session devoted to the concept of guest service.

A significant amount of information is provided and reviewed during employee training and orientation sessions. It is unrealistic to assume employees, particularly part-time employees, will make the effort necessary to comprehend and retain all of this information. Consequently, all employees should be provided with a copy of the employee manual that contains detailed information about which each employee should be knowledgeable. Both event-specific and general information should be contained in the manual. Some public assembly facilities use an Event Handbook that all employees must carry with them while working.

The IAAM has developed and/or endorsed several event staff training programs that are available to public assembly managers. For training event staff, IAAM publishes video training programs, most with instructors' guides and resource manuals on the following topics:

- Guest relations skills.
- Dealing with the problem patron.
- Providing services to guests with disabilities.
- Safety awareness.
- Basics of crowd management.
- Basics of emergency planning.

Other training and informational programs and materials are available from the IAAM and from the various other organizations and associations noted in Appendix D.

PUBLIC IMAGE

One of the most valuable assets of any public assembly facility is its public image; how the public feels about the facility. The facility's public image is also formed in part by its success in accommodating community needs through its programming and the level of maintenance and housekeeping afforded the facility and its adjacent grounds. Another very important aspect in determining the facility's public image is the quality of the interactions between the guest and the front-of-house event staff, a workforce primarily composed of part-time employees. Consequently training is absolutely critical. Every day, managers entrust the image of their public assembly facility to those employees who might be the least trained, marginally supervised, poorest paid, and least committed to the overall enterprise.

For many guests attending an event at a public assembly facility, the annoying parking guard, the stressed ticket seller, the surly ticket taker, the inattentive usher, or the employee unable to provide initial first aid or cardiopulmonary resuscitation (CPR) due to lack of training becomes "the facility." Negative encounters with these individuals may dramatically alter the guest's perception of that facility. The only way to reduce the potential for employees acting in a negative fashion (or not acting at all) is to have a training program that truly emphasizes the need for positive guest relations and that imparts in the employee a sense of ownership in the success of the event production.

SUMMARY

Event production starts with the selling of facility time and space. Event management requires the interaction of a variety of people generally associated with the facility operations department.

Management of the client/tenant relationship is crucial to event management. All public assembly facility managers must assume the responsibility of fostering and maintaining these relationships. Public assembly facilities generate income through the leasing or rental of their facility for events as well as through the ancillary revenue streams, including catering, food and beverage, novelties, and parking.

Every effort must be taken to prevent the occurrence of event day surprises. All anticipated problems and issues should be addressed and resolved prior to event day. To avoid these distractions requires cooperation from and effective communication among all units of the public assembly facility's organization.

Once an event has been booked and contracted, the planning and production of the event commences. It is important to have a promoters' packet available, especially for those promoters new to the facility. These packets need not be expensive, but must be informative, and may be available on the facility's web site.

Entertainment events should have a production rider, signed by the promoter and the performer/agency, detailing all elements required by the performer in order to provide a quality performance. Once the production rider is developed, it becomes the responsibility of the promoter to ensure the requirements are met. In most instances, the promoter relies upon the public assembly facility manager to fulfill these conditions. However, the facility manager should deny all requests of the promoter until the lease or rental agreement is completed.

Events undertaken by local groups, especially those produced by non-professionals, require special attention during the planning stage. All events should have detailed diagrams specifying room arrangements for meetings, dining functions, and other uses.

A schedule of event timelines should be created and adhered to. An event document similar to a diary should be maintained for each event. Everything about the event, including any incidents, should be recorded in a clear and detailed manner. This document is very valuable in evaluating the event and in future planning for the event.

In many instances, the public assembly facility manager is expected to assist in providing equipment and staff required by the event such as front- and back-of-house personnel, part time labor, and house or rental equipment. The cost of providing for these needs is billed to the event and its promoter.

Crowd management and crowd control issues must be discussed and planned for each event. Decisions must be made regarding the type and level of security necessary to ensure the safety of the guests, the performers, and the facility's personnel based on the event's history, the anticipated audience's demographic profile, the current political climate, and the facility's design and hardware. Security personnel, as well as all employees, should be trained in crowd management techniques. Each employee should know how to respond to crowd control issues, especially in the event an order is issued to evacuate the facility.

Each employee must be an ambassador for the public assembly facility. Interactions between guests and employees must be positive at all times. In making policy and procedure decisions, the effect upon guests must be seriously taken into consideration. It is especially important that policies and procedures directly affecting guests be communicated to them in order to avoid potential problems resulting from enforcement.

REFERENCES AND ADDITIONAL READINGS

Berlonghi, Alexander. 1990. *The Special Event Risk Management Manual.* Dana Point, CA: Event Risk Management.

Berlonghi, Alexander. 1996. *Special Event Security Management, Loss Prevention, And Emergency Services: The Guide for Planning and Documentation.* Dana Point, CA: Event Risk Management.

Cote', Ron, P.E. (Editor). 2003. *The Life Safety Code Handbook.* Quincy, MA: National Fire Protection Association.

Goldblatt, Joe. 2001. *Special Events: Twenty-First Century Global Event Management,* 3rd ed. Hoboken, NJ: John Wiley & Sons, Inc.

Goldblatt, Joe and Kathleen Nelson. 2001. *The International Dictionary of Event Management* Hoboken, NJ: John Wiley & Sons, Inc.

IAAM (International Association of Assembly Managers, Inc.). 1994. *IAAM Position Description Handbook.* Coppell, TX: IAAM.

_____. 2002. *Venue Security After September 11* Audioconference Package. Coppell, TX: IAAM.

_____. 2002. *Venue Emergency Planning After September 11* Audioconference Package. Coppell, TX: IAAM.

_____. 2003. *Convention Center Security Planning and Risk Management Update* Audioconference Package. Coppell, TX: IAAM.

_____. 2003. *Performing Arts Venue Safety & Security Update.* Coppell, TX: IAAM.

_____. 2003. *Emergency Planning at Public Assembly Facilities.* Coppell, TX: IAAM.

_____. 1999. *Managing the Crowd.* Coppell, TX: IAAM.

_____. 1997. *Customer Service Begins With Me: Superior Guest Relations at Public Assembly Facilities.* Coppell, TX: IAAM.

_____. 1995. *Safety Awareness at Public Assembly Facilities.* Coppell, TX: IAAM.

_____. 1993. *Service Excellence: Patrons With Disabilities.* Coppell, TX: IAAM.

_____. 1994. *Service Excellence: Dealing with Guests' Problems and the Problem Guest.* Coppell, TX: IAAM.

Maloy, Bernard P. and Charles R. Higgins. 2000. *No Excuses Risk Management.* Carmel, IN: Cooper Publishing.

Morrow, Sandra L. 2002. *The Art of the Show,* 2nd ed. Dallas, TX: IAEM Foundation.

Silvers, Julia Rutherford. 2003. *Professional Event Coordination.* Hoboken, NJ: John Wiley & Sons, Inc.

Tarlow, Peter E. 2002. *Event Risk Management and Safety.* Hoboken, NJ: John Wiley & Sons, Inc.

FACILITY SERVICES AND OPERATIONS

CHAPTER OUTLINE

INTRODUCTION

At its fundamental core, delivery and achievement of the public assembly facility's objectives depends on a solid facility maintenance and operation services department. Regardless of type, size, ownership, or number of events, common operations and engineering services activities must occur in order for the public assembly facility to function in a safe, efficient, and effective manner. Facility services/operations is generally responsible for the facility's physical environment that includes its state of repair, cleanliness, air quality, the logistical delivery of event production requirements, and the overlapping life safety/security control of the building(s).

Providing satisfying and rewarding experiences to the client and guests through the execution and delivery of the facility's commitment (in relation to the lease requirements) is the theme of this chapter as it focuses largely on the back-of-house operations or functions that facilitate the delivery of services to the customer. Ultimately, facility services and operations must have a concentrated focus on providing a clean, safe, and comfortable environment.

Understanding the dynamic impact the facility's physical environment has upon its ability to achieve positive financial, entertainment, and cultural objectives should encourage the public assembly facility manager to devote significant attention and support to the event services and operations department.

Generally, facility services and operations have two distinctively different components, both critical to the success of the organization and its mission. One is devoted to the maintenance and upkeep of the physical plant and the other is focused on event services. On the one hand, facility services must be continually keeping the facility clean and in good repair while they are facilitating building conversion to fulfill event-related requirements.

To achieve the facility's objectives, the facility services and operations department must be flexible and responsive to the varying needs of the organization and the clients/public it serves, while

- constantly maintaining and repairing the physical plant;
- attending to the cleanliness and aesthetics of the facility, its landscaping, and parking lots;
- inspecting, maintaining, and repairing the equipment necessary to produce the facility's events; and
- providing the services required to deliver the expected experiences.

Facility services and operations departments are usually responsible for housekeeping services, the ongoing process of keeping the facility and its equipment clean. In addition they may also be responsible for event production activities including event setup and/or staging activities, such as providing and positioning necessary equipment prior to an event's arrival and returning that equipment to its storage place following the event's departure. In many of the larger public assembly facilities, particularly exhibition, convention, and conference centers, the number of scheduled meetings and events may require a separate audiovisual unit. Audiovisual units are frequently located within the facility services and operations department with its director reporting to the department manager.

When facility services and operations are managed in-house, the organization of the department is generally based on the tasks to be performed. The facility services and operations manager is responsible for the supervision of the department's various unit managers. The number of unit managers depends upon the size of the facility, the extent and type of event activity, the number of facility services and operations employees and the responsibilities assigned to the facility services and operations department. It is not uncommon for a public assembly facility to employ individuals such as a maintenance supervisor, a housekeeping services supervisor, and a production (stage manager) supervisor. Each of these supervisors is charged with the responsibility for directing and supervising their workers who may be part- or full-time employees (or a combination of both) depending on the facility's event schedule. Although maintenance, housekeeping services, and event staging generally reside in the facility services and operations department, the tasks assigned these units can be significantly different. Consequently, each unit requires workers with skills and abilities specific to that unit. Each area of facility services and operations should be supervised by a manager who is knowledgeable about the specifics of the work to be performed, the workers who will perform the tasks, and the public assembly facility's objectives.

A major challenge for the public assembly facility manager may well be the cultivation of positive and cooperative relationships between the various groups of employees whose missions may appear to be contrary to one another. For example, conflicts sometimes arise between housekeeping services and concessions. Housekeeping services' tasks include keeping the facility clean. A task of the concessions department is to sell food, beverage, and novelty items, all of which tend to produce trash and other cleaning issues. Another example is the conflict that may arise between the maintenance unit and the stage unit. One maintenance responsibility might be to maintain and repair equipment used by the stage unit. Stage unit employees use, possibly damage, and eventually wear out equipment thereby creating additional work for the maintenance unit.

Allowing individual units to lose sight of the public assembly facility's overall mission tends to encourage the emergence of these and similar unfortunate, but inevitable, conflicts. Understanding this particular dynamic should encourage the public assembly facility manager to adopt management techniques that assist both full-time and part-time employees to focus on the facility's mission and to understand and appreciate their contribution to that mission. The facility manager may accomplish this objective by insisting that all full-time facility services supervisors implement the facility's recruiting, hiring, training, and rewards systems for all of their full-time and part-time employees. Some of the tools that may assist the manager in creating an efficient and effective workforce include having up-to-date job descriptions; providing manuals and handbooks that clearly explain the facility services and operations department's policies and procedures; scheduling required employee training sessions; requiring documentation of employee skill levels; and using effective employee evaluation and reward techniques.

MAINTENANCE AND THE PHYSICAL PLANT

One role of facility maintenance that is not generally recognized is its impact on customer service. The astute, capable manager recognizes that any decision to defer repair and renovation projects may negatively affect the facility's performance and the public's perception. Additionally, cleanliness and safety are paramount elements of the public's perception of the event environment. The public quickly perceives a poorly maintained public assembly facility as an unsafe facility and hesitates to attend events if they believe the facility puts them at a safety risk.

TRADES AND CRAFTSMEN

Maintenance unit personnel spend a substantial portion of their time maintaining and repairing the physical plant and its equipment. Job descriptions for maintenance workers vary depending on the job level. If the services of highly skilled personnel are available through another agency, maintenance workers may only be required to have a general knowledge of, rather than certified training in, areas such as carpentry, plumbing, painting, electrical and mechanical work. However, depending upon the needs of the physical plant, some maintenance workers may be required to hold certificates in one or more specific fields. Some facility operations are large enough to allow the hiring of workers as *helpers* and assign them to certified personnel for on-the-job training. Desirable attributes of maintenance workers include being a high school graduate with trade or technical training or having the equivalent training through on-the-job experience. The majority of maintenance workers are hourly employees who are eligible for overtime compensation, depending on the laws and regulations of the particular jurisdiction.

Certified personnel in carpentry, plumbing, refrigeration, electricity, mechanical systems, etc., are usually referred to as tradesmen or craftsmen. In many instances, they are the team leaders who supervise the non-certified workers often referred to as helpers. At one time, entry to the maintenance segment of the facility services and operations profession was through the helper position. After serving an apprenticeship and passing certification examinations in one or more of the traditional maintenance skills areas, the helper became eligible for promotion to a tradesman/craftsman position. The vocational/technical school training in a host of maintenance areas currently available in many countries has significantly altered the need for, and nature of, the apprenticeship system.

Today's maintenance worker/tradesman/craftsman often holds a certificate in one or more of the classic common maintenance areas such as plumbing, electrical, mechanical, or carpentry and is expected to have a general working knowledge of them all. These employees may also possess skills in general shop work, general mechanics, electrical and gas, milled steel welding, metal fabrication, heating/ventilation/air conditioning (HVAC), painting, and computer applications in the facility services and operations areas.

Maintenance assignments could include tasks such as inspecting and changing light bulbs, changing air filters in the facility's air handlers, checking and repairing seats, checking and maintaining safety hardware, and providing equipment maintenance and repair. A well-planned and documented preventive maintenance plan (PM program) is critical in providing timely and ongoing maintenance for the facility and its equipment. It is the facility services and operations manager's responsibility to produce adequate preventive maintenance schedules and to ensure and document the completion of all assigned maintenance tasks. A complicating factor in keeping to a maintenance schedule is the facility's schedule of event activities which must take precedence. However, a facility manager needs to intentionally schedule time on the event calendar for major maintenance projects, such as rigging inspections and floor maintenance.

MECHANICAL AND ENGINEERING

The term engineering services refers to those activities associated with the management of the facility's mechanical systems environment. Engineering services is also responsible for supplying electrical power, steam, water, compressed air, and other resources required by either the facility or the event being staged. In exhibition and convention centers, the engineering services department's responsibilities might include maintaining electrical power distribution equipment, determining the most efficient and effective ways to provide electricity to the facility's clients, and the installation and removal of temporary electrical outlets.

Exactly where the line is drawn between facility services and operations and engineering services depends on several variables: size of the facility, the facility's mission, the number and types of activities hosted, and whether the facility has access to other departments for required areas of support. In many facilities, the functions are combined in one department. A municipally-owned public assembly facility might well have an on-site facility services and operations department to deal with general maintenance and housekeeping services but rely completely upon the municipality's public works department for major repairs and HVAC environmental support. It is not unusual for a university-managed performing arts center, particularly one with a modest event schedule, to draw all of its maintenance and housekeeping support from the university's maintenance, grounds, and housekeeping departments. And, in all probability, the performing arts facility would receive its water, electrical power, and HVAC support from the respective university departments as well. In situations of this nature, the public assembly facility could employ a superintendent to oversee the facility's operation and to serve as a liaison between the facility and the *parent organization*. Most public assembly facilities have some level of in-house maintenance, staging, and housekeeping services support. That support might be actual in-house support, meaning the employees are directly employed and managed by the public assembly facility, or it might be provided by other departments (e.g. municipalities, universities, etc.) or through a contractual arrangement between the facility and a private contractor.

In public assembly facilities with an ice surface for hockey, traveling shows and/or public skating, it is not unusual for an ice engineer to be in charge of the ice and the ice-making equipment. The ice engineer is responsible for installing, maintaining, and removing the ice; painting and logo placement; maintaining the ice surfacing equipment (such as a Zamboni); and managing the maintenance program for the ice-making equipment. Depending on union contracts, the ice engineer or the stagehands might install and remove the dasher boards and glass that surround the hockey rink playing surface. In most cases, the ice engineer works under the supervision of the facility services and operations manager. The sheet of ice that the players skate on is, in effect, the stage for the event.

MECHANICAL SYSTEMS

Central control of the public assembly facility's physical plant environment is one of the key roles of engineering, and in today's public assembly facilities management, mechanical systems have become very sophisticated through technological advancements. For both the welfare of the patrons and the life extension of the facility's physical plant, programming and the operations of such critical support components require extensive training, skills, and experience. To provide for expedient oversight of these systems, many public assembly facilities have what is sometimes called the *motor control center*. This feature of the facility is where manual and automated control circuitry may be centralized for master control of the facility's life safety, security, and comfort environments. Typically located in the back-of-house near the loading dock or shipping/receiving zones, the motor control center may have surveillance security and alarming systems, fire detection and enunciator panels, and switch gear for HVAC and its monitoring, to name a few. Furthermore, computerized systems today assist engineers to save on utility consumption by automatically adjusting demand through load shed or by systematically sequencing motor startups. Newer lighting systems can be installed that will only come on when someone enters the rooms. From automatic timed shut off of water faucets to metered toilet flushing, today's public assembly facility has built-in systems that make it economically viable to operate from both the perspective of utility use and labor. Many of these programs are also operable remotely from computer laptops, providing even more flexibility to facility management. During inclement weather conditions when freezing temperatures or snow loads become a concern, engineers are capable of monitoring systems and making appropriate adjustments from remote locations that may avoid catastrophic outcomes.

Because of the training and licensing required for many of these specialized areas, it is often more cost efficient and effective to employ the services of outside companies to perform periodic maintenance tasks. Maintenance and repair of equipment requiring specialized service such as elevators, escalators, fire suppression equipment, security alarm and surveillance systems, air handlers, cooling towers, etc., are generally outsourced to private companies through contracts. Purchasing outside services in a publicly managed facility often requires bids from a minimum of three sources generated by a request for quotation (RFQ) or request for proposal (RFP) announcement.

FACILITY LIFE CYCLE

Understanding the life cycle of a facility is an important step in extending the life expectancy of its components. Adequate funding for public assembly facility maintenance is critical to the facility's life span. Some public assembly facility managers believe the facility services and operations department's annual budget should be at least one percent of the facility's current value; not its initial cost but its current value. Investing a minimum of one percent of the facility's current value annually into maintenance, repair, and renovation activities should provide sufficient resources to keep the physical assets updated and properly maintained.

Responsibility for the maintenance of a public assembly facility can be assigned to the facility's maintenance staff, the maintenance staff of a larger umbrella public works type of department or a private contractor. Exactly which approach best benefits the facility depends upon a number of variables such as the availability of services from an *umbrella group*, availability of skilled labor, costs of service, and type of maintenance and repairs anticipated. The best format for each public assembly facility is simply the one that, after careful examination of all options, produces desired results at an acceptable cost and on time.

PREVENTIVE MAINTENANCE

Extending the life of the facility and its operating equipment and systems can be a daunting task, particularly if the facility has been run-down and/or chosen to defer maintenance. Unfortunately, when public assembly facility owners are confronted with the need to reduce expenses, one of the first cuts tends to be the facility's maintenance budget. Deferred maintenance may be encouraged for one reason or another (usually financial), but will eventually take its toll on the public assembly facility. Clearly, deferring maintenance will reduce short-term operating costs. However, owners must understand that the cost of repairing or replacing neglected equipment becomes far more expensive than the cost of providing routine maintenance and that deferred maintenance decisions predictably result in very expensive long-term costs. Inevitably, it will affect what the guests experience.

A well designed preventive maintenance program takes into consideration the life cycle of the facility and its equipment as well as optimum maintenance activities necessary to maximize use with minimum cost. To initiate such a program, the facility services and operations department may categorize the various properties of the physical plant, e.g., equipment, hardware, painted surfaces, flooring, exterior, grounds, etc. A maintenance schedule for each category's elements can be assigned a timeline for attention and formalized in a departmental action plan. Graffiti, especially in restrooms can be reduced if a systematic cleaning and/or removal of same is diligently followed. The key is to have an orchestrated method and plan of upkeep to reduce the aging process.

CAPITAL REPLACEMENT

Regardless of how good the facility services and operations efforts may be, equipment eventually wears out. Whether it is door hinges and closures or mechanical bearings and motor windings, new equipment must be purchased and installed. Planning ahead for such inevitable replacement is an important role of the facility services and operations department. Knowledge of anticipated life span of equipment and facilities is an important step towards planning for replacement. If a carpeted area receives a lot of traffic, it will show the wear sooner. A plan that schedules such maintenance is called capital replacement and, viewed over a three- to five-year period, enables management to anticipate line-item expenses for each year's budget. Management may be inclined to establish a Reserve for Replacement fund with a three to five percent budget allocation annually.

RIGGING

Rigging for events poses special risks for facility managers. Each type of public assembly facility has specific types of rigging. In a performing arts venue, stage rigging is an integral element of the stage design. At arenas, stadiums and convention centers, temporary (arena-style rigging) is often used. In addition, nearly all facilities have some type of permanent rigging, such as scoreboards, speakers, chandeliers, etc. Facility management has liability responsibilities for all rigging that takes place in the facility, even if it is installed by lessees and their contractors. A rigging safety plan might include the following:

- Building load capacities.
- Fall protection plan and equipment.
- Training of riggers, event managers and management.
- Evaluation of safety and condition of rigging equipment.
- Procedures that require supervision and inspection of rigging by competent personnel on a regularly scheduled basis.

The facility's engineering services department and stagehands should always be involved when questions arise concerning facility structural issues. When a public assembly facility is being designed, the architect calculates the effects of additional weight and stress being placed on the facility's roofs, walls, floors, and structural beams. Appropriate safety margins are incorporated into the structural design for more recently constructed or renovated public assembly facilities to accommodate anticipated production and tension loads that may add stress to the structure. Once the construction phase is completed and the public assembly facility is nearly ready for occupancy, weight limits for the various aspects of the facility must be confirmed and documented by the contractor and submitted to the appropriate structural engineer for certification. It is the responsibility of the engineering services unit, or other designated individual(s), to monitor activities held in the facility in order to ensure these weight limits are not exceeded. The limits should be made known to the prospective promoter during the booking process. It is wise and prudent to periodically engage the services of an architectural or engineering firm to confirm the facility's ability to accommodate the load requirements of touring shows that hang equipment and to perform an overall structural audit of the facility.

HOUSEKEEPING AND CUSTODIAL

Of all the work that occurs in a facility, keeping the facility clean and presentable is undoubtedly the least glamorous activity of facility operations. However, housekeeping and custodial services are critical components to the successful management and operation of a public assembly facility. Although housekeeping services may be underappreciated and undervalued, a clean and inviting facility environment is one of the most essential elements to increasing patronage. Generally, housekeeping services relate to those tasks directed toward keeping the facility safe, clean, and appealing to guests, users, and owners.

The housekeeping services unit faces many challenges. One is to establish a standard for cleanliness for those areas not regulated by statute. Another is to successfully identify, recruit, train, and supervise competent and dependable employees. The many tasks that fall under the housekeeping services domain, if not properly performed, may result in the facility being sanctioned or closed by public health or safety agencies.

Within every public assembly facility, housekeeping services are required and each area may have its own standard by which acceptable cleanliness is measured. The cleanliness standard for the office area, for example, may be quite different from that for a private dining room. Housekeeping attention provided to open-air seating in a sports stadium is different from that afforded to box-seating areas in a performing arts center.

Housekeeping expectations for luxury suites in many of today's public assembly facilities differ from those for the general admission seating sections. As noted in the maintenance services section, the key dynamic affecting the level of housekeeping service provided beyond statutory requirements is based upon guests' and tenants' expectations. Consequently, it becomes the responsibility of the housekeeping services supervisor to recognize the different levels of expectations and to develop operating procedures for the housekeeping services staff that specify what must be done in order to meet these expectations.

As with the maintenance services supervisor, the housekeeping services supervisor's job includes information dissemination to custodial and housekeeping staff. The housekeeping services supervisor outlines the activities of the day and informs the service crews of particular challenges related to the day's events or activities. These meetings also represent an opportune time for supervisors to remind their crew of the facility's housekeeping services objectives and to reinforce the relationships that exists between housekeeping services and the facility's other units.

It is not uncommon for a public assembly facility to have full-time housekeepers in order to maintain the facility's offices and those areas generally open to the public during non-event periods. Keeping the general meeting rooms, the lobby, the main office space, and other public areas within the facility clean and presentable is normally a responsibility assigned to the full-time housekeeping services staff. Cleaning the arena, the stadium, the auditorium, convention, or exhibit center following an event usually requires more personnel than just the facility's full-time housekeeping services staff. Tasks of this magnitude are often assigned to cleaning crews employed on a part-time, as-needed basis. Some facilities use full-time staff to serve as crew leaders. To clean a public assembly facility after a concert in a larger facility may easily require a crew of 100 or more workers in order to perform the labor necessary to transform the facility back into one that is clean and presentable. Often such work begins after midnight and must be completed in sufficient time to allow the facility to host another event in the morning.

If not performed by in-house personnel, a common method often used by public assembly facilities to secure the services of part-time, as-needed cleaning crews is to contract with a private business that provides such labor. The contract between the public assembly facility and the labor contractor usually stipulates that the facility's housekeeping services supervisor must advise the contractor of the facility's labor needs within a specified advance notice timeframe. The contractor then provides the labor, and supervision if necessary, and subsequently bills the public assembly facility for the services rendered based upon the rates specified in the contract. It is important that the facility reserves management rights and quality control/evaluations in monitoring the work performed and the overall contract requirements.

CONVERSION AND EVENT PRODUCTION

The role of the production team is considered by some to be the more glamorous or exciting side of facility services and operations. This is the functional component of the facility's repertoire that is directly involved with the client or tenant's performance activity, without which the logistical deliverables that produce event outcomes could not exist. Fundamentally, the production team is responsible for assisting the client or tenant with producing the physical and technical environment required to achieve the desired objectives.

There are a number of similarities between a production services unit, sometimes referred to as the stage unit, and those of maintenance and housekeeping services, the chief example being the need for part-time labor. The stage unit is responsible for identifying, recruiting, training, and employing stagehands and part-time labor.

At the outset of the tenant taking possession of the facility, or any part thereof, management is obligated to make the appropriate changes from the occupancy of the previous tenant to the new tenant. Typically, this activity is known as "conversion." Conversion is the act of transformation that occurs between uses that provides the necessary foundation for next use.

In some cases, this may simply be the elimination of all barriers or obstacles by providing a clean and open space. Other situations, as in the conversion from a basketball sporting environment to ice hockey, may require significant conversion activities requiring engineering adjustments to the facility and physical arrangement changes to the venue.

PERFORMANCE (OR PRODUCTION) RIDER

As described in Chapter 8, the event promoter often provides a production rider that includes a detailed description of production assistance required to conduct their program or activity. Many of the specific requirements may be carried out by the facility services and operations department. The typical production rider may ask the public assembly facility to provide workers in one or all of the following categories: riggers to hang and detach equipment above the stage; stagehands to be responsible for the handling of event-related equipment; runners to perform pick-up and delivery tasks; equipment operators trained to operate forklifts, and other mechanical and hoisting equipment; electricians to handle power/energy distribution for the event; carpenters to build sets/props; wardrobe hands to help arrange, clean, organize, and sometimes repair costumes; and, first aid/emergency medical technicians (EMT) to deal with medical emergencies that may occur while the event is being set-up, during the event itself, or while the event is being broken down. (See Appendix A, Figure 9-1 for a sample production rider).

Touring attractions, concerts, circuses, exhibitions, etc., typically provide their own production crew leaders such as the production manager and the sound and lighting director, but they generally do not provide their own laborers such as loaders, drivers, riggers, wardrobe assistants, and the like. It is usually the public assembly facility's responsibility to provide such labor. Labor requirements are normally specified in the production rider. Unloading trucks, operating forklifts and hoists, assembling stage equipment, hanging and removing rigging, setting tables and chairs, and loading equipment are typical tasks required by traveling attractions and accomplished by the stagehands and/or part-time labor force. The expense of providing these workers is usually borne by the event's promoter.

STAGEHANDS AND SHOW LABOR

Virtually all public assembly facilities utilize a large number of part-time employees to produce the activities for which the facilities were designed. A performing arts theatre may have a professional manager and a small, full-time, non-event day staff. However, on event day, the number of staff personnel may swell considerably when the additional part-time stagehands, front-of-house staff, security and parking guards, catering employees, and others are included in the count.

Event-related labor, particularly for arenas and theatres, may be divided into two categories: move-in/move-out labor and production labor. In-and out-labor is that required to unload and load an event; organize and assemble equipment; dismantle and pack equipment at the end of the performance; and remove equipment from the facility. Production labor is that required during the course of the actual event and might be referred to as the *show call*. This type of labor may require the services of employees possessing higher skill levels than that normally available from in- and out-labor personnel. In such instances, these workers generally command a higher rate of pay.

Decorator is a labor category common to the convention center industry. Decorators are responsible for laying carpet, dressing and setting tables and chairs, piping and draping exhibit booths, etc. Larger, busy convention centers normally have a decorating unit within their organizational structure with its director reporting to the facility services and operations manager. In the same way that arenas, auditoriums, and theatres often rely on part-time stagehands, many convention centers rely upon part-time employees for food preparation, beverage service, and dining/banquet room wait service. Just as a union or private contractor may supply stagehands for the arena, the same arrangement may be used to provide part-time decorators, wait staff, or kitchen employees. Once again, the best arrangement for each public assembly facility depends upon its activities, size, local politics, regulatory laws, and mission statement.

The production rider may also request the presence of additional security guards in order to protect the attraction's equipment, buses, and vans along with the dressing rooms, back-of-house, and other areas. Additional housekeeping services employees may be requested as well. Supervision of housekeepers and security guards may be the responsibility of either the stage manager or the event supervisor depending upon the manner in which the unit is organized. Typically, the public assembly facility's manager provides this extra labor with the expense being charged to the promoter. Other labor requests that may be included in the production rider are deckhands/stagehands who actually work on stage during a performance; spotlight operators; house light operators trained to operate the facility's emergency lighting and general illumination; house electricians familiar with the facility's electrical equipment; and sound and lighting technicians to use the facility's sound and lighting equipment. Of course, the event may bring its own sound and lights and personnel to operate them.

SAMPLE EXPLODED RATE CARD

Title	Base Rate	Medi(1.45%)	FICA(6.25%)	H/W(5.0%)	PP(6.25%)	SDI(.01%)	UE/WC(3%)	Overhead(10%)	Billed Rate
Supr.	20.00	.29	1.25	1.00	1.25	.20	.60	2.00	26.59

Supr. = Supervisor
Medi = Medicare
PP = Pension Plan
UE/WC = Unemployment Insurance and Workmen's Compensation Insurance.

Positions may not have numbers in every column, e.g., FICA and PP (Pension Plan) columns.
H/W column may be union plans.
State may not have SDI (State Disability Insurance) or it may be an employee paid plan.

FINALLY - Facility may decide to absorb any or all of the add-ons to the base rate.

FIGURE 9-2

Temporary Employees

One of the stage manager's many responsibilities is to develop a pool of trained, reliable, and accessible personnel. The size and source of the pool that the public assembly facility draws from depends on a number of variables including the number and types of events the facility stages, the particular work skills required by the booked attractions, local labor union policies and regulations, regulatory laws, and the availability of qualified workers. The pool may come from the student body of the local university, volunteers, civic organizations, off-duty fire and police personnel, residents of the local community and surrounding areas, labor contractors, or the local theatrical and stage employees union.

A number of issues affect the decision as to how to best organize and manage the public assembly facility's staging labor pool. In some instances, development of this pool may be the direct responsibility of the public assembly facility's management. When this occurs, laborers might become part-time employees of the facility and work on an as-needed basis; are supervised by the facility's stage manager; are paid directly by the facility; and may be eligible for some elements of the facility's employee benefits package.

In this scenario, the event or tenant requiring the use of laborers submits their request to the stage manager who then fills the *labor call* from the facility's pool. Rates of pay are established by the facility along with other personnel costs charged to the promoter. The personnel recharge rates calculated, as shown in Figure 9.2, are carried forward onto a general rate card provided to the promoters. Other standard charges for equipment and other facility services might also be included on the same rate card.

The promoter is billed for the labor provided and the public assembly facility's management receives its payment at the event settlement meeting, less any advance deposit received. In this arrangement, workers are paid in accordance with the facility's regular payroll schedule. Labor management costs incurred by the facility, such as insurance, payroll preparation and distribution, training, records management, and overhead, are typically calculated and charged to the parties requesting the labor.

Commercial labor contractors are also a source for laborers. The public assembly facility may enter into a contract agreement with a labor contractor to provide the labor requested by event promoters. The contractor develops and maintains the labor pool, establishes the rate of pay as allowed or required under the contract, and provides the event with the requested labor workers. The public assembly facility usually provides supervision for the workers through its stage or facility services and operations departments and also guarantees the contractor payment for services rendered. After the labor requirements have been finalized, the stage manager informs the contractor of the event's labor needs. Thus, in this scenario, facility management makes the labor call and the provider fulfills the request. For each event, the public assembly facility manager submits a bill to the promoter for the labor provided and then collects the amount due on behalf of the contractor as part of the event settlement.

Some facilities may elect (others are legally obliged) to use the local stage employee worker's union for its labor requirements. In the United States, the International Association of Theatrical and Stage Employees union (IATSE) is capable of meeting all production-related labor requests for *production calls* while the Teamsters Union may coordinate *car loaders* for unloading trucks. The union's local business agent (BA) identifies and recruits potential employees, certifies skills and abilities, negotiates wages and rates of pay, and establishes working rules. The union may also provide worker supervision. Sometimes labor requests and requirements for an event scheduled in a union contracted public assembly facility can be submitted directly to the facility's union steward or the local union secretary. The union fills the labor call and the union bills the attraction's promoter directly or through the facility. In many instances, all financial activities between the promoter and the union might be separate and distinct from those between the public assembly facility and the promoter.

Prior to entering into a relationship with a union for the provision of labor, representatives of the public assembly facility's management and the union's management must negotiate a labor contract. This contract, which is generally subject to periodic renegotiation, establishes pay rate schedules and employee benefits, crew compositions, employee training, work rules and guidelines, and employee supervision. It is extremely important for the facility to retain management rights. It is also essential that the cost of using union employees is competitive with the cost of using non-union employees in order to keep costs in line with competing public assembly facilities.

Some shows, before they go on tour, contract with the union for providing stagehand service in every community throughout the tour. Known as *yellow card* shows, these shows are typically theatrical events like Broadway shows or family entertainment such as ice shows.

Again, the number and type of activities presented, local politics, and the facility's ownership type are usually the prime variables that determine which worker supply mode or combination of modes is used. In some jurisdictions the law will affect the labor supplier decision. In those jurisdictions with right to work statutes, it is illegal to require an employee or potential employee to hold union membership. In such jurisdictions, union members can be employed but non-union workers cannot be systematically excluded.

Guest/Client Services

Facility services and operations are critical to providing guests and clients with superior customer service and providing positive experiences that are clean, safe, and comfortable. This functional area also can be an important source of ancillary revenue for the facility. Today, with the patron experience expectations so extraordinarily high and shipping of equipment so costly, clients/tenants and promoters are increasingly dependent upon local suppliers and purveyors to provide necessary products and support services. Many of these support services are generic, off-the-shelf items that either can be obtained locally or provided in-house by the facility services and operations department.

Some of the more common services provided to clients are business- or production-related equipment, e.g., audiovisual services, decorating supplies, and office equipment such as fax machines, telephones, etc. For the facility, these extra services to the promoter can become business opportunities to generate additional revenue.

INVENTORY MANAGEMENT

Responsibilities that typically fall under the facility services and operations department in many public assembly facilities may include inventory control, shipping and receiving, grounds maintenance, periodic facility inspections, lock maintenance and key controls, surveillance and security systems, emergency power generation, fire/sprinkler and smoke detection systems, and ice and snow removal.

The creation and maintenance of production and operations inventory records documenting the existence, location, and condition of every piece and type of equipment owned or leased by the public assembly facility is a demanding task. Items contained in the inventory would include, but not be limited to mechanical equipment, tools, cleaning materials and equipment, napkins and table cloths, tables and chairs, sound and lighting equipment, carpeting, furniture, computers, audiovisual equipment, kitchen equipment and utensils, telephones, storage racks, lockers, etc.

In some public assembly facilities, the inventory control system includes a labeling and numbering scheme whereby each item to which a label and number can be affixed has one. These labels, in addition to identifying the item, may also display a barcode that when scanned provides additional information about the item such as its manufacturer, model number, date of purchase, date of service entry, etc. Some public assembly facilities hire personnel or contract with an inventory control specialist to manage their system.

Similar to an external auditor, the inventory control specialist may randomly spot check selected items from the facility's inventory list. In the event an item is found to be missing or unaccounted for, a thorough and complete accounting of the facility's entire inventory may be mandated. Larger facilities with extensive equipment inventories frequently employ their own full-time inventory control specialist. When this occurs, the inventory control specialist is able to immediately label, number, and barcode each new inventory item and add it to the control list thereby facilitating the ability to conduct periodic checks more frequently in order to verify the presence, location, and condition of all inventory items.

Establishing procedures that address the process for deleting (taking out of service) outdated, non-functional, sold, or traded items from the inventory control list is critical. Creating an inventory of all lock keys and to whom each key is issued is also very important to maintaining the facility's security and access control. A part of the key inventory may also include conducting periodic inspections of all locks and any required maintenance.

It is also important controls be in place for accounting for the receipt and use of materials and supplies. These would include paper goods for restrooms, cleaning supplies, grounds herbicides and fertilizers, office supplies, etc. An inventory system for these areas provides many benefits:

- It records materials when they arrive and informs administration a transaction is complete and payments may be made.

- It records the use of materials and therefore the need to re-order.

- In the case of event-related usage, such as restroom paper goods, the information can identify usage that can be calculated on a per capita (PC) basis. This information is an important management tool in determining the amount of product necessary for an event or series of events. It is also an excellent tool when creating an annual budget. For example, the PC for rock concerts, consumer shows, symphonies, etc., is $X. The budgets project Y number of such events with a total attendance of Z. It is a simple calculation that X times Z equals the amount to budget for these paper products. Of course the number for X would   include any increase or decrease in cost of goods projected during the budget year.

   On an individual event basis, if the product used is to be charged to the tenant, it provides the usage amount. The tenant might be charged on a PC basis, or if an event of several days, such as a religious convocation/convention or consumer show, on a re-stocking basis. The re-stocking approach is simply to be fully stocked at the beginning and end of an event, with the amount of product used to re-stock being the amount on which a charge is calculated.

- The knowledge an inventory system exists also acts as a deterrent to theft or misappropriation and holds management and supervisors responsible for exercising controls.

RISK MANAGEMENT

Together with the event management department and on behalf of the fiscal accountability of the facility's administration, the facility services and operations department is responsible for many safety and risk management tasks. As a part of their risk management duties, facility services and operations must be on continuous alert to remove hazards that may cause accidents. Such tasks might include installing and maintaining flo-rescent tape or paint on steps, de-icing of pedestrian walkways, storage of hazardous materials (HSMAT), maintaining lens screens over light bulbs, etc.

The facility services and operations department is often tasked with the responsibil-ity of being the "keeper" of emergency preparedness and crisis communications plans. Designing evacuation routes, emergency communications, and response systems is oper-ational in nature. Implementation of plans occurs whether the building is occupied or dark. Additional care must be taken to ensure that, in the event of a disaster, programs and records (electronic and hard copy) and/or their duplicates are secured. Business recovery may depend on backup information being stored separately off-site.

Maintaining the facility's compliance with a broad range of regulatory codes is often another responsibility of facility services and operations department. Local regulatory jurisdictions usually will oversee compliance of public assembly facilities in a number of ways, but invariably will refer to various national codes. In the United States, some of the more common are the Occupational Safety & Health Administration (OSHA) regula-tions, which seeks to protect safety and health of workers; the Americans with Disabilities Act (ADA), which protects both employees and patrons from discrimination; and fire, life safety, and building codes such as those developed and recommended by the National Fire Protection Association (NFPA). Other countries have similar code requirements. The facility management and its facility services and operations department are usually the entities assigned this responsibility.

Additionally, the facility services and operations department is responsible for a myr-iad of periodic inspections ranging from elevator maintenance certification to fire extin-guisher validations. Failure to comply with some of these responsibilities not only places the tenant and patron in danger, but also can put the facility in a liability position or financial jeopardy.

The facility services and operations department must pay careful attention to the removal of ice and snow, if present, in order to provide for the safety of employees, users, and guests. Many public assembly facilities do not have adequate equipment to deal with this removal task and consequently enter into a contract for this particular service.

The facility services and operations department should conduct periodic inspection of the electrical, surveillance, security, fire/sprinklers, and smoke detection systems. Auxiliary generators used to produce electric power for emergency lighting and public address systems during periods of electrical outages should be routinely tested and main-tained. It is imperative that, during periods of electrical outages, emergency power be available to provide for the safety of the facility's employees, users, and guests. Emergency power systems are a legal requirement for assembly occupancies in many jurisdictions.

SHIPPING AND RECEIVING

Public assembly facilities host trade shows, exhibitions, or similar activities that require vendors to ship their materials to the facility in advance of the event, and upon its conclusion, to ship their materials back to their place of business or to another site. Facilities of this nature might have a shipping and receiving unit and employ a clerk specifically to oversee the shipping and receiving operation.

The shipping and receiving unit should be adequately staffed and equipped to receive shipments of materials and equipment from delivery services in both a timely and organized manner; to manage an identification system that enables the clerk to connect the equipment with the correct exhibition activity; to stage the materials properly in order to maximize their efficient movement to the exhibition space; to organize the process of removing the materials from the exhibition space at the end of the event and prepare them for shipping; and to manage the required documentation activities associated with the receiving and shipping processes. It is not unusual for trade and/or exhibit events to use a private contractor to perform these functions.

MARSHALLING AND STAGING YARDS

Some events may require significant space dedicated to a support function for "staging" the event or performance. Such areas may be reserved for queuing purpose of contestants, such as in motor sports, herding or sorting of animal acts, or rodeo performers, or simply for overnight parking of touring circus vehicles.

Apart from managing advance shipments of exhibitor's materials, the shipping and receiving unit is usually responsible for accepting, inspecting, and certifying deliveries of materials and equipment related to the general operation of the public assembly facility. Providing a central location at the facility for receiving shipped materials is essential. In some cases, particularly with hazardous materials or under extreme security alerts, separate, even off-site, facilities will be dedicated to screening materials destined for the venue.

Having established policies and procedures for receiving, documenting, and distributing delivered shipments offers all parties an additional level of protection. Appropriate shipping and receiving policies and procedures also facilitate the transfer of item ownership and provides an additional monitoring opportunity for the shipping and receiving clerk, as well as the facility services and operations manager.

SUMMARY

It is the responsibility of the facility services and operations managers and staff to keep the public assembly facility safe, clean, and inviting. A well-maintained environment is critical to providing a satisfactory environment for guests and clients. Safety must be a first consideration in every facility services and operations decision, as well as providing event-related services with a high quality of guest relations skills. Management must create, implement, and monitor programs designed to train all full-time and part-time staff on how to meet and exceed client/guest expectations. Facility services and operations, as one of the "core components" of a venue, is the division or department of the public assembly facility responsible for delivering services promised to the client and guests. Charged with the care and stewardship of the physical plant, this department must maintain and plan for replacement of the physical assets of the facility. Risk management and emergency preparedness are core components of this department's mission.

REFERENCES AND ADDITIONAL READINGS

Convention Industry Council. 2000. *The Convention Industry Council (CIC) Manual,* 7th ed. McLean, VA: Convention Industry Council.

Donovan, Harry. 2002. *Arena Rigging: A Practical Guide for Riggers, Designers & Managers.* Seattle, WA: Rigging Seminars.

Feldman, Edwin B. 2000. *Managing Housekeeping and Custodial Operations Handbook.* Latham, NY: National Trade Publications.

Glerum, Jay O. 1997. *Stage Rigging Handbook,* 2nd ed. Carbondale, IL: Southern Illinois University Press.

Lewis, Bernard T. 1999. *Facility Manager's Operation and Maintenance Handbook.* New York, NY: McGraw-Hill.

Robbe, Deborah. 1999. *Expositions and Trade Shows.* New York, NY: John Wiley & Sons, Inc.

Rondeau, Edmond P., Robert Kevin Brown, and Paul D. Lapides. 1995. *Facility Management.* New York, NY: John Wiley & Sons.

Wireman, Terry. 1999. *Developing Performance Indicators for Managing Maintenance.* New York, NY: Industrial Press.

APPENDIX A

ILLUSTRATIONS

———— **FIGURE 3-5** ————

GLOBAL SPECTRUM
MANAGING FACILITIES WORLDWIDE
636-946-7776 • 800-366-2427

LICENSE APPLICATION

The following information is requested by the St. Charles Convention Center management to assist in the review and consideration of your request for lease of the Convention Center facilities. The accuracy and completeness of the information provided below are very important insofar as this information will be a critical factor in considering your request. Be as detailed and specific as possible. Until Convention Center management officially approves this application and a formal License Agreement is fully executed, there is no legal or binding commitment between the Convention Center and the rental applicant.

EVENT NAME: _____

TYPE OF EVENT: Consumer Show ☐   Trade Show ☐   Convention ☐   Other ☐ (describe below)

EVENT DESCRIPTION: _____

ESTIMATED DAILY ATTENDANCE: _____

SPACE REQUESTED: _____

DATES REQUESTED (specify ingress/egress and event): _____

REQUESTED EVENT AND INGRESS/EGRESS TIMES: _____

PAID ADMISSION EVENT: Yes ☐   No ☐   If yes, state ticket prices: $ _____

NAME OF LICENSING ORGANIZATION: _____

Address: _____

City: _____   State: _____   Zip: _____

Tax I.D. Number: _____   Or SSN: _____

NAME & TITLE OF PERSON WHO WILL SIGN THE LICENSE AGREEMENT: _____

HOW DID YOU LEARN OF THE CONVENTION CENTER? _____

LICENSE APPLICATION - PAGE 2

BANK & CREDIT REFERENCES:

1. _____
        Name   Telephone Number   Account Number

2. _____
        Name   Telephone Number   Account Number

3. _____
        Name   Telephone Number   Account Number

REFERENCES WITHIN INDUSTRY:

1. _____
        Name   Company   Telephone Number

2. _____
        Name   Company   Telephone Number

3. _____
        Name   Company   Telephone Number

PREVIOUS EVENTS:
(List name and type of show, when it was held, facility contact name and phone number)

1. _____

2. _____

3. _____

OTHER COMMENTS: _____

SIGNATURE: _____
                    Name   Title   Date

Reprinted with permission of Saint Charles Convention Center and Global Spectrum.

——— FIGURE 4-2 ———

Show Title
Marketing Settlement
Engagement Date

	GROSS	NET	
I. Advertising			
Print:			
1. Inquirer (Trade $41,032.44)		$ 33,771.48	
2. Courier Post		$ 3,964.90	
3. News Journal (Trade: $4,793.40)		$ 2,377.50	
4. Tribune		$ 1,133.76	
5. Metro		$ 650.00	
6. NIE		$ 3,500.00	
7. Times		$ 916.38	
Total Print		$ 46,314.02	$ 46,314.02
Television:			
1. ABC	$ 30,000.00	$ 25,500.00	
2. FOX	$ 30,000.00	$ 25,500.00	
3. WB17 (Trade $1,000)	$ 23,025.00	$ 19,571.25	
4. Comcast Cable (Trade $16,000)	$ 16,000.00	$ 13,600.00	
5. PBS	$ 3,000.00	$ 3,000.00	
Total Television:	$ 102,025.00	$ 87,171.25	$ 87,171.25
Radio:			
1. B101 ($1,325 Trade)	$ 13,000.00	$ 11,050.00	
2. 92.5 ($1,255 trade)	$ 4,995.00	$ 4,245.75	
3. Q102 ($5,500 Trade)	$ 12,000.00	$ 10,200.00	
Total Radio:	$ 29,995.00	$ 25,495.75	$ 25,495.75
Outdoor:			
1. Clear Channel Outdoor (Trade = $1,500)	$ 10,500.00	$ 8,925.00	
2. Printing		$ 4,178.65	
Total Outdoor	$ 10,500.00	$ 13,103.65	$ 13,103.65
Total Advertising			$ 172,084.67
II. Event Services			
1. Postage 5,750 Club Box Postcards @ $.20	$ 1,150.00		
2. Mailhouse production 6,000 Club Box Postcards	$ 790.00		
3. Postage 13,727 Group Brochures @ $.22	$ 3,019.94		
4. Mailhouse production 20,000 Group Brochures	$ 875.00		
5. Postage Scout Brochures @ $3.50	$ 87.50		
6. Graphic Services 10,000 Prefered Mailers	$ 1,001.48		
7. Market Data Retrieval for School Lists	$ 1,026.44		
8. Club Box/Group Order Forms	$ 1,000.00		
9. Postage 150 school reminders @ $.37	$ 52.50		
10. Postage 4,600 chamber club fliers @ $.37	$ 1,717.00		
11. Postage 1,589 past purchaser reminder fliers @ $.37	$ 587.93		
12. Event services mailing labels	$ 124.00		
13. Event services envelopes	$ 310.00		
14. AAA ad	$ 100.00		
15. 15,000 Copies of show fliers	$ 525.00		
16. Postage 5,000 Preferred Mailers @ $.22	$ 1,100.00		
17. Part time telemarketing	$ 1,440.00		
Total Event Services:	$ 14,906.79		$ 14,906.79
III. Public Relations			
1. Invitations 150 @ .37	$ 55.50		
2. Fed Ex Press invitations	$ 7.96		
3. Fed Ex B-roll	$ 9.64		
4. Add'l invitations	$ 3.17		
5. Press kit	$ 3.95		
6. Blast Service	$ 300.00		
7. Press Invitations	$ 540.00		

Continued on next page

Show Title
Marketing Settlement
Engagement Date

8. Aramark Press Breakfast	$ 516.00		
9. Aramark a.m. TV food	$ 279.40		
10. About Balloons	$ 196.18		
11. About Balloons	$ 107.30		
12. Publicity Trip 8/29	$ 101.50		
13. Publicity Trip 8/30	$ 86.50		
14. Expense Report #1	$ 21.60		
15. Expense Report #2	$ 54.23		
16. Expense Report #3	$ 214.46		
17. Expense Report #4	$ 390.95		
18. Expense Report #5	$ 9.72		
Total Public Relations	**$ 2,898.06**		**$ 2,898.06**
IV. Complex Marketing Miscellaneous:			
1. Graphic Services	$ 2,030.00		
2. Radio Production (2nd Street)	$ 360.00		
3. S.A.L.P.	$ 372.44		
4. Expense report #1	$ 11.75		
5. Expense report #2	$ 52.58		
6. Aramark- sponsor suite catering	$ 181.52		
7. Fed Ex Mailings	$ 768.11		
8. Grassroots Team	$ 2,000.00		
Total Miscellaneous	**$ 5,776.40**		**$ 5,776.40**
V. Promoter Miscellaneous\Promotional Expenses:			
1. Direct Mail	$ 27,099.98		
2. Prep Cost	$ 249.50		
3. Display Materials	$ 7,526.54		
4. General Printing	$ 23.50		
5. PR expenses	$ 681.29		
6. Group Sales expense	$ 4,231.23		
7. Misc. Promo expense	$ 4,092.82		
9. MSM expense	$ 50.62		
10. Ad Production	$ 9,987.00		
11. Newspaper	$ 6.00		
12. Outdoor	$ 410.12		
Total Promoter Misc.	**$ 54,358.60**		**$ 54,358.60**
VI. Agency Fee\Expenses:			
1. Agency Fee (flat or % of gross placed)	N/A		
TOTAL AGENCY:	**$ -**		**$ -**
VII. Creative Fee			
1. Creative Fee			
$ per show	N/A		
TOTAL CREATIVE	**$ -**		**$ -**
VIII. Shares/Donations			
1. Ronald McDonald House	$ 4,000.00		
Total Shares	**$ 4,000.00**		**$ 4,000.00**
Recap:			
I. Advertising	$ 172,084.67		
II. Event Services	$ 14,906.79		
III. Public Relations	$ 2,898.06		
IV. Miscellaneous	$ 5,776.40		
V. Promoter Miscellaneous	$ 54,358.60		
VI. Agency Fee	$ -		

Continued on next page

Show Title
Marketing Settlement
Engagement Date

VII. Creative Fee	$ -		
VIII. Shares/Donations	$ 4,000.00		
TOTAL EXPENSES:	**$ 254,024.52**		
Advertising Add Backs			
1. ABC CO	$ 15,750.00		
2. XYZ CO	$ 3,250.00		
3. MMM CO	$ 1,250.00		
4. WILL CO	$ 7,000.00		
Total Advertising Add Backs	**$ 27,250.00**		
Reimbursable to Promoter:			
1. Promoter Miscellaneous\Production	$ 54,358.60		
2. Creative Fee	$ -		
Total Promoter Reimbursement	**$ 54,358.60**		
Reimbursable to Agency:			
1. Advertising	$ 172,084.67		
2. Event Services	$ 14,906.79		
3. Public Relations	$ 2,898.06		
4. Complex Miscellaneous	$ 5,776.40		
5. Shares/Donations	$ 4,000.00		
6. Agency Fees/Commissions	$ -		
TOTAL COMPLEX REIMBURSE:	**$ 199,665.92**		
TOTAL MARKETING EXPENSES	**$ 254,024.52**		
LESS SPONSORSHIP AD BACKS	**$ 27,250.00**		
Total expenses less adbacks:	**$ 226,774.52**		

Approved by Promoter:

_____

Signature   **Date**

_____

Print Name and Title

—————— FIGURE 4-3 ——————

RUN OF SCHEDULE

MEDIA	THU 1	FRI 2	SAT 3	SUN 4	MON 5	TUE 6	WED 7	THU 8	FRI 9	SAT 10	SUN 11	MON 12	TUE 13	WED 14	THU 15	FRI 16	SAT 17	SUN 18	MON 19	TUE 20	WED 21	THU 22	FRI 23	SAT 24	SUN 25	MON 26	TUE 27	WED 28	THU 29	FRI 30	Daypart	Total # Spots	Rate / Unit	Total Gross
KBUL 98.1 FM					5	5	5					5	5	5					5	5	5										ROS	45X	$43.00	$1,935
KOH 780 AM					5	5	5					5	5	5					5	5	5										ROS	45X	$40.00	$1,800
KRNO 106.9 FM												5	5	5					5	5	5										ROS	30X	$42.00	$1,260
KTHX 100.1 FM					5	5	5					5	5	5					5	5	5										ROS	45X	$35.00	$1,575
KJZS 92.1 FM					7	7	7					7	7	7					7	7	7										ROS	63X	$10.00	$630
KOZZ 105.7 FM					5	5	5					5	5																		ROS	25X	$40.00	$1,000
TOTAL																																253X		$8,200

ACPS=$32.41

FIGURE 5-4

SCALING THE HOUSE

Concert Hall
Capacity 2812
with Pit Seats

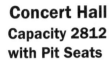

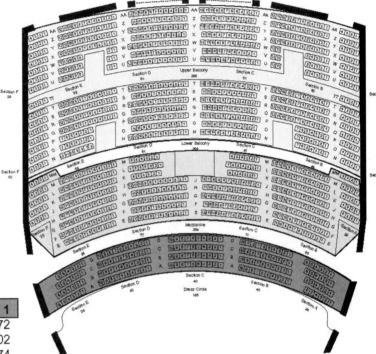

Three Tier
Pricing Option

Price Level 1
Dress Circle 172
Main Floor Rows A-L 402
Total Seats = 574

Price Level 2
Main Floor Rows M-Z 696
Mezzanine 384
Total Seats = 1,080

Price Level 3
Main Floor Rows AA-JJ 406
Lower Balcony 364
Upper Balcony 356
Total Seats = 1,126

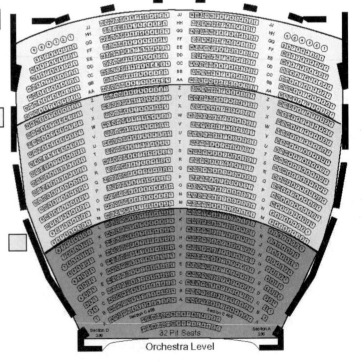

Orchestra Level

—————— FIGURE 5-5 ——————

ADA ACCESS SEATS

The Center
Access Seats

We have installed sixty two (62) ADA access seats in the Auditorium.

First, it is necessary to put the Access Seats in a hold status when tickets go on sale in order to serve those who need this particular accommodation.

Second, it is necessary to put additional seats, adjacent to the Access Seats, in a hold status when tickets go on sale in order to provide companion seating.

It is The Center's policy to hold the Access Seats as long as possible. This is interpreted to mean until:
1. They are requested by a qualified individual.
2. They are the last unsold seats in
    a. that price range.
    b. that location (main floor or balcony).

It is The Center's policy to hold Companion Seats as long as possible. This is interpreted to mean until:
1. They are requested by an individual qualified to purchase an Access Seat and are purchased in conjunction with an Access Seat.
2. They are the last unsold seats in
    a. that price range and are released when the adjacent Access Seat is released.
    b. that location (main floor or balcony) and are released when the adjacent seat is released.

Enclosed is a list of the actual Access Seats, in which the armrest can be lifted to allow the access, and the Companion Seats. Please note some seats are accessible from the right side of the seat and some from the left side of the seat.

Companion Seats to hold are listed under the Companion Seat column.

We appreciate your attention to this information and help in meeting the requirements of the Americans with Disabilities Act.

MAIN FLOOR

Left Hand Arm (24)			Companion Seats			Right Hand Arm			Companion Seats		
Section	Row	Seat	Section	Row	Seat	Section	Row	Seat	Section	Row	Seat
3	D	7	3	D	5	3	E	1	3	E	3
	F	11		F	9		G	1		G	3
	H	13		H	11		H	1		H	3
	K	15		K	13		L	1		L	3
	M	17		M	15		N	1		N	3
	O	19		O	17		P	1		P	3
	R	21		R	19		R	1		R	3
	T	25		T	23						
						4	D	8	4	D	6
4	E	2	4	E	4		F	12		F	10
	G	2		G	4		H	14		H	12
	H	2		H	4		K	16		K	14
	L	2		L	4		M	18		M	16
	N	2		N	4		O	20		O	18
	P	2		P	4		R	22		R	20
						5	D	1	5	D	3
5	D	7	5	D	5		G	1		G	3
	F	9		F	7	6	F	10	6	F	8
	H	13		H	11		G	12		G	10
	K	15		K	13		J	14		J	12
	M	17		M	15		L	16		L	14
	O	19		O	17		M	18		M	16
	R	21		R	19		P	20		P	18
	T	23		T	21		S	24		S	22
6	H	2	6	H	4		U	26		U	24

FIGURE 5-6

Civic Center
Box Office Statement

ngagement____   Play Dates_____November 14, 200X
how_____Saturday, November 15, 200X

le pac	Manifest Cap	Free Passes	Passes and Special Rates G-Type	T-Type	TOT Not Sold at Full Price	TOT Sold	Tick Price	House Receipts
	2226	32			55	2139	22.75	48662.25
	5468	209			1130	4129	18.75	77418.75
								00.00
								00.00
								00.00
								00.00
								00.00
								00.00
tal	7694	241	0	0 0	1185	6268		

	Total House Receipts	126081.00

t cket Price	State Tax	TOT State Tax	City Tax	TOT City Tax
.06	1.26	2695.14	0.42	898.38
.36	1.04	4294.16	0.35	1445.15
00	0.00	0.00	0.00	0.00
00	0.00	0.00	0.00	0.00
00	0.00	0.00	0.00	0.00
00	0.00	0.00	0.00	0.00
00	0.00	0.00	0.00	0.00
00	0.00	0.00	0.00	0.00
00	0.00	0.00	0.00	0.00

Less State Amusement Tax	6989.30
Less City Amusement Tax	2343.53
Total Net	116748.17
Less City B & O Tax	583.74
Total Final Net	116164.43

eather: Cold/Cloudy   Temp: 28 degrees

	Number	Dollars
vance	6268	126081.00
sh	0	0.00
al	6268	126081.00

endance

	Today	To Date
d	6268	6268
mp	241	241
al	6509	6509

	Total	Total To Date
Gross Receipts	126081.00	126081.00
St. Amuse. Tax	6989.30	6989.30
Ct. Amuse. Tax	2343.53	2343.53
Total Net	116748.17	116748.17
City B&O Tax	583.74	583.74
Final Net	116164.43	116164.43

We certify that we have personally checked
the above statement and it is in every way correct.

_____

—————— FIGURE 6-1 ——————

IAAM ARENA
INCOME STATEMENT
APRIL 30, 200X

OPERATNG REVENUES	MONTH ENDING	YEAR TO DATE
RENT	60,000	400,000
REIMBURSED EXPENSES	26,000	310,000
CONCESSIONS	80,000	520,000
CATERING	24,000	280,000
ADVERTISING	10,000	100,000
COMMISSIONS	6,000	40,000
MISCELLANEOUS	0	5,000
TOTAL OPERATING REVENUES	206,000	1,655,000
OPERATING EXPENSES		
EXPENSES	185,000	1,485,000
INCOME FROM OPERATIONS	21,000	170,000
NON-OPERATING INCOME / DEDUCTIONS		
INTEREST INCOME	3,000	29,000
HOTEL / MOTEL TAX	16,000	141,000
CC RENEWAL / REPLACEMENT FUND	(3,000)	(30,000)
TOTAL NON-OPERATING	16,000	140,000
INCOME / DEDUCTIONS		
NET INCOME (LOSS)	37,000	310,000
PRIOR SURPLUS	2,248,000	2,100,000
HOTEL / MOTEL TAX	(16,000)	(141,000)
SURPLUS	2,269,000	2,269,000

FIGURE 6-2

IAAM ARENA
BALANCE SHEET
MONTH ENDING APRIL 30, 200X

ASSETS

CURRENT ASSETS
CASH	36,000
PETTY CASH	1,000
PAYROLL FUND	0
TEMPORARY INVESTMENT	8,000
ACCOUNTS RECEIVABLE	334,000
INVENTORY	128,000
	33,000

TOTAL CURRENT ASSETS 540,000

SUNDRY ASSETS
PREPAYMENTS	20,000
DEPOSITS	8,000

TOTAL SUNDRY ASSETS 28,000

FIXED ASSETS
BUILDING EQUIPMENT	190,000
KITCHEN EQUIPMENT	218,000
CONCESSION EQUIPMENT	132,000
TOOLS	24,000
BOX OFFICE EQUIPMENT	16,000
OFFICE EQUIPMENT	36,000
COMMUNICATIONS EQUIPMENT	51,000
TRANSPORTATION EQUIPMENT	64,000
BUILDING IMPROVEMENTS	4,801,000

TOTAL FIXED ASSETS 5,532,000

TOTAL ASSETS 6,100,000

LIABILITIES AND EQUITY

CURRENT LIABILITIES
ACCOUNTS PAYABLE	164,000
NOTES PAYABLE	100,000
LOAN PAYABLE	60,000
CONSUMER SALES TAX	4,000
F.I.C.A.	2,000
WORKERS COMPENSATION	1,000
ADVANCE DEPOSITS	0

TOTAL CURRENT LIABILITIES 331,000

EQUITY
HOTEL / MOTEL TAX	2,000,000
CONTRIBUTIONS	1,500,000
SURPLUS	2,269,000

TOTAL EQUITY 5,769,000

TOTAL CURRENT LIBABILITIES AND EQUITY 6,100,000

──────── FIGURE 6-3 ────────

IAAM Arena
Detail Revenue/Expense Statement

ACC#	Account Title	This month	Year to Date
	Operating Revenues		
500	Rent	60,000	400,000
510	Concessions	80,000	520,000
515	Catering	24,000	280,000
520	Reimbursed Expenses	26,000	310,000
530	Advertising	10,000	100,000
540	Miscellaneous	0	5,000
550	Commissions	6,000	40,000
	TOTAL OPERATIONS REVENUE	206,000	1,655,000
	Operating Expenses		
	Building Maintenance		
601	Supervision	4,000	48,000
602	Labor	10,000	120,000
603	Building Maintenance	100	8,000
604	Equipment Maintenance	1,000	8,000
605	Operations	1,700	35,000
606	Office Expenses	100	300
607-A	Electric	7,000	88,000
607-B	Water/Sewer/Etc.	1,100	12,700
607-C	Gas	13,600	50,000
	TOTAL BUILDING MAINTENANCE	38,600	370,000
	Concessions		
611	Supervisions	2,000	20,000
612	Labor	5,000	28,500
614	Equipment Maintenance	500	800
615	Operations	300	300
616	Office Expenses	200	400
617	Food Supplies	22,000	160,000
	TOTAL CONCESSIONS	30,000	210,000
	Catering		
621	Supervision	2,000	20,000
622	Labor	5,000	68,800
624	Equipment Maintenance	400	1,000
625	Operations	300	16,000
626	Office Expenses	100	200
627	Food Supplies	8,200	94,000
628	Contracted Services	0	0
	TOTAL CATERING	16,000	200,000
	Event Operations		
631	Supervision	1,500	15.000
632	Ushers	4,000	34,000
633	Ticket Takers	5,000	36,000
634	Equipment Rentals	1,000	4,000
635	Operations	6,000	60,000
636	Security	3,500	21,000
637	Materials & Supplies	2,000	42,000
638	Spots & Stagehands	16,400	81,000
	TOTAL EVENT OPERATIONS	39,400	293,000

Continued on next page

REVENUE/EXPENSE STATEMENT - CONTINUED

	Box Office		
641	Supervision	2,500	20,000
642	Labor	5,000	28,000
643	Outlet Expenses	300	600
644	Equipment Maintenance	200	500
646	Office Expenses	300	900
647	Advertising/Promotion Expenses	17,700	50,000
648	Contract Fees	0	0
649	Equipment Rental	0	0
	TOTAL BOX OFFICE	26,000	100,000
	Administrative		
661	Supervision	6,000	45,000
662	Labor	4,000	28,000
663	Insurance	5,400	58,000
664	Equipment Maintenance	200	400
665	Telephone	1,000	12,000
666	Office Expenses	600	8,000
667	Travel	750	6,000
668	Legal Services	0	2,200
669	Misc. Administrative Expenses	50	400
	TOTAL ADMINISTRATIVE	18,000	160,000
	Accounting		
671	Supervision	500	10,000
672	Labor	1,800	7,000
673	Payroll Services	300	7,000
674	Equipment Maintenance	100	1,000
676	Office Expenses	200	1,000
677	Audit Expenses	100	6,000
679	Federal / State Tax Expense	0	0
	TOTAL ACCOUNTING	3,000	32,000
	Employee Welfare Expenses		
681	Vacation / Holiday	0	0
682	Sick Leave	400	1,200
683	Unemployment Insurance	700	3,000
684	Group Insurance	4,000	34,000
685	FICA	4,800	37,400
686	Workers Compensation	2,800	21,000
687	Education / Seminars	300	7,400
688	Pension	1,000	6,000
689	Miscellaneous	0	10,000
	TOTAL EMPLOYEE WELFARE EXP.	14,000	120,000
	TOTAL OPERATING EXPENSES	**185,000**	**1,485,000**

──────── FIGURE 6-4 ────────

EVENT FINANCIAL SETTLEMENT STATEMENT

MID-SIZE ARENA EVENT SETTLEMENT STATEMENT			
EVENT: HEAVY METAL ROCK 'N ROLL CONCERT DATE: PROMOTER:			
DESCRIPTION OF ACTIVITY		AMOUNT	TOTALS
INCOME			
Gross Ticket Sales		322,204.50	
TOTAL INCOME			$ 322,204.50
EXPENSES			
Facility Rental Fee (12% capped @ $18,000)		18,000.00	
Box Office Commission (4% capped @ $2,000)		2,000.00	
Stage Labor-Hands, Riggers, Electrician, Runners		7,511.89	
Custodial-Set-Up, Show, Clean-Up		2,880.15	
Guest Services-Ushers, Ticket Takers, T-Shirt Security		4,980.20	
Uniformed Police		3,030.00	
Parking Services-Attendants		1,014.25	
Emergency Medical Services		450.00	
City Fire Expenses		551.20	
Show Expenses:		-	
Forklift Rental		298.25	
CO-2 Refills		155.06	
Telephone Line Installation		600.00	
Pyro Technicial		300.00	
Vehicle Rental #1		150.00	
Vehicle Rental #2		30.00	
Vehicle Rental #3		190.00	
Dressing Room Furniture Rental		282.00	
City Business License		65.00	
City Floor Plan Approval		120.00	
City Pyro Permit		150.00	
TOTAL EXPENSES		$ 42,758.00	
NET INCOME			$ 279,446.50
TOTAL AMOUNT DUE AT FINAL SETTLEMENT			$ 279,446.50
AGREED			
Promoter		Facility Management	
Date		Date	

———— FIGURE 7-5 ————

EVENT EVALUATION FORMS TO DETERMINE ALCOHOL SALES

Toby Keith Concert

Event Date(s):   Doors Open at: 7:00 p.m.   Event Starts at: 8:00 p.m.

Event Ends at: 10:00 p.m.

	Sport	Flat Show	O Ent.	Concert*
Type				x
Comment				

	Rock	Pop	C&W	Other
Concert Type*			x	

	Low Key	Variable	Exciting	
Intensity			x	
Comment				

	Light	Competitive	Aggressive
Energy	x		
Comment			

	Lax	Informal	Formal
Decorum		x	
Comment			

	Under 25	25-35	Over 35
Age		x	
Comment			

	Male	Female	Non-Specific
Gender		x	
Comment			

	No Alcohol	Neutral	Alcohol
Expectation			x
Comment			

	Under 2,000	2-3,000	3-4,000	4-5,000	Over 5,000
Attendance Projected					x
Comment					

	Family	Couple	Friend Group
Attendance Pattern		x	
Comment			

	Flat	Floor Only	Balcony Only
Seating Configuration			
	Festival Floor	Seated Floor	Tables Floor
	x		

Reported Incidents
History: No reported incidents, high energy show, sell-out crowds.
Other Comments/Factors: Beer Garden area is too small to control and accommodate a sell-out crowd.

Toby Keith Concert
Security Needs and Alcohol Sales

EVENT PROFILE

Type	C&W Con.	**History:**	
Intensity	Exciting	No reported incidents, high energy show, sell-out crowds.	
Energy	Light		
Decorum	Informal		
Age	25-35		
Gender	Female	**Other Comments:**	
Expectation	Alcohol	Beer Garden area is too small to control and accommodate crowd.	
Attendance Projected	Over 5,000	Recommendation: Allow patrons to carry beverages to balcony	
Attendance Pattern	Couple	seats but not to floor.	
Seating Configuration	S - Floor		
Will Alcohol Be Sold?	Y N		

If yes:

Alcohol Sales

# of POS	POS Locations/	ID Checking	Products Sold	Start Sales	End Sales
1	Sky Club	at bar	all	w/ doors	10:00 PM
1	B Concourse	assisted	b&w only		9:30 PM
1	C Concourse	assisted	b&w only		9:30 PM
Total 3					

Security

	Uniformed Officers	T-Shirt Security	Professional Event Staff
Number:	6	2 0	0
Stations:	Roaming	Floor - 6	
		Vomitories -10	
		Lobby - 4	

These forms were authored by Mary Muse, Executive Director for The Adams Center at The University of Montana, Missoula in 2003, published in 2004.

———— **FIGURE 8-9** ————

DEFINING CROWD MANAGERS

IAAM conducted a study on staffing responsibilities for crowd management and identified the following roles:

Four levels of crowd management responsibility were identified:

1. *Crowd Assembly Facilitator (CAF)*—front-line event staff providing direct services to patrons. Example job titles are usher, ticket taker, parking attendant, peer security.

2. *Crowd Assembly Supervisor*—During an event, CAFs report to the Crowd Assembly Supervisor, who oversees activities of CAFs during an event.

3. *Crowd Management Administrator*—Professional staff person with necessary experience and expertise to design and implement all facility security, crowd management, and emergency preparation activities.

4. *Crowd Management Instructor*—A crowd management professional, trained under an IAAM-endorsed curriculum, who has the knowledge and skills to develop and conduct in-facility training programs for Crowd Assembly Facilitators and Crowd Assembly Supervisors. Instructors may be regular staff or consultants.

Staffing Definition
Crowd Assembly Facilitator
Crowd assembly facilitators assist facility or event administrators in providing a safe and enjoyable environment for their guests by implementing the facility/event policies and procedures. Crowd assembly facilitator duties include contributing to the safety of facility and event, managing the movement and activities of crowd/guests, assisting in emergencies, assisting guests with specific concerns related to their enjoyment and/or involvement with the event by communicating with the guests in a polite and professional manner.

Duties of a Crowd Assembly Facilitator
<u>Training</u>
Knowledge of event and facilities.
Perform communications function.
Risk management.
Crowd dynamics management.
Assist guests.
Implement facility/event policies and procedures.
Conflict identification and mitigation.
Major emergency response.

<u>Assisting Guests</u>
Maximize accessibility to guests.
Anticipate guests' needs.
Use good guest service techniques.
Answer questions or assist to find answers.
Provide direction to appropriate locations.
Respond to guest concerns.

Continued on next page

Implement Facility/Guest Policies and Procedures
Learn and apply appropriate policies and procedures.
Observe violations of policies and procedures and report to supervisor.
Inform guests of violations of policies and procedures and ensuing consequences.
Review policies and procedures as appropriate.
Proactively monitor changes to policies and procedures.
Report problems not addressed in policies and procedures to supervisor.

Risk Management
Participate in pre-event orientations.
Conduct pre-event review of assigned work area.
Review check-list of safety hazards.
Identify and mitigate safety hazards and report to supervisor.
Confirm assigned work area and equipment readiness to supervisor.
Operate and maneuver equipment in safe manner.
Report incidents and property damage to supervisor.
Identify, mitigate and report medical emergencies to supervisor.
Return assigned equipment in good working order.

Crowd Dynamics Management
Adjust to crowd demographics.
Anticipate crowd activities and behavior.
Maintain the usability of means of egress.
Make guests aware of their responsibilities.
Observe crowd for potential problems and report to supervisor.
Monitor flow of crowd during duration of event.
Identify changing crowd behavior and demeanor and report to supervisor.

Knowledge of Event and Facilities
Review schedule of event activities.
Review venue/event diagram.
Review event specific policies and procedures.
Review event specific alcohol policies and procedures.
Review specific event ticketing and credentialing policies.
Familiarize oneself with event seating requirements.
Familiarize oneself with type and activities of the event.
Identify key event/facility personnel.
Maintain control of limited access areas.

Conflict Identification and Mitigation
Identify credential/ticketing/seating problems.
React according to policies and procedures regarding problem guests.
Mitigate credential/ticketing/seating problems.
Resolve guest complaints/problems.
Avoid arguments with guests.
Avoid physical contact with guests.

Continued on next pa

Training
Attend employment orientation.
Fulfill certification as legally required.
Attend facility/event orientation.
Fulfill specific facility training requirements.
Read assigned and posted material.
Attend pre and post event briefing sessions.
Participate in job assignment training from supervisor at events.
Maintain focus on role during event.
Share competence with other employees.
Interact positively with guests and employees.
Follow chain of command.
Attend continuing education as appropriate.
Participate in on-going training.
Participate in performance evaluation.

Perform Communications Function
Employ good listening skills.
Adapt communication to crowd diversity.
Adhere to proper written and verbal communication channels.
Follow supervisor instruction.
Utilize proper written, verbal, and non-verbal communication techniques.
Report communication breakdowns to supervisor.
Be competent with communication equipment.
Keep communication relevant.
Utilize event/facility terminology.
Communicate with all personnel associated with the event.
Maintain the integrity of confidential information.
Recognize non-verbal crowd communication.
Utilize signage in communication process.
Respond appropriately to all public address announcements.
Complete required written documentation.

Major Emergency Response
Maintain guest safety as a priority.
Assist guests with special needs.
Follow appropriate instructions applicable to fire, weather, earthquake,
crowd incidents, terrorism, hazardous materials, transportation mishaps, and power loss.
Participate in drills.
Report all fires immediately regardless of size.
Permit individual guests to leave if they wish during an emergency.
Execute assigned tasks or responsibilities as provided in event of emergency.
Provide appropriate information.

Definitions for other staff roles can be found at: http://www.iaam.org/CVMS/CVMSsafety.htm

FIGURE 8-10

INCIDENT REPORT

DATE ___April 4, 1997___   TIME OF INCIDENT _8:00 p.m._
                                  TIME OF REPORT _8:05 p.m._

LOCATION: (Lower Level)   Sect. ___12___
             Mezzanine Level   Row _____
             Upper Level   Seat(s) _____
             Bleachers   Concourse _____
             Parking Lot _____
             Concession Stand _____
             Other _____

TYPE: Altercation   T.E.A.M. Player
             Foul Ball   Abusive Language
             Alcohol Possession   Other _____
             (Fall)

EMPLOYEE   Bob Smith   BADGE # _234_

DESCRIPTION OF SUBJECT

RACE _____   SEX _____   HEIGHT _____   WEIGHT _____
HAIR COLOR _____   EYE COLOR _____

SUBJECT AND WITNESS INFORMATION

SUBJECT'S NAME _Jan Mason_____
ADDRESS ___1234 Bay Street, Apt. 4_____
CITY ___San Francisco_____ STATE _CA__ ZIP CODE _94904_
PHONE NUMBER _____
STATEMENT _"I slipped on some kind of liquid. I hurt my back."_
_____
_____
_____

WITNESS' NAME __John Mason___ RELATION TO SUBJECT __Husband__
ADDRESS _Same as above_____
CITY _____ STATE _____ ZIP CODE _____
PHONE NUMBER ___( ) same_____
STATEMENT __"I heard a noise and looked back and she was on the__
_____ground."_____

This sample incident report was excerpted from the TEAM Training Manual.
TEAM (Techniques for Effective Alcohol Management) Coalition is a non profit
organization promoting responsible drinking and positive fan behavior at sports
and entertainment facilities.

FIGURE 9-1

PRODUCTION RIDER

SHOW ADVANCE

SHOW DATE(S): _____   VENUE: _____   CITY: _____

LABOR CALLS

LOAD IN: 9:00 AM	SECOND CALL: _____	SHOW CALL: 6:00 PM	LOAD OUT: 10:00 PM

STEWARD: _____	HANDS: _____	STEWARD: _____	STEWARD: _____
HEADS: _____	RUNNERS: _____	DECK HANDS: 6	HEADS: _____
LOADERS: 4	PROD. ASST. _____	HOUSE SPOTS: 4	LOADERS: 4
HANDS: 18		ELEC/HSE LTS: 1	HANDS: 22
UP RIGGERS: 4			UP RIGGERS: 4
DN RIGGERS: 1			DN RIGGERS: 1
ELECTRICIAN: 1		LOAD OUT: 9:00 PM	ELECTRICIAN: 1
FORK OPS: 1			FORK OPS: _____
RUNNERS: 3		FORK OPS: 1	
		LOADERS: 4	

RUNNING TIMES

SOUND CHECK NFG:	3:00 PM	Band 1	6:30 PM - 6:50 PM
SOUND CHECK GC:	4:00 PM	Band 2	7:10 PM - 7:40 PM
SOUND CHECK OP:	5:00 PM	Band 3	8:10 PM - 9 PM
DOORS:	5:30 PM	Headliner	9:30 PM - 10:20 PM
SECURITY MEETING:	4:00 PM	CURFEW:	10:30 PM

STAGE AND FOH RISERS / POWER / SPOTS / BARRICADE

STAGE SIZE:	60'w x 40'd x 5'h	FOH SOUND POSITION:	16'w x 16'd x 0'h
SL WING:	16'w x 24'd x 4'h		on floor at 75' from DS
SR WING:	16'w x 24'd x 5'h		
	wings recessed 4'	FOH LIGHT RISER:	12'w x 8'd x 2'h
			directly behind sound
UPSTAGE WING:			
		RIGGING POINTS:	14 Lights, 6 Sound
AUDIO POWER:	200 Amp & 50 Amp	BARRICADE:	tour carrying 120'
LIGHTING POWER:	400 Amp & 200 Amp		we will need bike rack for FOH
	120/208 Volt 3Phz, 5 Wire		
		SPOTS:	Require 4 FOH spots

VEHICLE INFO / PARKING

# PRODUCTION TRUCKS:	3	# BAND BUSES:	2
# MERCH TRUCKS:	2	# CREW BUSES:	2
# SPONS FOH TRUCKS:	2	# SPONSOR BUSES:	1
TRAILER ON BUS:	1	# SUPPORT BUSES:	1
AND:	Van & Trailer	RUNNER VEHICLES:	3

Page 1

PRODUCTION RIDER - CONTINUED

CATERING

	TIMES	NUMBERS*	NOTES
BREAKFAST:	8:30 AM - 10:30 AM	35	
LUNCH:	12:00 PM - 3:00 PM	45	9 vegetarian, 3 vegans
DINNER:	5:00 PM - 8:00 PM	60	12 vegetarian, 4 vegans

*note -- these are tour numbers only

HEADLINER 1
DR SET-UP   12 Noon   NOTES: _____

HEADLINER 2
DR SET-UP   11:00 AM   NOTES: _____

*Please have 4 Dozen towels & 8 Bars of Soap to production office at load in and additional 6 dozen by 5 pm

SECURITY/FIRST AID

BACKSTAGE	NUMBER	TIMES	FOH	NUMBER	TIMES
BACKSTAGE DOOR:	1	Load In	SOUND CHECK:		
TRUCKS & BUSSES	1	Load In	FOH MIX:	1	Doors
STAGE AREA			WINGS:	2	Doors
BAND DR:	1	Noon	BARRICADE:	8	Doors
BAND DR:			EMTS:		
ROVERS:			SUPERVISOR:		
SUPERVISOR:					

(These are suggested minimums, # to be determined in advance)

DRESSING ROOMS AND OFFICE NEEDS

TOUR PRODUCTION OFFICE
Four tables, Eight chairs
3 Phone lines, 1 Fax line

ACCOUNTING OFFICE
One table, Four chairs
1 Phone line

TOUR SPONSOR OFFICE
Two tables, Six chairs
2 Phone lines

BAND 2 BAND ROOM
Large enough for 8 people
Love seat, armchairs.

OPENER BAND ROOM
Large enough for 8 people
Catering table, Ten Chairs

Headliner BAND ROOM
Real furniture for 8 people
Couches, armchairs, lamps, tables.

Headliner 2 BAND ROOM
Real furniture for 8 people
Couches, armchairs, lamps, tables.

Hedliner 1 PRACTICE ROOM
Large enough for 8 people
Needs 110 power and Four chairs.

Headliner 2 PRACTICE ROOM
Large enough for 8 people
Needs 110 power and Four chairs.

MEET & GREET ROOM
Large enough for 50 people
Two tables, Ten chairs

THANK YOU FOR HELPING US MAKE THIS A SUCCESSFUL TOUR AND A GOOD DAY IN YOUR VENUE!

B

APPENDIX B

CORE COMPETENCIES OF PUBLIC ASSEMBLY FACILITY MANAGERS

CORE COMPETENCIES OF PUBLIC ASSEMBLY FACILITY MANAGERS

Developed in 1999-2000 by IAAM Body of Knowledge Task Force

I. Facility Services
    1. Admission
        a. Control System (Patrons, Employees/Vendors)
            1. Box office
            2. Labor
            3. Training
            4. Hiring
            5. Supervising
            6. Bonding
            7. Uniforms
            8. Accounting
            9. Auditing
            10. Ticket Sales (Advance, Gate)
                a. Ordering
                b. Groups
                c. Trades/Comps
                d. Phone Center
                e. Cash Handling Skills
            11. Settlements
            12. Line Controls
            13. Will Call
            14. Vault (Security)
            15. Ticket Type
            16. Trouble Seats (Relocates, Duplicates)
        b. Credentials
    2. Production
        a. Stages, Fixed and Portable
        b. Sound, Public Address, Internal/External
        c. Lights, House, Theatrical
        d. Seating, Types, Configuration
        e. Curtains, Portable, Backdrops
        f. Stagehands (Labor)
        g. Equipment
        h. Truck/Bus Parking for Events
        i. Portable Floors
        j. Directional Signage
        k. Dressing Rooms

      l.   Catering/Hospitality
      m. Press Location
      n.   Utilities (Electric, Gas, Compressed Air)
      o.   TV Production (Locations, Hookups)
      p.   Advancing Shows (Technical Rider)
      q.   In-House Communications
      r.   Phone Lines

3. Rigging
    a. Weight Limitations
    b. Safety
    c. Load Bearing Capacities
    d. Equipment (Types, Conditions)
    e. Ground Riggers
    f. Up Riggers
    g. Risk Management/Legal Limitations
    h. Certifications
    i. Trade Specific Knowledge

4. Physical Plant
    a. Interior Maintenance
    b. Exterior (Building, Grounds, Seeds, Ice/Snow)
    c. Groundskeeping (Event Preparations)
    d. HVAC
    e. Mechanical
    f. Ice-Making & Maintenance
    g. Capital Improvement Implementation
    h. Products (Inventory, Purchasing Determination)
    i. Service Contracts
    j. Loading Docks
    k. Trucks & Bus Parking

5. Housekeeping
    a. Custodial
    b. Products
    c. Equipment
    d. Labor (Hiring, Training, Supervising)
    e. Scheduling (Changeovers)
    f. Event vs. Daily
    g. OSHA
    h. Risk Management
    i. Inventory Control
    j. Trade Specific Knowledge (Carpet Care)

6. Food & Beverage
    a. Labor (Hire, Train, Supervise)
    b. Health Department Regulations
    c. Alcohol, Licensing

     d.   Catering

     e.   Concessions

     f.   Uniforms

     g.   Products Selection (Basic, Branded)

     h.   Pricing

     i.   Contract (Negotiations, Compliance/Management, Benchmarking)

     j.   Cleaning/Sanitation

     k.   Signage

     l.   Pest Control

     m.   Service System (Point of Sale)

     n.   Accounting (Audit, Cost Controls)

     o.   Staffing Levels

     p.   Stand presentation

     q.   Options-In-House vs. Outsource

     r.   Legal/Risk Management Issues/Insurance

     s.   Cash Handling Skills

7.   Merchandise

     a.   Labor (Hire, Train, Supervise)

     b.   Negotiate Commissions (Contract)

     c.   Signage

     d.   Locations — Sales & Inventory

     e.   Pricing

     f.   Presentation

     g.   Product Approvals

     h.   Staffing Levels

     i.   Cash Handling Skills

     j.   Service System (Point of Sale)

8.   Event Management

     a.   Labor (Hire, Train, Supervise)

     b.   Ushers, Sellers, Ticket Takers, Security, Police, Medical, Event Custodial

     c.   Equipment

     d.   Incident Reports

     e.   Event Reports

     f.   Event Briefing

     g.   Parking/Traffic

         1.   Cash Control

         2.   Ticketing

         3.   Labor

         4.   Training

         5.   Uniforms

         6.   Ingress/Egress

         7.   Equipment

         8.   Lot Maintenance

9.   Communication
10. Traffic
11. Signage

II. Administration
  1.   Capital Improvement
     a.   Funding
     b.   Budgeting/Forecasting Expense
     c.   Identifying the Need
  2.   Construction Management
     a.   Understanding the Bidding Process
     b.   Technical Specifications
     c.   Blueprints/Drawings/Schematics/Terminology
     d.   Supervision (On-Site and Administration)
  3.   Technology
     a.   Computer (Basic Skills)
     b.   Terminology
     c.   Types
        1.   Computer
        2.   Wireless
        3.   Networks
        4.   Management Systems
        5.   Control Systems
        6.   Event Management
     d.   Ability to Identify Appropriate Technologies
     e.   Ability to Evaluate Emerging Technologies
  4.   Insurance/Risk Management
     a.   Terminology
     b.   Assessment
     c.   Evaluation of Risk
     d.   Cost/Benefit Analysis
     e.   Administration/Understanding
  5.   Emergency Management
     a.   Evacuation Plans
     b.   Communication Strategies
     c.   Emergency Service Coordination (Police, FBI, Fire, EMT)
     d.   Staff Training and Preparedness (CPR, First Aid)
     e.   Media Relations
     f.   Knowledge of Emergency Equipment
        1.   Radios
        2.   Lighting
        3.   Generators
        4.   First Aid
        5.   Fire Equipment
        6.   Life Safety

6. Crisis Management
    a. Response Procedures
        1. Bomb Threat
        2. Fire
        3. Weather-Related
        4. Chemical
        5. Natural Disaster
        6. Terrorist
    b. Staff Training and Preparedness
    c. Media Relations
    d. Appropriate Decorum of Staff
    e. Contractual Issues
    f. Insurance Issues
    g. Proper Notification
7. Human Resources/Labor Relations
    a. Legal and Regulatory
        1. Workers Comp
        2. Fair Labor Standards
        3. Right to Know
        4. Unemployment Compensation
        5. Applicable Federal Laws
        6. Applicable State Laws
        7. Recruitment
    b. Training
    c. Retention
    d. Creating and Maintaining Workplace Morale
    e. Employee Counseling
        1. Substance Abuse
        2. Stress Management
        3. Employee Support/Assistance Programs
    f. Conflict Management & Resolution
    g. Union Relations
        1. Contracts
        2. Negotiations
        3. Grievances
        4. Work Rules
    h. Workplace Safety
        1. Carpal Tunnel
        2. Ergonomics
        3. Protective Equipment
    i. Equal Employment Opportunities
8. Contract Administration
    a. Terminology
    b. Negotiation

     c.   Legal issues

     d.   Communication

9. Governance

     a.   Communication & Information

     b.   Understanding the Operating Policies

     c.   Knowledge of the Environment and the Players

10. Tenant Management

     a.   Landlord Responsibilities (Contract Management)

     b.   Long-Term vs. Short-Term

     c.   Understanding Tenant Needs

     d.   Communication and Feedback

     e.   Creating a Happy Marriage

     f.   Facilitating Activities

     g.   Partnering (Mutually Beneficial)

11. Training and Development

     a.   Needs Assessment of Staff and Facility

     b.   Evaluation of the Training

     c.   Types (Skills, Emergency, Customer & Guest Services)

     d.   Knowledge of Available Resources (Internet, IAAM, Chamber of Commerce)

12. Legal Issues

     a.   Laws Affecting Facilities

         1.   Labor

         2.   Liability

         3.   Workers

         4.   Employment

         5.   Patrons

         6.   Public Safety

         7.   Applicable State and Federal Laws

         8.   BOCA

         9.   NEC

     b.   Available Resources

13. Disability Services

     a.   Needs Assessment

     b.   Accessibility (Elevator, Entrances)

     c.   Programmatic Compliance

     d.   Staff Training

     e.   Resources (State, Federal, Local, IAAM)

     f.   Legal Responsibilities/Requirements

     g.   Communications and Feedback

14. Public and Private Management

     a.   Understanding the Difference and Application

     b.   Meeting Expectations

III. Fiscal Management
    1.   Budgeting and Financial-GAAP
            1.   Goals
            2.   Coordination
            3.   Measurement
        a.   Budget Estimate
        b.   General Budgeting
            1.   Ledger
            2.   P&L Statements
            3.   Receivables
            4.   Payables
            5.   Payroll
        c.   Audit Controls
    2.   Inventory Control
    3.   Cost Accounting
        a.   Cost Systems
        b.   Production
        c.   Allocating Expenses
        d.   Fixed & Variable
    4.   Investments
        a.   Cash Flow Management
    5.   Capitalization
        a.   Bonding
    6.   Forecasting
IV. Sales & Marketing
    1.   Sponsorship
    2.   Perceived Value to Buyer
        a.   Effective Presentation
        b.   Uses of Sponsorship Dollars
        c.   Sponsor vs. Advertising Exclusivity
        d.   Pre-emption rights
        e.   Value to Sponsor Annual Reports
        f.   Market Demographic
        g.   Parking/Fulfillment
        h.   Understanding the Difference Between Advertising and Sponsorship
    3.   Community Relations
        a.   Sensitivity and Understanding of Community
        b.   Community Influence on Facility Governing Officials
        c.   Know Direct and Indirect Impact of Facility
        d.   Job Impact
        f.   Programming Sensitivity to Community
    4.   Public Relations
        a.   PSA
        b.   Free Advertising

    c.   Comp Tickets
    d.   Web Site
    e.   Press Release
5.   Advertising
    a.   Knowledge of Media
        1.   Print
        2.   Video
        3.   Technology
    b.   External
        1.   In-House Services
        2.   Efficient Use of Media
    c.   Internal
        1.   Naming & Pouring Rights
        2.   Signage, Branding/Sales Premium Seating
        3.   Scoreboard/Marquee
        4.   In-House Publications
        5.   Ticket Stock
        6.   Parking Lots
        7.   Gift Certificates
        8.   Event Acquisition
        9.   Booking & Scheduling
       10. Fund Raising
       11. Premium Seating
6.   Marketing (Creating a Demand)
    a.   Demographics
    b.   Research & Analysis
    c.   Campaign Development
    d.   Strategic Planning
    e.   Product Packaging
    f.   Understanding and Directing Image
    g.   Contingency Plan
7.   Booking & Scheduling
    a.   Event Knowledge
    b.   Event Relationship-Promotions, Agents, Talent & Production
    c.   Contract Knowledge
    d.   Negotiation Skills
    e.   House Limitations
    f.   Knowing Competition
8.   Event Programming
    a.   Talent Buying
        1.   In-House
    b.   Event Acquisition
        1.   Standard Rental
        2.   Co-promotion

3. Program Development
4. Series
5. Prime Tenants
6. Non-Profit/Public Service
7. Yield Management
8. Ancillary Income Impact
9. Sponsorship Potential
   a. Retail
   b. Corporate
   c. Media
   d. Gross potential

9. Fund Raising
   a. Identify Potential
   b. Balance Fund Raising with Other Sources of Revenue
   c. Endowment
10. Premium Seating
    a. Golden Circle
    b. Suites
    c. Leases
    d. Sales & Marketing
    e. Concierge Services
    f. Rights
    g. Parking
    h. Revenue Sharing with Tenants
    i. Standing Room Only
    j. Mosh Pits/Festival Seating
11. CVB Relations
    a. Shared Marketing
    b. Booking \Priorities
    c. Economic Impact Studies
    d. Sports Components
    e. Joint Sales/Marketing/Advertising
    f. Urban Development

V. Leadership & Management
   1. Principles of Leadership
      a. Value and Vision
      b. Risk Taking
      c. Empowerment
      d. Collaboration
   2. Use of Power & Authority
      a. Balance the Power
      b. Achieve More With Less
      c. Team Development
   3. Strategic Planning

     a.   Mission Statements
     b.   Goals and Objectives
4. Knowing the Ground Rules
     a.   History
     b.   Laws
     c.   Rules
     d.   Boundaries
5. Staff Development
     a.   Use Job Descriptions Effectively
     b.   Evaluations
     c.   Define New Focus
6. Mentoring
     a.   Guidance
     b.   Impart Knowledge, Experience, Confidence
7. Morals & Ethics
     a.   Professional Empowerment
     b.   Lead by Example
     c.   Fairness
     d.   Give Respect
8. Motivation
     a.   Accessibility
     b.   Problem Solving Skills
9. Decision Making
10. Sense of Humor
11. Communication
12. Assertive Communication
13. Policy Communication
14. Time Management
15. Crisis Management
16. IAAM Membership & Participation

APPENDIX C

CONTRACT COMPONENTS

CONTRACT COMPONENTS TENTATIVE COMMITMENTS/CONTRACTUAL OBLIGATIONS

A tentatively held date becomes a firm commitment when a formal contractual instrument is issued. It becomes a contract when properly signed by all parties. The scope and importance of the event will usually dictate whether any serious negotiating will be required. Many facilities utilize standard form contracts or license agreements with a "fill in the blank" type format. These types of instruments allow the process to be streamlined and somewhat consistent in format.

Negotiated contracts or license agreements require advance preparation. The assistance of an attorney is certainly a must for the original standard facility document. Whether or not an attorney is needed for individual event contracts is a decision to be made by the manager unless there is a policy requiring a sign-off by the facility's attorney. In addition to the "boiler plate" information that usually appears in most documents, several areas must be addressed prior to negotiation. A comprehensive "laundry list" must be developed with major deal points outlined. Armed with the information, the facility negotiator can focus on items such as special terms, condition, and benefits to be obtained by the parties.

COMPONENTS OF A CONTRACT

A contract is defined as an agreement of two or more parties to do or refrain from doing some lawful thing. The agreement must create obligations on the part of all parties. Every contract must meet four basic requirements:

1. Mutual assent of all contracting parties.
2. The parties must possess the legal rights and capacity to make the contract.
3. Proper and fair consideration of services or provisions must be received by all contracting parties.
4. Offer of terms of the agreement.

The contract must have a lawful objective and a legal method for accomplishing it. In law, a contract is a promissory agreement between two or more parties to establish, change, or rescind a legal relationship. The public assembly facility manager should understand that the prime purpose of a contract is to provide protection to:

1. The owner of the public assembly facility.
2. The organization or individual using the facility.
3. The patron attending the event (whatever that event might be).

There are some very basic components that should be contained in the facility use contract. These items will, in nearly all cases, be seen as a part of the basic contract form:

1. **Form of Legal Document** - i.e., Is it a Contract, License, Lease, Permit, etc.?
2. **Facility Identification** - Include name, address, city, state, zip code, telephone and fax number of the facility. Be sure to include legal nomenclature such as Municipal Corporation, Incorporated, Partnership, Joint Venture, etc.
3. **User Identification** - Include business name, address, city, state, zip code, event contact person, telephone and fax number of the contracting organization. Be sure to include legal nomenclature such as Corporation, Partnership, Sole Owner, D.B.A., Joint Venture, etc.
4. **Event Identification** - What space is being rented for what purpose and the name of the event.
5. **Event Date(s)** - List date(s) of use, including move-in and move-out.
6. **Event Time(s)** - List time(s) of use, including move-in and move-out.
7. **Event Schedule** - State what will be going on during specific date/time frames.
8. **Venue Identification** - List the exact space(s) which will be rented. This is particularly important when the facility being rented has many spaces. The User must know that he/she is only renting specific areas and not the whole building, unless that is the case. Be sure to also include language which states that the organization will, or will not, also have use of the common public areas for ingress and egress to the event(s).
9. **User Fees and Revenue Sources** - State the specific amount of money which will be paid for rental of the space or a percentage of ticket sales, or even a combination of base rent against a percentage of ticket sales. Other User Fees and Revenue Sources include:
   - Equipment use.
   - Labor charges.
   - Merchandise.
   - Parking.
   - Food/beverage.
   - Catering.
   - Flowers, etc.
   - Videotaping, etc.
10. **Payment Schedule** - State a precise schedule of when payments are due for:
   - Advance/Contract Deposit.
   - Minimum Base Rental.
   - Percentage Balance (if appropriate).
   - Commission on Sales (if appropriate).
   - Service/Labor Costs.
   - Equipment Rental Costs.
   - Other.

11. **Insurance Requirements** - Include language to identify the exact type of coverage, limits of liability and scope, and qualified insurance companies required by the facility. Note a Certificate of Insurance will be required by the facility X days prior to the event. Specific wording of any requirement for making the facility or the governing authority an "additionally named insured" should also be included here. Facility should have right to AUTOMATICALLY provide coverage at User's expense if user fails to provide on time.

12. **Indemnity Clause** - Include specific language holding the facility, its manager, employees, agents and guests harmless from legal action caused by the acts or omissions of the User.

13. **Cancellation Clause** - Definite and specific language must be in place which spells out the allocation of risk between the parties in the event of cancellation by either party.

14. **Attorney Fees** - Most attorneys will insist on a clause which obligates the payment of attorney fees and court costs by the non-prevailing party to the prevailing party in the event of a lawsuit.

15. **Force Majeure** - This is a clause which states that the facility will not be obligated in any way in the event of an act of God, fire, civil riot, strike, lockout, flood, war or other situations over which the facility has no control.

16. **No Partnerships** - Unless there is specific language to the contrary, there should be a section which simply states that there is no partnership relationship between the facility and the User.

17. **Obstruction/Alterations** - Include language with regard to the specifics of not blocking, for example, sidewalks, ramps, entries, doors, corridors, passageways, galleries, vestibules, hallways, lobbies, stairways, elevators, aisles, driveways, fire hose cabinets, heating and air conditioning vents, lighting fixtures and fire prevention water sprinkler systems, to ensure patron safety. No physical alterations to the facility should be allowed without prior written consent of management.

18. **Signature Lines and the Corporate Seal** - There should be sufficient room at the end of the document to allow for all signatures required by the governing authority in addition to that of the User. If the User is a corporation, a corporate seal may need to be affixed to the document over the signature of the corporate secretary.

19. **Personal Requirements** - A mention should be made with regard to any personnel that are necessary to set up, operate, and tear down the event and who will provide those personnel. Note that worker's compensation law varies from state to state. If union personnel are required, this should be stated.

20. **Basic Services Provided by the Facility** - Reference should be made for the provision of heat, light, air conditioning, cleanliness, water, sewer, natural gas, if the facility normally supplies these services as a part of the rental agreement. It should be stated if the facility does not provide these services or only provides them at a fee.

21. **Control of Building** - The building should always be under the ultimate control of the facility manager and it should be specifically spelled out in the document.

22. **Changes to Agreement** - Changes to the agreement must be in writing and signed by all parties.

This is not meant to be a complete listing of each clause which should be in a facility use contractual document. In addition to the foregoing, each facility manager should regularly seek the counsel and advise of the facility's attorney to be sure that all requirements of federal, state and local law are properly covered.

In addition, there are many operating aspects and other items involved in the use of a public assembly facility that need to be addressed, although trying to include them in a contract document may be too complex and cumbersome. Many facilities address this issue by developing "policies and procedure" and/or "rules and regulations" documents which are made a part of the contractual agreement by a statement in that latter document so stating. Some areas that might be addressed in the policies and procedures if that approach is used, could include, but not be limited to:

1. *Concessions* - Revenue and expenses connected with food and beverage, merchandise, photography, flowers, etc. would be addressed.

2. *Exhibits* - The terms and conditions for exhibits, including storage, freight, locations, local laws, etc.

3. *Alterations/construction* - Requirements for either approval or prohibitions against nails, balloons, adhesives, etc., if applicable.

4. *Capacity* - State maximum seating, floor loads and rigging requirements, among other items.

5. *Broadcasting/filming* - Specify who has rights to these, under what conditions, and at what formula for determining costs and revenue distribution.

6. *Tickets* - Specify who sells and through what resources, collects money, prints tickets, manifest requirements, box office staffing and statements, seating configurations, complimentary tickets, and trade tickets.

7. *Evacuation of facility in case of Emergency* - Who controls, diagrams, etc.

DEFINITIONS

a. **Contract**: A contract is defined as an agreement upon sufficient consideration to   do or refrain from doing some lawful thing. The agreement must create an obligation. Every contract must have at least the following four elements:
   1. Mutual assents.
   2. Parties with the capacity to contract.
   3. Consideration and valid subject matter.
   4. Term.

b. **Warranties**: Warranties are assurances that are part of a contract.

c. **License**: A license or certificate is a form of written approval to do a lawful thing, often issued by a division of government. Additional elements or provisions are usually added to define the extent and limits of such license. It usually gives the licensee the right to obtain certain space but not possession; therefore, the individual/organization does not become a tenant. To be a tenant, one must have exclusive possession, not mere use alone.

d. **Lease**: A lease is a contract whereby, for a consideration called rent, one party agrees to give possession of premises to another. A lease must contain five essential elements:
   1. Contract.
   2. Exclusive Possession.
   3. Subordinate Holding.
   4. Reversion in the Landlord.
   5. Reservations of Rent.

   Other formal provisions usually found in a lease include the following:
   1. Term of duration.
   2. Description of premises.
   3. Purpose for which premises may be used.
   4. Repairs and improvements.
   5. Insurance.
   6. Assignment.
   7. Security Deposit.
   8. Default and Remedies.
   9. Quiet enjoyment.

e. **Permit**: A permit is a written acknowledgment of consent to do some lawful thing without command; it grants a liberty and professes to tolerate all legal action.

f. **Agreement**: All contracts are agreements, but all agreements are NOT contracts. Agreements that do not include the essentials of a contract are not enforceable as a contract by law. The use of agreements therefore, should be for arrangements which are simpler in nature and duration.

g. **Ultimate terms and conditions**: For very large and complex operations, it is advisable to include many more terms and conditions in the contract. The enforcement of certain provisions can become extremely difficult. In all cases, it will require supervision of at least one individual representing the party granting the privilege.

APPENDIX D

RELATED
ASSOCIATIONS AND
ORGANIZATIONS

RELATED ASSOCIATIONS AND ORGANIZATIONS

ABRACCEF www.abraccef.org.br
Brazilian Association of Conference Centers (Associacao Brasileira dos Centros de Convencoes e Feiras)
Rua Barao do Rio Branco 370
CEP 80010-180 Curitiba, Parana
BRAZIL
Phone: 55-41-322-8955, Fax: 55-41-322-8955
Email: abraccef@abraccef.org.br

ACCED-I www.acced-i.colostate.edu
Association of Collegiate Conference and Event Directors Intl.
Colorado State Univ., Tiley House
Fort Collins CO 80523-8037
Phone: 970/491-5151, Fax: 970/491-0667

ACME www.acmenet.org
Association for Convention Marketing Executives
2965 Flowers Road South, Ste. 105
Atlanta GA 30341
Phone: 770-454-6111, Fax: 770-458-3314
Email: assnhq@mindspring.com

ACOM www.acomonline.org
Association for Convention Operations Management
2965 Flowers Road South, Ste. 105
Atlanta GA 30341
Phone: 770/454-9411, Fax: 770/458-3314
Email: info@acomonline.org

AIPC www.aipc.org
Association Internationale des Palais de Congrès (International Association of Congress Centres)
55 Rue de l'Amazone
1060 Brussels
BELGIUM
Phone: 32-2-534-59-53, Fax: 32-2-534-63-38
Email: secretariat@iapc.org

ALSD www.alsd.com
Association of Luxury Suite Directors
636 Northland Blvd., Ste. 250
Cincinnati OH 45240
Phone: 513/674-0555, Fax: 513/674-0577

AMPROFEC www.amprofec.org.mx
Association of Mexican Professionals in Fairs, Exhibitions & Conventions
Ave. Benjamin Franklin, Num 166-4
Col. Escandon Mexico, 11800 D. F.
MEXICO
Phone: (55) 5273 1103, Fax: (55) 5273 1103

APAP www.artspresenters.org
Association of Performing Arts Presenters
1112 16th St., NW, Ste. 400
Washington DC 20036
Phone: 202/833-2787, Fax: 202/833-1543
Email: artspres@artspresenters.org

APECC www.apecc.org
Asia Pacific Exhibition & Convention Council
PO Box 1871
Toowong QLD 4066
AUSTRALIA
Phone: 61-7-3780-4777, Fax: 61-7-3780-4666

APPA www.appa.org
APPA: The Association of Higher Education Facilities Officers
1643 Prince St.
Alexandria VA 22314-2818
Phone: 703/684-1446, Fax: 703/549-2772

ArenaNetwork www.arenanetwork.net
ArenaNetwork
5750 Wilshire Blvd., Suite 501
Los Angeles, CA 90036
Phone: 323/930-7180, Fax: 323/930-7181
Email: bparsons@arenanetwork.net

ASAE www.asaenet.org
American Society of Association Executives
1575 I St., NW
Washington DC 20005-1103
Phone: 202/626-2723, Fax: 202/371-8825
Email: pr@asaenet.org

CEIR www.ceir.org
Center for Exhibition Industry Research
SmithBucklin Headquarters
401 N. Michigan Ave.
Chicago, IL 60611
Phone: 312/527-6735, Fax: 312/673-6722
Email: info@ceir.org

CIC www.conventionindustry.org
Convention Industry Council
8201 Greensboro Dr., Ste. 300
McLean VA 22102
Phone: 703/610-9030, Fax: 703/610-9005
CMA www.cmaworld.com

Country Music Association
One Music Circle South
Nashville TN 37203
Phone: 615/244-2840, Fax: 615/726-0314
Email: international@CMAworld.com

EAA www.eaaoffice.org
European Arenas Association
Sarphatikade 12
Amsterdam 1017 WV
THE NETHERLANDS
Phone: 31-20-530-4717, Fax: 31-20-530-4711
Email: eaa@eaaoffice.org

ESCA www.esca.org
Exposition Service Contractors Association
2260 Corporate Circle, Suite 400
Henderson NV 89074-7701
Phone: 702/319-9561, Fax: 702/450-7732
Email: askus@esca.org

ESMA www.esmastadium.org
European Stadium Managers Association
10 Rue De Paris
Boulogne- Billancourt 92100
FRANCE
Phone: 00 33 1 46 04 42 10; Fax: 00 33 1 46 04 42 35

ESTA www.esta.org
Entertainment Services and Technology Association
875 Sixth Ave., Ste. 1005
New York NY 10001
Phone: 212/244-1505, Fax: 212/244-1502
Email: info@esta.org

EVVC www.evvc.org
European Association of Event Centers
Thueringer avenue 12, House 3, OG
14052 Berlin
GERMANY
Phone: 30-30-38-58-00, Fax: 30-30-38-58-02
Email: info@evvc.org

IAAM www.iaam.org
International Association of Assembly Managers
635 Fritz Drive, Suite 100
Coppell TX 75019
Phone: 972/906-7441, Fax: 972/906-7418
Email: info@iaam.org

IAAPA www.iaapa.org
International Association of Amusement Parks & Attractions
1448 Duke St.
Alexandria VA 22314
Phone: 703/836-4800, Fax: 703/836-9678

IACC www.iacconline.org
International Association of Conference Centers
243 N. Lindbergh Blvd., Ste. 315
St. Louis MO 63141
Phone: 314/993-8575, Fax: 314/993-8919
Email: info@iacconline.org

IACVB www.iacvb.org
International Association of Convention & Visitor Bureaus
2025 M Street NW, Ste. 500
Washington DC 20036
Phone: 202/296-7888, Fax: 202/296-7889
Email: info@iacvb.org

IAEM www.iaem.org
International Association for Exposition Management
P O Box 802425
Dallas TX 75380-2425
Phone: 972/458-8002, Fax: 972/458-8119
Email: news@iaem.org

IAFE www.fairsandexpos.com
International Association of Fairs & Expositions
Box 985
Springfield MO 65801
Phone: 417/862-5771, Fax: 417/862-0156
Email: iafe@fairsandexpos.com

IAPCO www.iapco.org
International Association of Professional Congress Organizers
42 Canham Road
London W3 7SR
UNITED KINGDOM
Phone: 44 20 8749 6171, Fax: 44 20 8740 0241
Email: iapco@xs4all.be

IATSE www.iatse.lm.com
Intl. Alliance of Theatrical Stage Employees & Moving Picture Technicians of the US and Canada
1430 Broadway, 20th Floor
New York New York 10018
Phone: 212/730-1770, Fax: 212/730-7809

ICCA www.icca.nl
International Congress & Convention Association
Entrade 121
NL - 1096 EB Amsterdam
THE NETHERLANDS
Phone: 31-20-398-1919, Fax: 31-20-699-0781
Email: icca@icca.nl

ICMA www.icma.org
International City/County Management Association
777 North Capitol St., NE, Ste. 500
Washington DC 20002
Phone: 202/289-4262, Fax: 202/962-3500

IEDC http://www.iedconline.org/index.html
International Economic Development Council
734 15th Street Ste. 900
Washington DC 20005
Phone: 202/223-7800, Fax: 202/223-4745

IFEA www.ifea.com
International Festival & Events Association
2601 Eastover Terrace
Boise, ID 83706
Phone: 208/433-0950 Fax: 208/433-9812

IFMA www.ifma.org
International Facility Management Association
1 East Greenway Plaza, Suite 1100
Houston TX 77046-0194
Phone: 713/623-4362, Fax: 713/623-6124
Email: ifmahq@ifma.org

INTIX www.intix.org
International Ticketing Association
250 West 57th St., Ste. 722
New York NY 10107
Phone: 212/581-0600, Fax: 212/581-0885
Email: info@intix.org

ISES www.ises.com
International Special Events Society
401 North Michigan Avenue
Chicago IL 60611-4267
Phone: 312/321-6853, Fax: 312/673-6953
Email: info@ises.com

ISPA www.ispa.org
International Society for the Performing Arts
17 Purdy Avenue, P.O. Box 909
Rye NY 10580
Phone: 914/921-1550, Fax: 914/921-1593
Email: info@ispa.org

LHAT www.lhat.org
The League of Historic American Theatres
616 Water Street, Ste. 320
Baltimore MD 21202
Phone: 410/659-9533, Fax: 410/837-9664

MPI www.mpiweb.org
Meeting Professionals International
4455 LBJ Freeway, Ste. 1200
Dallas TX 75244-5903
Phone: 972/702-3000, Fax: 972/702-3070
Email: confmtgs@mpiweb.org

NAA www.ilmc.com/naa
National Arenas Association
27 Friary Avenue
Shirley Solihull, West Midlands B90 4SZ
UNITED KINGDOM
Phone: 44-121-744-2211, Fax: 44-121-774-2211

NAAC
National Association of Accessibility Consultants
1154 Fort Street Mall, Suite 204
Honolulu Hawaii 96813
Phone: 808/523-3344, Fax: 808/523-3008
Email: naac@aloha.net

NAC www.nacoline.org
National Association of Concessionaires
35 E. Wacker Drive
Chicago IL 60601
Phone: 312/236-3858, Fax: 312/236-7809
Email: info@naconline.org

NACA www.naca.org
National Association for Campus Activities
13 Harbison Way
Columbia SC 29212-3401
Phone: 803/732-6222, Fax: 803/749-1047

NACDA http://nacda.ocsn.com/
National Association of Collegiate Directors of Athletes
P.O. Box 16428
Cleveland OH 44116
Phone: 440/892-4000, Fax: 440/892-4007

NACS www.publicshows.com
National Association of Consumer Shows
147 S.E. 102nd Ave.
Portland OR 97216
Phone: 503/253-0832, Fax: 503/253-9172
Email: info@publicshows.com

NAIA www.naia.org
National Association of Intercollegiate Athletics
23500 W. 105th St., P O Box 1325
Olathe KS 66051
Phone: 913/791-0044, Fax: 913/791-9555

NAPAMA www.napama.org
National Association of Performing Arts Managers & Agents
459 Columbus Ave., Ste. 133
New York NY 10024
Phone: 888/745-8759, Fax: 212/580-5438
Email: info@napama.org

NBA www.nba.com
National Basketball Association
Olympic Tower, 645 Fifth Ave., 15th Fl
New York NY 10022
Phone: 212/826-7000, Fax: 212/826-0579

NCAA www.ncaa.org
National Collegiate Athletic Association
700 W. Washington Avenue
Indianapolis IN 46206-6222
Phone: 317/917-6222, Fax: 317/917-6888

NCBMP www.ncbmp.com
National Coalition of Black Meeting Planners
8630 Fenton St., Ste. 126
Silver Spring MD 20910
Phone: 202/628-3952, Fax: 301/588-0011

NFL www.nfl.com
National Football League
280 Park Ave., Ste. 12-West
New York NY 10017
Phone: 212/450-2000, Fax: 212/681-7559

NFPA www.nfpa.org
National Fire Protection Association
1 Batterymarch Park, P.O. Box 9101
Quincy MA 02269-9101
Phone: 617/770-3000, Fax: 617/770-0700
Email: public_affairs@nfpa.org

NHL www.nhl.com
National Hockey League
1251 Ave. of the Americas, 47th Fl.
New York NY 10020
Phone: 212/789-2000, Fax: 212/789-2020

NLC www.nlc.org
National League of Cities
1301 Pennsylvania Ave., NW, Ste. 550
Washington DC 20004-1763
Phone: 202/626-3000, Fax: 202/626-3043
Email: inet@nlc.org

PCMA www.pcma.org
Professional Convention Management Association
2301 South Lake Shore, Ste. 1001
Chicago IL 60616-1419
Phone: 312/423-7262, Fax: 312/423-7222

PRCA www.prorodeo.com
Professional Rodeo Cowboys Association
101 Prorodeo Drive
Colorado Springs CO 80919-9989
Phone: 719/593-8840, Fax: 719/548-4876

RCMA www.rcmaweb.org
Religious Conference Management Association
One RCA Dome, Suite 120
Indianapolis IN 46225
Phone: 317/632-1888, Fax: 317/632-7909
Email: rcma@rcmaweb.org

SC www.sportengland.org
Sport England
16 Upper Woburn Place
London WC1H 0QP
ENGLAND
Phone: 020 7273 1500, Fax: 020 7383 5740
Email: info@sportengland.org

SCMP www.scmp.org
Society of Corporate Meeting Professionals
2965 Flowers Road South, Ste. 105
Atlanta GA 30341
Phone: 770/457-9212, Fax: 770/458-3314
Email: info@scmp.org

SGMP www.sgmp.org
Society of Government Meeting Planners
908 King Street, Lower Level
Alexandria VA 22314
Phone: 703/549-0892, Fax: 703/549-0708

SMA www.stadianet.com
Stadium Managers Association
525 SW 5th St., Ste. A
Des Moines IA 50309
Phone: 515-282-8192, Fax: 515-282-9117
Email: sma@assoc-mgmt.com

UFI www.ufinet.org
Union des Foires Internationales
35bis, rue Jouffroy d'Abbans
F-75017 Paris
FRANCE
Phone: (33) 1 42 67 99 12, Fax: (33) 1 42 27 19 29
Email: info@ufinet.org

USITT www.usitt.org
USITT: U.S. Institute for Theater Technology
6443 Ridings Road
Syracuse NY 13206-1111
Phone: 315/463-6463, Fax: 315/463-6525
Email: info@office.usitt.org

VMA www.vma.org.au
Venue Management Association
PO Box 1871
Toowong QLD 4066
AUSTRALIA
Phone: 61-7-3780-4777, Fax: 61-7-3780-4666

WCVM www.venue.org
World Council for Venue Management
635 Fritz Drive, Suite 100
Coppell TX 75019
Phone: 972/255-8020, Fax: 972/255-9582

APPENDIX E

GLOSSARY OF TERMS

GLOSSARY OF TERMS

A

advertising campaign - The plan for advertising, promotions, and other means by which tickets for events are advertised and promoted in electronic media (radio and TV), in print, over the Internet, via direct mail, or by other means of general and/or direct contact.

ancillary revenue - Generally refers to income earned from events other than rent and expense reimbursements. Typical examples of ancillary income include concessions and catering, merchandise (novelties), parking and decorating.

ancillary revenue streams - Revenue source in addition to facility charges of rent, labor and equipment to include, but not limited to food/beverage sales, catering commissions, novelty/souvenir sales, parking fees, advertising commissions, ticket/facility surcharges, naming rights fees, sponsorships, etc.

ancillary services - Revenue sources available to facility managers by providing basic services such as food and beverage, merchandising and novelty sales, and parking services. Additional services such as equipment rentals, computer cafes, freight handling (drayage), providing box office services to other organizations, event advertising, and automatic teller machines (ATM), are just a few additional examples of such revenue generators.

audit stub - A portion of a ticket created by perforations that are retained by a ticket seller to document that the ticket was sold and at what price. Audit stubs are an inventory control device and accounting tool that identifies the price at which a ticket was sold: discount, child, full price.

avails - Dates that are available for booking.

B

back-of-house - That portion of the facility where public assess is not permitted, usually behind the stage, production area and/or other restricted areas such as mechanical rooms, dressing rooms, kitchen, etc. Beyond the physical location this term can be used in conjunction with building functions.

banquet event order (BEO) - A document that confirms a food/beverage service for a select group of people.

bar coded tickets - Tickets bearing a series of vertical bars of varying widths conforming with the Universal Product Code used especially for computerized inventory control. Bar coded tickets are now used during the admission process at numerous facilities.

billed back - The process by which one party that provides goods or services to another party bills for and receives reimbursement for the goods and/or services provided.

box office advance - Funds advanced to an event promoter from revenue derived from event ticket sales and paid in advance of the event settlement; the fulfillment of the contract by the event promoter or prior to the conclusion of the event.

box office statement - An itemized accounting of tickets distributed (sold or complimentary), or unsold and the corresponding monies collected for a specific event.

branding - Usually refers to a relationship whereby a food and/or beverage product is given exclusivity in return for agreeing to purchase advertisements and generally promote its presence at the facility via its own advertising, marketing and point-of-sale promotions in the general market area.

break-even operation - Generally refers to a public assembly facility that does not require an operating subsidy from its owner to cover annual operating expenses; operating revenue is sufficient to cover operating expenses. Debt service, capital improvement reserves and taxes are typically excluded as operating expenses.

bundling - A marketing strategy used to help promote events in public assembly facilities and used to encourage patrons and fans to make a long-term commitment by purchasing a number of events in bulk. The season ticket or subscription series of events is offered at the bulk price which is usually less than the combined individual rates of each event.

C

car-loader - A person that is hired temporarily, often a union employee (Teamsters, IATSE), to unload/load freight to and from a truck or railcar.

casual labor - Employees not holding regular positions and working only as opportunity opens (on-call). These employees may be released or furloughed when there is no work for them to perform.

certificate of insurance - Written verification of types, terms, and amounts of insurance carried by the named insured which are sent to those who require proof of such coverage.

change order - In construction or renovation, formal change made to final construction documents. A change order may affect the final cost of a construction or renovation project up or down or not al all, or it may change the length of the construction time. For a banquet, a formal change made to a Banquet Event Order changing a food service event.

changeover - The activities required to change from one stage set-up, seating configuration, etc. within a public assembly facility to another, different set-up or configuration necessitated by the requirements of different types of events or tenant's production needs.

commissaries - A warehouse or production room for food, beverage and/or merchandise. The term is also used to describe a vending room that supplies products to the hawkers selling in the seats of a venue.

complimentary tickets - Tickets to an event issued at no charge to the recipient. Complimentary tickets are specially marked, punched or printed tickets which have no monetary value. Some contracts require the promoter to pay the facility rent as if the tickets had been sold. Usually this is limited to only the number of tickets issued as complimentary in excess of the number allowed in the contract.

confirmed contract - A contract that has been negotiated, agreed to and is awaiting signatures.

contract - A written agreement between two or more parties in which it is agreed that one party will perform a desired work or provide a service for which the other will pay some form of compensation.

contracted - Contract that has been signed and returned, usually with a rent deposit.

co-promoted - Generally is a term to describe an event that the facility becomes involved with on at least a partially at-risk basis. In a co-promoted arrangement, the facility might not charge a guaranteed rent, and in some cases expenses, and earns a negotiated percentage of gross ticket sales. Some events are only willing to book a facility if the facility is willing to become an active promotional partner. By sharing in the downside risk, facilities can possibly earn more revenue through a co-promotion than a standard rental relationship.

cost accounting - Method of accounting which emphasizes the determination and the control of costs, particularly the costs of production and the final product. It deals with actual costs to be reported on financial statements. One of the principal functions is to assemble and interpret cost data, both actual and prospective, for the use of management in controlling current operations and in planning for the future.

cost estimate - A written or verbal estimate provided by a party providing goods or services to another of the resources required to provide said goods or services.

crisis management - The plan and process of responding to an emergency situation and minimizing damage to property or injuries to persons once an emergency or crisis has occurred.

cross-bounce coupon - A marketing tool used to increase sales of tickets to an event or retail product by offering a value-added benefit for the customer either in the form of a discount on the price of a ticket to an event or a discount on a retail item at a participating retail outlet or on something offered by some other promotional partner. Cross-bounce coupons are usually printed as part of a print ad for an event, but can be separately printed advertising/promotion collateral.

crowd control - General term for the combined services involved in managing the direction and demeanor of an audience.

crowd management - The planning of, and the work performed by ushers, ticket takers, peer-group security, medical teams and facility management to provide the safety and security for the general public attending events.

D

dark - A date without a performance or event and not usually available for booking.

deadwood - Unsold tickets that remain in inventory.

donor - Refers to a business, organization or individual who gives money to a fundraising drive, often to a performing arts center itself and/or one or more of its shows or to a university athletic department.

drop count - The number of ticket stubs collected for a single event at the entry point(s) of a facility. If bar coded tickets are used, a report is provided in place of the physical ticket stubs.

E

egress - The act of leaving or exiting a public assembly facility or other location.

emergency preparedness - Maintaining a plan and performing regular training to best respond to any incident, situation, or occurrence that could possibly result in the injury/death of employees, patrons, clients or visitors at a facility and/or cause any damage to the facility, equipment and its contents.

event management - The process of planning and disseminating information and communicating pertinent event production requirements to a facility's staff which results in the coordination of activities that leads to the successful production of an event.

event operations - When used as a verb, the process of running an event. When used as a noun, the various units needed to operate the event and facility, including, but not limited to, technical staff, sound and lighting operators, laborers, electricians, changeover crews, maintenance staff, etc.

event timeline - An outline or timeline used to help manage an event that lists dates when important event production details are scheduled to occur in the event management process.

exhibition - An event at which products and services are displayed.

external audit - An audit conducted by an individual or firm that is independent of the company being audited. Auditors typically are called in for an annual audit, after the completion of the company's fiscal year. Their role is to give an opinion of the financial statement's reflection of the status and operations of the company being audited. Based on what they witness during the audit, they will also produce, for management and board use, a management letter.

F

fixed assets - Those assets of a permanent nature required for the normal conduct of a business, and which will not normally be converted into cash during the ensuing fiscal period. For example, furniture, fixtures, land and buildings are all fixed assets. However, accounts receivable and inventory are not. Sometimes call PLANT.

fixed overhead - Ongoing administrative expenses of a business that cannot be assigned to a specific business activity and that tend to stay the same whether sales go up or down, e.g. rent, utilities, telephone, insurance, etc.

followspot - Spotlight mounted on a swivel socket in order to produce a sharp moveable beam of light which can travel with the subjects on a stage or ice surface as they move from place to place.

front-of-house - The area in a facility which the public typically occupies. This area typically includes lobbies, concession stands, public restrooms, ticket office and the seating area.

full-service venue - Usually refers to a facility that provides all critical support services necessary for the tenant to successfully present/produce their event.

G

golden circle - The condition in which the best seats in the house are set-aside and are sold at a significantly higher price. The difference between the golden circle price and the next highest priced ticket is considered a donation. Often used for charity sponsored fund raising events.

governing body - Typically refers to the highest authority of a facility's ownership level. Examples include city councils, county commissions, university board of regents, or a board of directors of a private corporation.

gross revenue - Total revenue generated before any expenses or taxes are applied or paid.

group ticket sales - Refers to the process of selling blocks of tickets to groups. Group tickets are usually offered for specific performances at a discount.

H

helpers - In the context of this text, entry level apprentice workers employed to assist professional craftsmen.

hotel nights - Nights in a hotel reserved and/or actually used by convention or meeting delegates. One room rented for one night is a hotel night or room night.

I

incident report - Documentation of what occurred during a situation and what steps were taken in response. Such documentation is usually made by a member of a facility's staff on a pre-printed form.

ingress - The act of entering a public assembly facility or other location.

in-house - An activity that is conducted within, coming from or being within an organization. Refers to services provided by the facility itself rather than through outside, third-party contractors. Food and beverage concessions and advertising services to event promoters are common examples.

internal audit - An independent appraisal of the financial health of a company's operation by its own employees. Employees who carry out this function are called internal auditors.

L

labor call - A specified list of required temporary personnel that must be available at a specified time and place, including stagehands with specific skills.

license application - Form completed by potential facility user demonstrating the necessary financial resources, prior experience and ability to produce an event.

limited contract - An agreement between two parties that is restricted to specific issues, such as purposes, date and time and that usually expires at the conclusion of an event.

limited view seats - Seats in a public assembly facility that offer only a partial or restricted view of the stage, performance area or playing field where the event is being held or staged.

luxury suites - Refers to a form of premium or VIP seating sold in arenas and stadiums. Suites are physically separated from the general seating and might typically offer cushioned seats, standing room for additional guests, catered meals and drinks, closed circuit TV, special VIP access including parking, restroom facilities, concierge services and other amenities.

M

market position - Refers to the relative competitive standing of a facility in its general market area.

mission statement - A mission statement defines a facility's basic public purpose, often in two powerful statements.

motor control center - That portion of the facility that is devoted to engineering and mechanical switch gear.

N

naming rights - Refers to a form of advertising and marketing whereby a business, organization, or individual, places its (his/her) name on the facility for a fixed amount of money over a period of years - or often with universities in perpetuity. In return, the naming rights sponsor is guaranteed benefits such as luxury suites, club seats, name also on the scoreboard and other inside advertising signage inventory, name on tickets, brochures, event advertising, the right of first refusal to sponsor certain events, employee group discounts and the like.

net operating surplus - Revenue that is generated and retained in excess of the total operating expenses of a facility.

O

obstructed view seats - Seats in a public assembly facility from which the view of the stage, performance area or playing field for an event is blocked or hidden from sight. Such seats my provide a view of the stage, performance area or playing field on video screens.

outsource - The act of assigning work to an outside provider.

P

packaging - Generally refers to the process whereby the facility, individually or with one or more of its prime tenants, packages respective inventory through a combined sales staff in order to offer clients the broadest possible means by which to become advertising and sponsorship partners. Income received is simply allocated on a pre-determined basis.

panic hardware - A door latching assembly incorporating an unlatching device, the activating portion of which extends across at least one half the width of the door leaf on which it is installed. (UBC) Panic hardware allows anyone to open a door to permit exiting/egress even if the door is locked from the entry/ingress side.

parent organization - Refers to owner or oversight authority/entity of which the facility or operations is a subsidiary thereof.

personal seating license - Is typically used at the outset to raise funds to help finance a public assembly facility. The buyer essentially "buys" a seat(s) and has the right of first refusal to then buy tickets for all events.

petty cash - An account and location where a small amount of cash is stored for incidental expenses in purchasing or the reimbursing of inexpensive out-of-pocket expenditures.

physical plant - Refers to the equipment commonly associated with the heating, ventilation and air conditioning (HVAC) system, electrical distribution system, plumbing/sewage system, etc. within a public assembly facility.

pipe and drape - Pipe material with fabric draped from it to make up side rails and the back wall of a trade show booth or a temporary barrier.

pouring rights - Generally refers to the award of exclusive soft drink rights in return for an annual rights payment to the facility. It is generally against federal and most state laws to solicit advertising payments in return for exclusive arrangements involving beer, wine and/or alcohol.

premium seating - In arenas and stadiums, premium seating refers to the sale of individual "club" seats, the cost of which generally include tickets to all prime tenant sporting events. All other tickets must be purchased on a right of first refusal basis.

private management - Generally refers to a publicly owned facility contracting with an outside operator that specializes in the management, marketing and operation of public assembly facilities. The motivation for entering into such a relationship is often because it offers the owner the opportunity to operate, market and compete in a "business-like" manner not generally possible within their own system.

production call - A specified list of required personnel, many of whom may be temporary, that are needed to run the equipment or perform duties during the actual performance.

production rider - A document detailing an event's specific technical requirements in terms of stage location and size, sound and lighting equipment, mixer location, catering, etc. and other pertinent information.

promoter - Contracted person(s) or company(ies) responsible for costs, production and promotion of an event.

promoter packet - A pamphlet or brochure designed to familiarize a new promoter with the features and services of a public assembly facility. The contents of a promoter packet frequently includes information such as line drawings of spaces available for rent, seating diagrams, meeting room layouts, list of house-owned equipment, fire and safety codes, labor rates, maps of the area, etc. Promoter "packets" are increasingly being hosted on a facility's web site where the level of information provided is only limited by the creativity of the facility's management.

R

reconciliation - Audit reports conducted to reconcile cash and financial performance statements.

request for proposal - Process by which an outline of desired goods or services is responded to by vendors.

request for qualifications - Document issued prior to a request for proposal. The purpose is to ascertain that the respondent is qualified by knowledge, experience and financial capability to provide specified goods or services.

reserve - A date that has been tentatively held by a potential client for an event awaiting final contract negotiations. Also called a "tentative hold".

resident companies - Organizations for which the facility is their home. In a performing arts facility, it might include symphony orchestra, opera and/or theatrical drama companies. In arenas and stadiums it typically includes sports franchises.

revocable permit - The consent or authorization to enter, occupy or for other purposes remain upon a premises that can be revoked, recalled or withdrawn.

rigger - A person who installs rigging.

rigging - General term for the rope and pulley arrangement in the grid of a theater or the chain motors and wire cables used in an arena or amphitheater.

risk assessment - The process of evaluating the severity and frequency of loss associated with a particular activity or event.

risk management - The process of identification of risk, analysis of risk as to its likelihood, frequency and severity, risk reduction/elimination and transfer, to the extent possible, of the remaining risk.

runner - Also known as Production Assistant, is usually someone familiar with the community who is employed locally by the act or promoter to provide a means of transportation for crew members and to serve as a "go for" for the acquisition of various services and sundry items needed during an event's stay in a facility.

running schedule - A schedule used to help manage an event that lists important event production elements with corresponding times when they are scheduled to occur. Elements of a running schedule for a concert include the length of time an opening act performs, intermission beginning and ending times, and the time a headliner is scheduled to appear and how long they will perform.

S

scale-the-house - The process of assigning different ticket prices to different seating areas within a public assembly facility whereby prices vary depending on the seat location.

self-sustaining - A public assembly facility that does not require an operating subsidy from its owner to cover annual operating expenses and is similar to a "break-even operation."

settlement sheet - A detailed itemization of ticket sales, production expenses, building rent, box office costs and all other event-related expenses.

show call - A specified list of required personnel, many of whom may be temporary, that are needed to run the equipment or perform duties during the actual performance.

signage - Advertising display typically located in arenas and stadiums and to a lesser extent in convention centers, performing arts center and other public assembly facilities. Signage is typically located on scoreboards and electronic message boards, outdoor marquees, interior fascia between seating levels, on concourse walls over concession stands, etc.

sponsor - Refers to a business, organization or individual that pays fees to associate its name with a special event. Various sponsorship levels are available including, for example, "presenting," "associate," and "media."

stagehand - Generic term for backstage production personnel not performing in front of the audience.

subsidized operation - Refers to a facility that has operating expenses greater than the revenue it can generate and which, therefore, requires annual financial assistance (subsidy) from its owner.

T

tentative contract - Contract that is in the process of being negotiated during the time the date is on reserve/tentative hold.

ticket broker - An individual or agency reselling tickets in a locale where selling a ticket for more than face value is legal under specified conditions.

ticket manifest - A document that is used as evidence to prove the number of tickets printed for an event when hard tickets are preprinted. Also, a statement generated by a computerized ticketing system. Both document the number of seats programmed for a specific event and includes the number of tickets sold, unsold, held, killed and issued as complimentary for a specific event or series of events.

trade show - Exposition held for members of a common or related industry and not open to the general public.

trade tickets - Tickets for an event that are offered by an event promoter in exchange for event-related goods or services such as advertising, equipment, etc.

turnstile - Device that can keep the flow of an entering crowd at a controllable level, count the number of guests passing through, and discourage or prevent unauthorized entry, usually in the form of a rotating set of arms, permitting only one guest per arm. They can be either permanent or portable.

turnstile count - The number of customers or guests who enter the facility for an event as recorded by a turnstile.

U

umbrella group - Organization that links together a larger consortium of entities.

union shop - A facility which has a contract with a union and is able to hire any person without regard to union membership, but said employee must then join the union within a specified period of time and pay dues. This does not apply in Right to Work states.

V

variable expenses - Those business expenses that usually fluctuate in direct proportion to a level of activity, such as units of production or sales volume.

volunteers - Persons who perform or offer to perform a service of his or her own free will, usually at no charge.

Y

yellow card - Refers to a union contract agreement for stagehands between show producer and organized labor which applies to traveling, touring shows.

Z

Zamboni - The given name (manufacturer) of a maintenance vehicle used for preparing ice surfaces. Often used generically.

INDEX

A

accounts payable, 122
accounts receivable, 122
administration, 24
admission control, 178
advertising, 78, 83
alcohol sales, 148, 221, 222
American Marketing Association (AMA), 67
Americans with Disabilities Act (ADA), 60, 101
amphitheatre, 3
arena, 3
associations
    AMA, 67
    IAAM, 36
    related, 247
attachment to contract, 162
auditorium, 3
audits, 122

B

bomb threat, 180
booking, 48
    manager, 42
    memo, 58
    pitfalls, 57
booking priorities, 46
booking process, 48, 51
    avails, 51, 56, 260
    block booking, 56
    confirmed, 51
    contracted, 51
    date protection, 54
    hold dates, 51 - 54
    reserved, 51
    tentative, 58

C

D

E

F

G

NOTES